Paralegal Ethics and Regulation

Second Edition

Paralegal Ethics and Regulation

Second Edition

William P. Statsky

West Publishing Company

Minneapolis/St. Paul ■ New York ■ Los Angeles ■ San Francisco

Text Design: Rosyln Stendahl, Dapper Design
Composition: Parkwood Composition
Illustrations: Randy Miyake
Cover: Patricia Boman
Photos: p. 13, Anne Dowie; **p. 26,** Susan Spann Photography

WEST'S COMMITMENT TO THE ENVIRONMENT

In 1906, West Publishing Company began recycling materials left over from the production of books. This began a tradition of efficient and responsible use of resources. Today, up to 95 percent of our legal books and 70 percent of our college texts are printed on recycled, acid-free stock. West also recycles nearly 22 million pounds of scrap paper annually—the equivalent of 181,717 trees. Since the 1960s, West has devised ways to capture and recycle waste inks, solvents, oils, and vapors created in the printing process. We also recycle plastics of all kinds, wood, glass, corrugated cardboard, and batteries, and have eliminated the use of styrofoam book packaging. We at West are proud of the longevity and the scope of our commitment to our environment.

Product, Prepress, Printing and Binding by West Publishing Company.

COPYRIGHT ©1988   By WEST PUBLISHING COMPANY
COPYRIGHT ©1993   By WEST PUBLISHING COMPANY
                    610 Opperman Drive
                    P.O. Box 64526
                    St. Paul, MN 55164-0526

00 99 98 97 96 95 94 93   8 7 6 5 4 3 2 1 0

Library of Congress Cataloging-In-Publication Data

Statsky, William P.
    Paralegal ethics and regulation / William P. Statsky—2nd ed.
        p.   cm.
    Includes index.
    ISBN 0-314-01209-5 (soft)
    1. Legal assistants—United States.   2. Legal ethics—United States.   I. Title.
KF320.L4S745   1993   92-18128
274'.3'0973—dc20   CIP ∞

■ Also by William P. Statsky

Case Analysis and Fundamentals of Legal Writing, 3d ed. St.Paul: West Publishing Company, 1989 (with J. Wernet)

Essentials of Paralegalism, 2d ed. St. Paul: West Publishing Company, 1993

Family Law, 3d ed. St. Paul: West Publishing Company, 1991

Inmate Involvement in Prison Legal Services: Roles and Training Options for the Inmate as Paralegal. American Bar Association, Commission on Correctional Facilities and Services, 1974

Introduction to Paralegalism: Problems, Perspectives and Skills, 4th ed. St. Paul: West Publishing Company, 1992

Legal Desk Reference. St. Paul: West Publishing Co., 1991 (with B. Hussey, M. Diamond & R. Nakamura)

The Legal Paraprofessional as Advocate and Assistant: Roles, Training Concepts and Materials. Center on Social Welfare Policy and Law, 1971 (with P. Lang)

Legal Research and Writing: Some Starting Points, 4th ed. St. Paul: West Publishing Company, 1993

Legal Thesaurus/Dictionary: A Resource for the Writer and Computer Researcher. St. Paul: West Publishing Company, 1985

Legislative Analysis and Drafting, 2d ed. St.Paul: West Publishing Company, 1984

Paralegal Employment: Facts and Strategies for the 1990s, 2d ed. St. Paul: West Publishing Company, 1993

Torts: Personal Injury Litigation, 2d ed. St. Paul: West Publishing Company, 1990

Rights of the Imprisoned: Cases, Materials and Directions. Indianapolis: Bobbs-Merrill Company, 1974 (with R. Singer)

What Have Paralegals Done? A Dictionary of Functions. National Paralegal Institute, 1973

For Gabriel

■ Contents

■ Preface

A paralegal is a person with legal skills who works under the supervision of an attorney or who is otherwise authorized to use those skills; this person performs tasks that do not require all the skills of an attorney and that most legal secretaries are not trained to perform.

Ethics and other regulation issues continue to be "hot" topics in the paralegal field. They are regularly discussed and debated in a wide variety of settings throughout the country. The settings include paralegal newsletters, paralegal conferences, bar association meetings, bar association journals, courtrooms, and legislative committees. Not long ago, many individuals had to ask the question, "What's a paralegal?" While that day has long passed, there are still many unresolved questions about how the paralegal fits within the legal community. A primary mission of this book is to address these questions.

Changes in the Second Edition:

- There are new sections on the major issues of limited licensing, associate bar membership, conflict of interest, and malpractice liability insurance.
- There is more extensive coverage of the ethical rules governing attorneys.
- A paralegal perspective has been added to the discussion of each ethical rule governing attorneys.
- There is a greater emphasis on Model Rule 5.3 and ethical opinions on the use of paralegals.
- Each chapter includes a chapter outline, chapter summary, and key terms.
- A glossary has been added.

Acknowledgments

Valuable guidance and suggestions were made by a very talented team in the College Division of West Publishing Company: Elizabeth Hannan, acquisitions editor; Sandy Gangelhoff, production editor; and Carrie Kish, promotion manager. In addition, the contributions of the adopters and reviewers of the prior edition are gratefully acknowledged.

CHAPTER

1

The Regulation of Paralegals

▦ Chapter Outline

▦ Section A. Kinds of Regulation

The activities of paralegals could be regulated in seven important ways:

- Laws on the unauthorized practice of law and on the *authorized* practice of law by nonattorneys
- State licensing
- Regulation of education
- Self-regulation
- Fair Labor Standards Act
- Tort Law (e.g., the negligence of paralegals and of attorneys who employ them)
- Ethical rules

The first six of these methods of regulation are covered in this chapter. Ethics will be examined in the next chapter. As we explore these methods, you should keep in mind the terminology of regulation outlined in Figure 1.1.

FIGURE 1.1   The Terminology of Regulation

Accreditation is the process by which an organization evaluates and recognizes a program of study (or an institution) as meeting specified qualifications or standards.

Approval means the recognition that comes from accreditation, certification, licensure, or registration. As we will see, the American Bar Association uses the word "approval" as a substitute for "accreditation" of paralegal education programs.

Certification is the process by which a nongovernmental organization grants recognition to an individual who has met qualifications specified by that organization. Three of the most common qualifications are:

Graduating from a school or training program, or

Passing a standard examination, or

Completing a designated period of work experience.

Once certification has been bestowed by one or a combination of these methods, the individual is said to have been *certified.* If the certification comes from a school or training program, some prefer to say that the person has been *certificated.* (Occasionally a government agency will have what it calls a certification program. This program may be similar to those described above, or it may in fact be a license program.)

Code is any set of rules that regulates conduct.

Ethics are rules that embody standards of behavior to which members of an organization are expected to conform.

Guideline is suggested conduct that will help an applicant obtain accreditation, certification, licensure, registration, or approval.

Licensure is the process by which an agency of government grants permission to persons meeting specified qualifications to engage in an occupation and/or to use a particular title.

Limited Licensure (also called *specialty licensure*) is the process by which an agency of government grants permission to persons meeting specified qualifications to engage in designated activities that are customarily (but not always exclusively) performed by another license holder. (If, in the future, paralegals are granted a limited license in a particular state, they will be authorized to sell designated services—now part of the attorney monopoly— directly to the public in that state.)

Registration or *enrollment* is the process by which individuals or institutions list their names on a roster kept by an agency of government or by a nongovernmental organization. There may or may not be qualifications that must be met before one can go on the list.

Regulation is any governmental or nongovernmental method of controlling conduct.

▌ Section B. Unauthorized and Authorized Practice of Law

(a) Defining the Practice of Law

Every state has laws on who can be an attorney and on the *unauthorized practice of law.* In many states it is a *crime* to practice law illegally. It is not a crime to represent yourself, but you risk going to jail if you practice law on behalf of someone else. Why such a harsh penalty? Legal problems often involve complicated, serious issues. A great deal can be lost if citizens do not receive competent legal assistance. To protect the public, the state has established a system of licensing attorneys to provide this assistance and to punish anyone who tries to provide it without the license.

The *practice of law* involves three major kinds of activities:

- Representing someone in court or in an agency proceeding
- Preparing and drafting legal documents for someone
- Providing legal advice on someone's rights and obligations

The essence of legal advice is to relate the law to an individual's specific legal problem.

Suppose that you write a self-help book on how to sue your landlord. The book lists all the laws, provides all the forms, and gives precise guidelines on how to use the laws and the forms. Are you practicing law? No, since you are not addressing the *specific* legal problem of a *specific* person. It is not the practice of law to sell legal books or similar materials to the general public even if a member of the public uses them for his or her specific legal problem. Now suppose that you open an office in which you sell the book and even type the forms for customers. Practice of law? No, *unless you provide individual help in filling out the forms.* You can type the forms so long as the customer does all the thinking about what goes in the forms! So too:

- It is proper for a nonattorney to charge citizens a fee to type legal forms in order to obtain a divorce. But it is the unauthorized practice of law to provide personal assistance on how to fill out the forms.
- It is proper for a nonattorney to charge citizens a fee to type their will or trust. But it is the unauthorized practice of law to provide personal assistance on what should go in the will or trust.

For years, attorneys have complained that large numbers of individuals were crossing the line by providing this kind of personal assistance. Bar associations often asked the state to prosecute many of them. Yet some charged that the attorneys were less interested in protecting the public than in preserving their own monopoly over the practice of law. Perhaps the most famous recent case involving this controversy was that of Rosemary Furman and the Florida Bar.

Rosemary Furman: Folk Hero?

Rosemary Furman, a former legal secretary, believes that you should be able to solve simple legal problems without hiring an attorney. Hence she established the Northside Secretarial Service in Jacksonville, Florida. She compiled and sold packets of legal forms (for $50) on divorce, name changes, and adoptions. The price *included her personal assistance in filling out and filing the forms.* The Florida Bar Association and the Florida courts moved against her with a vengeance for practicing law illegally. She was convicted and sentenced to 30 days in jail.

Widespread support for Ms. Furman developed. Her case soon became a cause célèbre for those seeking increased access to the legal system for the poor and the middle class.[1] Many were outraged at the legal profession and the judiciary for their treatment of Ms. Furman.

The CBS program *60 Minutes* did a story that was favorable to her cause. Other national media, including *Newsweek,* covered the case. Warner Brothers considered doing

---

1. Peoples & Wertz, *Update: Unauthorized Practice of Law,* 9 Nat'l Paralegal Reporter 1 (Nat'l Federation of Paralegal Associations, February 1985).

a docudrama on the story. Rosemary Furman struck a responsive chord when she claimed that for every $50 she earned, an attorney lost $500. An editorial in the *Gainesville Sun* said, "Throw Rosemary Furman in jail? Surely not after the woman forced the Florida bar and the judiciary to confront its responsibility to the poor. Anything less than a 'thank you' note would indeed show genuine vindictiveness on the part of the legal profession" (Nov. 4, 1984). There were, however, other views. An editorial in *USA Today* said, "If she can give legal advice, so can charlatans, frauds, and rip-off artists" February 2, 1984).

The events in the Rosemary Furman story are as follows:

- 1978 & 1979: The Florida Bar Association takes Rosemary Furman to court, alleging that she is practicing law without a license.
- 1979: The Florida Supreme Court rules against her. She is enjoined from engaging in the unauthorized practice of law.
- 1982: The Florida Bar Association again brings a complaint against her business, alleging that she was continuing the unauthorized practice of law.
- 1983: Duval County Circuit Judge A. C. Soud, Jr. finds her in contempt of court for violating the 1979 order. The judge makes this decision in a nonjury hearing. She is then ordered to serve 30 days in jail.
- 1984: The United States Supreme Court refuses to hear the case. This has the effect of allowing the state jail sentence to stand. The Court is not persuaded by her argument that she should have been granted a jury trial of her peers rather than have been judged solely by members of a profession (attorneys and judges) that was biased against her.
- Her attorneys ask the Florida Supreme Court to vacate the jail sentence if she agrees to close her business.

- The Florida Bar Association tells the Florida Supreme Court that the jail term is a fitting punishment and should be served.
- November 13, 1984: The Florida Supreme Court orders her to serve the jail sentence for practicing law without a license. (451 So.2d 808)
- November 27, 1984: Rosemary Furman is granted clemency from the 30-day jail term by Florida Governor Bob Graham and his Clemency Board. She does not have to go to jail.
- Furman and her attorneys announce that they will work on a constitutional amendment defining the practice of law to make it easier for citizens to avoid dependency on attorneys in civil cases. Says Ms. Furman, "I have only begun to fight."

This case has had an impact in Florida and elsewhere in the country. Recently, for example, Florida has been considering a dramatic change in the definition of unauthorized practice of law. Under this proposal, it "shall not constitute the unauthorized practice of law for nonlawyers to engage in limited oral communications to assist a person in a completion of a legal form approved by the Supreme Court of Florida. Oral communications by nonlawyers are restricted to those communications reasonably necessary to elicit factual information to complete the form and inform the person how to file the form."[2] Later in this chapter, we will discuss the even more dramatic concept of *limited licensing* for paralegals, which is being considered in a number of states. Some have referred to these developments as "the long shadow of Rosemary Furman."

---

2. Florida Bar News 12 (August 1, 1989).

■ ASSIGNMENT 1.1

(a) Define the practice of law in your state. Quote from your state code, court rules, or other official authority that is available.

(b) Would Rosemary Furman have been prosecuted for the unauthorized practice of law in your state today?

> Legal Assistant regulation is on the horizon in one form or another, [and possibly in many forms]. It is imperative that we approach the regulation "can of worms" from an informed and knowledgeable vantage point, and that we participate in the formative process.
> Gail White Nicholson, Vice-President, Greenville Association of Legal Assistants, 1991

The Furman case involved direct competition with attorneys. More indirect competition comes from people engaged in law-related activities, such as accountants, claims adjusters, real estate agents, life insurance agents, and officers of trust departments of banks. For years, bar associations complained about such activities. In many instances, they challenged the activities in court as the unauthorized practice of law. The problem was so pervasive that some bar associations negotiated a "statement of principles" (sometimes called a treaty) with these occupations in an attempt to identify boundary lines and methods of resolving difficulties. Most of these treaties, however, have been ineffective in defining the kinds of law-related activities that can and cannot be performed by nonattorneys. A tremendous amount of effort and money is needed to negotiate, monitor, and enforce the treaties. The resources are simply not available. Furthermore, there is a concern that such efforts by attorneys to restrain competition might violate the antitrust laws, as we will see later in the chapter.

Some practitioners of law-related occupations have gone directly to the legislature to seek enactment of statutes that authorize what would otherwise be the unauthorized practice of law. In many instances, they have been successful. For example:

Ga. Code Ann. § 9-401 (Supp. 1970). § 9-401. . . . Provided that, a title insurance company may prepare such papers as it thinks proper, or necessary, in connection with a title which it proposes to insure, in order, in its opinion, for it to be willing to insure such title, where no charge is made by it for such papers.

Utah Code Ann. 1968, 61-2-20. § 61-2-20. Rights and privileges of real estate salesmen—brokers.—It is expressly provided that a real estate salesman shall have the right to fill out and complete forms of legal documents necessary to any real estate transaction to which the said broker is a party as principal or agent, and which forms have been approved by the commission and the attorney general of the state of Utah. Such forms shall include a closing real estate contract, a short-form lease, and a bill of sale of personal property.

Tenn. Code Ann. § 62-1325 (1955). § 62-1325. Licensed Real Estate Brokers may draw contracts to option, buy, sell, or lease real property.

The effect of such statutes is to allow members of designated occupations to perform certain legal tasks that are intimately related to their work without having to hire attorneys or without forcing their clients to hire them.

(b) Authorized Practice of Law

Examine the following phrase closely: unauthorized practice of law by nonattorneys. If there is such a thing as the *un*authorized practice of law, then, by implication, there must be an *authorized* practice of law. And indeed there is. The treaties and statutes discussed above are examples of this. There are also other areas where nonattorneys are given a special authorization to practice law. Occasionally attempts are made to call what they do something other than the *practice of law*, but as we will see, these attempts conflict with reality since the nonattorneys are doing what attorneys do within the sphere of the special authorization. These special authorizations have been vigorously opposed by attorneys on the ground that the authorizations conflict with the privileged domain of attorneys. The latter are not always this blunt in stating their opposition. The objection is usually couched in terms of "protection of the public," but in large measure, the opposition has its roots in turf protection. Attorneys are not above engaging in battles for economic self-preservation.

Some members of the public view attorneys as fighters, people who will pursue an issue to the bitter end. While this trait may place attorneys in a favorable light in the eyes of clients for whom they are doing battle, many feel that the aggressive inclination of the attorney can be counterproductive. Administrative agencies, for example, are often suspicious of the involvement of attorneys. They are viewed as combatants who want to turn every agency decision into an adversarial proceeding. Agencies often see courtroom gymnastics and gimmicks as the attorney's primary mode of operation. The attorney is argumentative to a fault.

This image of the attorney as someone who complicates matters is best summed up by an old accountant's joke that taxation becomes more and more complex in direct proportion to attempts by attorneys to *simplify* the tax law. Whether or not this view of the attorney is correct, it has accounted for some erosion of the legal profession's monopoly over the practice of law.

The unavailability of attorneys has also helped produce this result. A vast segment of our population has legal complaints that are never touched by attor-

neys. This is due, in part, to the fact that most of these complaints do not involve enough money to attract attorneys.

We now turn to a fuller exploration of these themes under the following headings:

1. Court "representation" by nonattorneys

2. Attempted restrictions on the activities of the "jailhouse lawyer" and the broader policy considerations raised by such restrictions

3. Agency representation by nonattorneys

(1) Court Representation

In the vast majority of courts in this country, only attorneys can represent someone in a judicial proceeding. There are, however, some limited—but dramatic—exceptions.

In Maryland, a nonattorney employee of a nonprofit legal service office can represent tenants in a summary ejectment proceeding in the District Court of Maryland! A special Lay Advocacy Program oversees this form of court advocacy by nonattorneys.[3] Another extraordinary example exists in North Dakota where lay advocates assist women who are petitioners seeking protective orders in domestic violence cases. Some judges "encourage and allow" the lay advocate "to conduct direct and cross-examination of witnesses and make statements to the court." A proposal has been made to formalize this activity by creating a new position called a Certified Domestic Violence Advocate. Under this proposal, the following activities of this nonattorney would *not* be considered the unauthorized practice of law: helping a petitioner fill out printed forms, sitting with the petitioner during court proceedings, and making written or oral statements to the court.[4]

There are some lower courts in the country, particularly in the West, where parties can have nonattorneys represent them. Examples include Justice of the Peace Courts, Magistrates Courts, and Small Claims Courts. It is relatively rare, however, for parties to have any representation in such courts.

Tribal Courts on Indian reservations have jurisdiction over designated civil and criminal matters involving Native Americans. In many of these courts, both parties are represented by nonattorney advocates.

Government employees occasionally act in a representative or semi-representative capacity in court proceedings, even though they are not attorneys. In North Carolina cases involving the termination of parental rights, for example, the United States Supreme Court has noted the role of nonattorneys:

In fact, . . . the North Carolina Departments of Social Services are themselves sometimes represented at termination hearings by social workers instead of by lawyers.[5]

---

[3]*Lay Advocacy Program Defends Indigent Tenants*, 6 Bar Bulletin 3 (Maryland Bar Ass'n, January 1991). Annotated Code of Maryland . 10–101 (1991 Supp).

[4]*Role of Lay Advocates in Domestic Violence Proceedings*, 15 Note Pad 1 (State Bar Ass'n of North Dakota, April 5, 1991).

[5]*Lassiter v. Dept. of Social Services*, 452 U.S. 18, 29, 101 S.Ct. 2153, 2161, 68 L.Ed.2d 640, 651 (1981).

It is well known that attorneys waste a good deal of pretrial time traveling to court and waiting around simply to give documents to the judge and to set dates for the various stages of pretrial and trial proceedings. Another problem is that an attorney may have to be in two different courtrooms at the same time. For example, the time spent at an early morning hearing may be unexpectedly extended so that the attorney cannot appear at a previously scheduled mid-morning proceeding in another courtroom on a different case. In such situations, wouldn't it be helpful if the attorney's paralegal could "appear" in court for the limited purpose of delivering papers to the judge, asking for a new date, or presenting some other message? *In most states, such activity is strictly prohibited.*

On August 16, 1982, a Kentucky paralegal learned about this prohibition in a dramatic way. Her attorney was involved in a trial at the Jefferson Circuit Court. He asked the paralegal to go to another courtroom during "Motion Hour," where attorneys make motions or schedule future proceedings on a case. He told her to ask for a hearing date on another case that he had pending. She did so. When the case was called during "Motion Hour," she rose, identified herself as the attorney's paralegal, and gave the message to the judge, asking for the hearing date. Opposing counsel was outraged. He verbally assaulted the paralegal in the courtroom and filed a motion to hold the paralegal and her attorney in contempt of court for the unauthorized practice of law. When a hearing was later held on this motion, members of a local paralegal association packed the courtroom. Tensions were high. When the judge eventually *denied* the motion, after a hearing on the matter, the audience broke out into loud applause. "Apparently the judge concluded that [the paralegal] had rendered no service involving legal knowledge or advice, but had merely transmitted to the court [the attorney's] message regarding disposition of the motion, that is, she had been performing a function that was administrative, not legal in nature." [6]

About twenty years earlier, a celebrated Illinois opinion, *People v. Alexander*, [7] took a position similar to this Kentucky court. In this opinion, the defendant was an unlicensed law clerk who appeared before the court to state that his employing attorney could not be present in court at the moment because he was trying a case elsewhere. On behalf of his employer, the law clerk requested a continuance. The defendant's actions were challenged. It was argued that any appearance by nonattorneys before a court in which they give information as to the availability of counsel or the status of litigation constitutes the unauthorized practice of law. The Illinois court took the unique position that this was not the practice of law. The reasoning of the court is presented in the excerpt from the opinion printed at the top of page 9.

It must be emphasized that most states would *not* agree with Kentucky and Illinois. Most states would prohibit nonattorneys from doing what was authorized in these two states. Fortunately, however, there are at least a few additional states that have begun to move in the direction of the minority view.

---

[6]Winter, *No Contempt in Kentucky*, 7 Nat'l Paralegal Reporter 8 (Nat'l Federation of Paralegal Associations, Winter 1982).
[7]53 Ill. App. 2d 299, 202 N.E.2d 841 (1964).

People v. Alexander

Appellate Court of Illinois, First District
53 Ill. App. 2d 299, 202 N.E.2d 841 (1964)

. . .

In the case of People ex rel. Illinois State Bar Ass'n v. People's Stock Yards State Bank, 344 Ill. 462, at page 476, 176 N.E. 901, at page 907, wherein a bank was prosecuted for the unauthorized practice of law, the following quotation is relied upon:

"According to the generally understood definition of the practice of law in this country, it embraces the preparation of pleadings, and other papers incident to actions and special proceedings, and the management of such actions and proceedings on behalf of clients before judges and courts * * *."

Since this statement relates to the appearance and management of proceedings in court on behalf of a client, we do not believe it can be applied to a situation where a clerk hired by a law firm presents information to the court on behalf of his employer.

We agree with the trial judge that clerks should not be permitted to make motions or participate in other proceedings which can be considered as "managing" the litigation. However, if apprising the court of an employer's engagement or inability to be present constitutes the making of a motion, we must hold that clerks may make such motions for continuances without being guilty of the unauthorized practice of law. Certainly with the large volume of cases appearing on the trial calls these days, it is imperative that this practice be followed.

In Toth v. Samuel Phillipson & Co., 250 Ill.App. 247 (1928) the court said at page 250:

"It is well known in this county where numerous trial courts are sitting at the same time the exigencies of such a situation require that trial attorneys be represented by their clerical force to respond to some of the calls, and that the court acts upon their response the same as if the attorneys of record themselves appeared in person."

After that opinion was handed down, the number of judges was substantially increased in the former Circuit and Superior Courts and the problem of answering court calls has at least doubled. We cannot add to the heavy burden of lawyers who in addition to responding to trial calls must answer pre-trial calls and motion calls—all held in the morning—by insisting that a lawyer must personally appear to present to a court a motion for a continuance on grounds of engagement or inability to appear because of illness or other unexpected circumstances. To reduce the backlog, trial lawyers should be kept busy actually trying lawsuits and not answering court calls.

The Allen County Bar Association of Indiana has taken the bold move of permitting paralegals to perform what hitherto had been considered attorney functions in court. A paralegal is authorized:

- To "take" default judgments
- To "set" pretrial conferences, uncontested divorces, and all other hearing dates
- To "file" stipulations or motions for dismissal
- Etc.

The paralegal, however, must perform these tasks with court personnel other than judges; nonattorneys cannot communicate directly with judges.

The vast majority of attorneys in the country would be amazed to learn what is going on in Allen County. Once the shock subsides, however, these attorneys will probably see the wisdom and common sense of what Allen County has done and begin to think of ways to try it themselves.

The rules of the Allen County program are as follows:

Paralegal Rules of Practice
Allen County Bar Association (Indiana)

1. Generally, a legal assistant employee shall be limited to the performance of tasks which do not require the exercising of legal discretion or judgment that affects the legal right of any person.

2. All persons employed as legal assistants shall be registered [see Figure 1.2] by their employer law firm with the Allen County Circuit and Superior Court Administrator and the Clerk of the Allen Superior and Circuit Courts. Said law firm shall, by affidavit, state that it shall be bound and liable for the actions of its legal assistant employee, and that any and all actions or statements made by such personnel shall be strictly and completely supervised by his employer member of the Bar. All documents the legal assistant presents or files must contain the attorney's signature, either as an attorney for the petitioning party, or a statement affixed indicating that the documents were prepared by said attorney. Each law firm shall certify in writing that the legal assistant employee is qualified in each field in which they will act with the Courts (probate, dissolution of marriage, collection, etc.). A copy of such statement and certification shall be given to such legal assistant and shall be carried by such person whenever activity with the Court is pursued by such person. There shall be one legal assistant certified by each law office desiring same, but [an] alternate shall be allowed in case of illness, vacation or unavailability. However, in those instances where a single law firm has more than one full time legal assistant, each of whom operate in separate specialized areas, a certification can be had by more than one person, showing that such person's specialization on a full time basis is limited to one specific area. Otherwise, there should be a limit of one person certified as a legal assistant per law firm.

3. Such employee shall be limited to the following acts:

   (a) Such employee may take default judgments upon the filing of an affidavit in each case stating the amount of damages and that proper service was obtained sworn to by affidavit.

   (b) Such employee shall have authority to set Pre-Trial Conferences, Uncontested Divorces, and all other hearing dates.

   (c) Such employee shall have authority to obtain trust account deposits at the Allen County Clerk's Office but only in the name of his employer firm.

   (d) Such employee shall have authority to file stipulations or motions for dismissal.

   (e) Such an employee shall have the authority to do all filing of documents and papers with the Clerk of the Allen Superior Courts and Circuit Court where such documents and papers are not to be given to anyone authorized to affix a judge's signature or issue Court orders.

   (f) Notwithstanding the limitations of subparagraph (e) above, such employee shall have the authority to obtain from the law clerk the signature stamp of the judge on non-discretionary standard orders and notices, such as notice of hearing, and orders to appear and to answer interrogatories on the filing of a Verified Motion for Proceedings Supplemental. Note: Standard orders which depart from the usual format, restraining orders, suit and support orders, bench warrants, and body attachments must be secured by an attorney.

   (g) Such employee is not to negotiate with opposing litigants within the Courthouse nor confer with a judge on legal matters. Matters requiring communications with a judge, require an attorney.

   (h) Where circumstances permit, attorneys shall take precedence over such employees in dealings with courts and clerks.

FIGURE 1.2   Allen County Circuit and Superior Court Certification of Legal Assistants

---

STATEMENT OF CERTIFICATION

This is to certify that _____

is employed by the law firm of _____.

Said law firm binds itself and takes full responsibility and liability for the actions of its legal assistant employee above-named and that any and all actions or statements made by such personnel shall be strictly and completely supervised by a member of the Bar of the State of Indiana. This is to certify that the above-mentioned legal assistant is qualified to assist an attorney in the _____ area of law.

LAW FIRM OF:_____

BY:_____

STATE OF INDIANA, COUNTY OF ALLEN, SS:

Subscribed and sworn to before me, a Notary Public in and for said County and State, this _____ day _____, 19_____.

_____

Notary Public

Note again that the above program does not allow the paralegal to talk directly with a judge in performing the authorized tasks. ("Matters requiring communications with a judge, require an attorney.") Why such a restriction? Wouldn't it make sense to allow paralegal-judge communication on some procedural matters that are of a routine nature? *No,* would be the response of most bar associations.

Yes, however, is the refreshing response of several county bar associations in the state of Washington. Under the sponsorship of the Seattle-King County Bar Association and the Tacoma-Pierce County Bar Association, paralegals are allowed to "present" certain orders to judges. The orders must be those that the parties have already agreed on, or must be ex parte (which means involving one party only). In presenting such orders to a judge, the paralegal must obviously deal directly with—and perhaps even communicate with—an almighty judge! The prohibition in Allen County, Indiana on communicating with a judge does not exist in these two counties of Washington state.

(2) The Jailhouse Lawyer

A *jailhouse lawyer* is a nonattorney who helps fellow prisoners with their legal problems. Some prisons attempted to prevent the jailhouse lawyer from providing this legal assistance even though no meaningful alternatives for such assistance were provided by the prisons. This prohibition was struck down, however, by the United States Supreme Court in *Johnson v. Avery* in 1969. The basis of the opinion was that without the jailhouse lawyer, prisoners may not have access to the courts. The concurring opinion of Justice Douglas has become one of the most widely quoted and influential statements in the field of paralegalism.

Johnson v. Avery

Supreme Court of the United States, 1969.
393 U.S. 483, 89 S.Ct. 747, 21 L.Ed.2d 718

Mr. Justice DOUGLAS, concurring.

While I join the opinion of the Court [in striking down the prohibition on the activities of jailhouse lawyers] I add a few words in emphasis of the important thesis of the case.

The increasing complexities of our governmental apparatus at both the local and the federal levels have made it difficult for a person to process a claim or even to make a complaint. Social security is a virtual maze; the hierarchy that governs urban housing is often so intricate that it takes an expert to know what agency has jurisdiction over a particular complaint; the office to call or official to see for noise abatement, for a broken sewer line, or a fallen tree is a mystery to many in our metropolitan areas.

A person who has a claim assertable in faraway Washington, D.C., is even more helpless, as evidenced by the increasing tendency of constituents to rely on their congressional delegation to identify, press, and process their claims.

We think of claims as grist for the mill of the lawyers. But it is becoming abundantly clear that more and more of the effort in ferreting out the basis of claims and the agencies responsible for them and in preparing the almost endless paperwork for their prosecution is work for laymen. There are not enough lawyers to manage or supervise all of these affairs; and much of the basic work done requires no special legal talent. *Yet there is a closed-shop philosophy in the legal profession that cuts down drastically active roles for laymen. . . . That traditional, closed-shop attitude is utterly out of place in the modern world where claims pile high and much of the work of tracing and pursuing them requires the patience and wisdom of a layman rather than the legal skills of a member of the bar.* [Emphasis added.]

"If poverty lawyers are overwhelmed, some of the work can be delegated to sub-professionals. New York law permits senior law students to practice law under certain supervised conditions. Approval must first be granted by the appellate division. A rung or two lower on the legal profession's ladder are laymen legal technicians, comparable to nurses and lab assistants in the medical profession. Large law firms employ them, and there seems to be no reason why they cannot be used in legal services programs to relieve attorneys for more professional tasks." Samore, Legal Services for the Poor, 32 Albany L.Rev. 509, 515–516 (1968).

The plight of a man in prison may in these respects be even more acute than the plight of a person on the outside. He may need collateral proceedings to test the legality of his detention or relief against management of the parole system or against defective detainers lodged against him which create burdens in the nature of his incarcerated status. He may have grievances of a civil nature against those outside the prison. His imprisonment may give his wife grounds for divorce and be a factor in determining the custody of his children; and he may have pressing social security, workmen's compensation, or veterans' claims.

While the demand for legal counsel in prison is heavy, the supply is light. For private matters of a civil nature, legal counsel for the indigent in prison is almost nonexistent. Even for criminal proceedings, it is sparse. While a few states have post-conviction statutes providing such counsel, most states do not. Some states like California do appoint counsel to represent the indigent prisoner in his collateral hearings, once he succeeds in making out a prima facie case. But as a result, counsel is not on hand for preparation of the papers or for the initial decision that the prisoner's claim has substance.

Notes

1. "Jailhouse lawyers, or *writ writers,* as they are sometimes called, have always been part of prison society. But in recent years their numbers as well as the amount of litigation they generate, his increased substantially. In 1985, prisoners filed 33,400 petitions in federal and state courts. . . ." One

Jailhouse lawyer, Fernando Jackson, Soledad Prison, California

jailhouse lawyer at Soledad prison "devotes sixteen hours a day to his legal work, subscribes to dozens of legal publications (at a cost of $1,800 a year), and files a steady stream of lawsuits." Suing "has become almost a national pastime. Prisoners act no differently from other citizens in a litigious society." Kroll, *Counsel Behind Bars: Jailhouse Lawyers . . .*, 7 California Lawyer 34 (June 1987).

2. The *Johnson* opinion stressed that the prison provided *no* alternative to the jailhouse lawyer. If alternatives had been available, the inmate would not be allowed to practice law. In *Williams v. U.S. Dep't of Justice*, 433 F.2d 958 (5th Cir. 1970), the court held that the presence of law students in the prison could be an alternative, but only if it is demonstrated that the students are meeting the need for inmate legal services. If the inmates had to wait a considerable period of time, for example, before they could be interviewed by the law students, then no alternative existed and the jailhouse lawyer could not be prevented from helping other inmates.

3. In *Gilmore v. Lynch*, 319 F. Supp. 105 (N.D. Cal. 1970), affirmed by the United States Supreme Court in *Younger v. Gilmore*, 404 U.S. 15 (1971), the court held that California either had to satisfy the legal needs of its prisoners or expand the prison law library to include a more comprehensive collection of law books. See also *Bounds v. Smith*, p. 15.

4. Finally, the right of an inmate to assist a fellow inmate in legal matters does *not* extend to representing the inmate in court. *Guajardo v. Luna*, 432 F.2d 1324 (5th Cir. 1970). Nor can a nonattorney represent an inmate in court even if this nonattorney is not an inmate himself or herself. This latter point

was decided by the United States Supreme Court in *Hackin v. Arizona,* 389 U.S. 143 (1967).

5. How far can the rationale of *Johnson* be extended? Suppose, for example, it is demonstrated that many claimants before state administrative agencies are not receiving legal services because attorneys cannot be afforded. Would the *Johnson* opinion permit paralegal representation before such agencies even if the latter prohibited it? What is the difference between an inmate's right to have access to the courts and *anyone's* right to complain to an agency? How do you think Justice Douglas would handle the case if it came before him?

"Although the *Johnson* case is admittedly narrow in scope, it does nevertheless, give aid and comfort to the view that whenever lawyers are unavailable for whatever reason, society will sanction alternative systems for the delivery of legal services. The paramount consideration will not be ethics nor the exclusivity of the right to practice law, but rather it will be the facilitation of access routes to the grievance machinery set up for the resolution of claims. If lawyers are not available to assist the citizenry with these claims, then the question arises as to whether skilled nonlawyers represent a viable alternative. The inevitability of this question becomes clear when we listen to the statistics on the demand for the services of a lawyer. Estimates have been made to the effect that if every lawyer devoted full time to the legal needs of the poor, there would still be a significant shortage of lawyers for the poor. If the legal needs of the middle class are added, the legal service manpower shortage becomes overwhelming." Statsky, W. and Lang, P., *The Legal Paraprofessional as Advocate and Assistant: Roles, Training Concepts and Materials,* 49–50 (1971).

See also Statsky, W., *Inmate Involvement in Prison Legal Services: Roles and Training Options for the Inmate as Paralegal* (American Bar Association, Commission on Correctional Facilities and Services, Resource Center on Correctional Law and Legal Services, 1974).

• • • • • • • • • • • • • •

Two other important Supreme Court cases involving nonattorneys in prison need to be considered: *Procunier v. Martinez* and *Bounds v. Smith.* Excerpts from these opinions are reprinted below:

Procunier v. Martinez

Supreme Court of the United States, 1974.
416 U.S. 396, 94 S.Ct. 1800, 40 L.Ed.2d 244

The District Court also enjoined continued enforcement of Administrative Rule MV-IV-02, which provides in pertinent part:

"Investigators for an attorney-of-record will be confined to not more than two. Such investigators must be licensed by the State or must be members of the State Bar. Designation must be made in writing by the Attorney."

By restricting access to prisoners to members of the bar and licensed private investigators, this regulation imposed an absolute ban on the use by attorneys of law students and legal paraprofessionals to interview inmate clients. In fact attorneys could not even delegate to such persons the task of obtaining prisoners' signatures on legal documents. The District Court reasoned that this rule constituted an unjustifiable restriction on the right of access to the courts. We agree.

The constitutional guarantee of due process of law has as a corollary the requirement that prisoners be afforded access to the courts in order to challenge unlawful convictions and to seek redress for violations of their constitutional rights. This means that inmates must have a reasonable opportunity to seek and receive the assistance of attorneys. Regulations and practices that unjustifiably obstruct the availability of professional representation or other aspects of the right of access to the courts are invalid. Ex parte Hull, 312 U.S. 546, 61 S.Ct. 640, 85 L.Ed. 1034 (1941).

The District Court found that the rule restricting attorney-client interviews to members of the bar and licensed private investigators inhibited adequate professional representation of indigent inmates. The remoteness of many California penal institutions makes a personal visit [by attorneys] to an inmate client a time-consuming undertaking. The court reasoned that the ban against the use of law students or other paraprofessionals for attorney-client interviews would deter some lawyers from representing prisoners who could not afford to pay for their traveling time or that of licensed private investigators. And those lawyers who agreed to do so would waste time that might be employed more efficaciously in working on the inmates' legal problems. Allowing law students and paraprofessionals to interview inmates might well reduce the cost of legal representation for prisoners. The District Court therefore concluded that the regulation imposed a substantial burden on the right of access to the courts.

Bounds v. Smith
Supreme Court of the United States, 1977
430 U.S. 817, 97 S.Ct. 1491, 52 L.Ed.2d 72

[In this opinion the Supreme Court is again concerned with the need of prisoners to have access to the courts and the use of nonlawyers in helping to obtain that access. The Court held that prisons must assist inmates in the preparation and filing of meaningful legal papers by providing the inmates with adequate law libraries or adequate assistance from persons trained in the law. The Court rejected the claim that nonlawyer inmates were ill-equipped to use the "tools of the trade of the legal profession." In the Court's experience, nonlawyer petitioners are capable of using law books to file cases raising claims that are "serious and legitimate" whether or not such petitioners win the cases. In outlining the options available to a prison, the Court specifically referred to paralegals:]

It should be noted that while adequate law libraries are one constitutionally acceptable method to assure meaningful access to the courts, our decision here . . . does not foreclose alternative means to achieve that goal. Nearly half the States and the District of Columbia provide some degree of professional or quasi-professional legal assistance to prisoners. . . . Such programs take many imaginative forms and may have a number of advantages over libraries alone. Among the alternatives are the training of inmates as para-legal assistants to work under lawyers' supervision, the use of paraprofessionals and law students, either as volunteers or in formal clinical programs, the organization of volunteer attorneys through bar associations or other groups, the hiring of lawyers on a part-time consultant basis, and the use of full-time staff attorneys, working either in new prison legal assistance organizations or as part of public defender or legal services offices.

ASSIGNMENT 1.2

Jim Mookely is an attorney who represents fifty inmates on a consolidated case in the state court. The inmates are in fourteen different institutions throughout the state. Jim asks the director of the state prison system to allow his paralegal, Mary Smith, to interview all fifty inmates at a central location. The director responds as follows:

- He refuses to transport the inmates to one location. The inmates would have to be interviewed at the institutions where they are currently living.

- He refuses to let anyone in any institution unless the individual has either a law degree *or* has been through the prison's two-week orientation program totaling twenty hours in the evening at the state capital.

Mary Smith has not taken the orientation program, and it would be very inconvenient for her to do so since she lives 150 miles from the capital. How would *Johnson, Procunier,* or *Bounds* apply to this problem?

---

(3) Agency Representation

A considerable number of administrative agencies will permit a paralegal or other nonattorney to represent clients at the agency. These individuals are usually called agents, practitioners, or representatives. They engage in informal advocacy for their clients at the agency or formal advocacy, including representation at an adversarial administrative hearing. (A proceeding is adversarial if another side appears in the controversy, whether or not the other side is represented. If there is no other side present in the matter before the agency, the proceeding is considered nonadversarial.) Often the issues before the agency are economic, statistical, or scientific, but legal issues are also involved. It is clear that in conducting an adversarial hearing before an agency, the nonattorney can be practicing law in a manner that is remarkably similar to an attorney's representation of a client in court. Our study of this phenomenon will begin with federal administrative agencies, and then we will cover state agencies.

Nonattorney Practice before Federal Administrative Agencies. For federal agencies, Congress has passed a statute, the Administrative Procedure Act, that gives each federal agency the power to decide for itself whether only attorneys can represent clients before it:

> **Administrative Procedure Act 5 U.S.C.A. § 555 (1967).** (b) A person compelled to appear in person before an agency is entitled to be accompanied, represented, and advised by counsel or, if permitted by the agency, by other qualified representative. . . .

When a federal agency decides to use this power to permit nonattorney representation, it can simply allow anyone to act as the agent or representative of another before the agency, or it can establish elaborate qualifications or standards of admission to practice before it. If the agency takes the latter course, its qualifications or standards could include a specialized test to demonstrate competency in the subject matter regulated by the agency, minimum educational or experience requirements, registration or enrollment on the agency's approved roster of representatives, and an agreement to abide by designated ethical rules of practice—a violation of which could result in suspension and "disbarment."

The United States Patent Office has established criteria for individuals to practice (as *registered agents*) before this agency by drafting and filing applications for patents, searching legal opinions on patentability, etc.[8] In 1982, there were approximately 12,000 registered agents who had met this criteria at the agency. Of this number, about 1,900 (or 15.8%) were nonattorneys. At the

---

[8] 37 C.F.R. 1.341–1.348 (1983).

Interstate Commerce Commission, close to 10,000 nonattorney "practitioners" have been authorized to represent clients at ICC proceedings that often involve issues such as rate increases and service extensions for railroads and other transportation carriers.[9] Perhaps the largest use of nonattorneys in federal agencies is at the Internal Revenue Service within the Treasury Department.[10] Any certified public accountant is authorized to practice before the IRS. There are over 190,000 members of the American Institute of Certified Public Accountants, most of whom are not attorneys.[11] In addition, the IRS has enrolled, i.e., registered, thousands of nonattorneys to represent taxpayers at all administrative proceedings within the IRS. These individuals, called *enrolled agents,* charge clients fees for their services. (Once a dispute goes to court, however, an attorney must take over.) To become an enrolled agent, an individual must either pass a written IRS examination or prove that he or she once worked at the IRS for five years interpreting and applying tax laws. In most states there are organizations of enrolled agents; the major national organization is the National Association of Enrolled Agents.

While many federal agencies allow nonattorney representation, it is not true that extensive numbers of nonattorneys actually use the authority they have. A recent study by the American Bar Association of thirty-three federal administrative agencies reached the following conclusion: "We found that the overwhelming majority of agencies studied permit nonlawyer representation in both adversarial and nonadversarial proceedings. However, most of them seem to encounter lay practice very infrequently (in less than 5% of adjudications), while only a few encounter lay practice as often as lawyer practice. Thus, although universally permitted, lay practice before federal agencies rarely occurs." [12]

One agency where nonattorney representation is fairly high (about 15%) is the Social Security Administration. Paralegals are frequently appointed by clients (see Figure 1.3) to represent them before the agency. In 1983, a study compared the success of clients at hearings based upon the kind of representation they received. The results were as follows:

- 59% of clients were successful when represented by attorneys.

- 54.5% of clients were successful when represented by nonattorneys.

- 43.7% of clients were successful when they represented themselves.[13]

Fees can be charged by attorneys or paralegals for these services, but the agency must specifically approve the fee. This is not to say, however, that attorneys and paralegals are treated alike. If an attorney successfully represents a claimant,

---

[9]49 C.F.R. 1103.1–1103.5 (1983).

[10]31 C.F.R. 10.3–10.75 (1983); 20 U.S.C. 1242 (1975).

[11]Rose, *Representation by Non-Lawyers in Federal Administrative Agency Proceedings* (Administrative Conference of the United States, 1984); Vom Baur, *The Practice of Non-Lawyers before Administrative Agencies,* 15 Federal Bar Journal 99 (1955).

[12]ABA Standing Committee on Lawyers' Responsibility for Client Protection, *Report of 1984 Survey of Nonlawyer Practice before Federal Administrative Agencies* (October 19, 1984).

[13]DSS/OHA *Participant Involvement in Request for Hearing Cases for Fiscal 1983,* Table 6, (May, 1984).

FIGURE 1.3 Appointment of Representative

DEPARTMENT OF
HEALTH AND HUMAN SERVICES
SOCIAL SECURITY ADMINISTRATION

NAME (Claimant) (Print or Type) | SOCIAL SECURITY NUMBER

WAGE EARNER (if different) | SOCIAL SECURITY NUMBER

Section I   **APPOINTMENT OF REPRESENTATIVE**

I appoint this individual _____
                                            (Name and Address)

to act as my representative in connection with my claim or asserted right under:

☐ Title II   ☐ Title XVI   ☐ Title IV FMSHA   ☐ Title XVIII
  (RSDI)   (SSI)   (Black Lung)   (Medicare Coverage)

I authorize this individual to make or give any request or notice; to present or elicit evidence; to obtain information; and to receive any notice in connection with my pending claim or asserted right wholly in my stead.

SIGNATURE (Claimant) | ADDRESS

TELEPHONE NUMBER | DATE

(Area Code)

Section II   **ACCEPTANCE OF APPOINTMENT**

I, _____, hereby accept the above appointment. I certify that I have not been suspended or prohibited from practice before the Social Security Administration; that I am not, as a current or former officer or employee of the United States, disqualified from acting as the claimant's representative; and that I will not charge or receive any fee for the representation unless it has been authorized in accordance with the laws and regulations referred to on the reverse side hereof. In the event that I decide not to charge or collect a fee for the representation, I will notify the Social Security Administration. (Completion of Section III satisfies this requirement.)

I am a / an _____
                    (Attorney, union representative, relative, law student, etc.)

SIGNATURE (Representative) | ADDRESS

TELEPHONE NUMBER | DATE

(Area code)

Section III (Optional)   **WAIVER OF FEE**

I waive my right to charge and collect a fee under Section 206 of the Social Security Act, and I release my client (the claimant) from any obligations, contractual or otherwise, which may be owed to me for services I have performed in connection with my client's claim or asserted right.

SIGNATURE (Representative) | DATE

WAIVER OF DIRECT PAYMENT

I ONLY waive my right to direct certification of a fee from the withheld past-due benefits of my client (the claimant). I do NOT, however, waive my right to petition for and be authorized to charge and collect a fee directly from my client.

SIGNATURE (Representative) | DATE

Form SSA-1696-U4 (3-88)   (See Important Information on Reverse)
Destroy prior editions

FILE COPY

---

the agency will deduct up to 25% of the claimant's award, which will be paid directly to the attorney to cover fees. On the other hand, if a paralegal successfully represents a claimant, the paralegal must collect the fee directly from the client, since the Social Security Administration will not deduct anything from the award in such cases.[14]

---

[14]42 U.S.C. 406 (1975).

Nonattorney Practice before State Administrative Agencies.   At the *state* level, there is often a similar system for authorizing nonattorneys to provide representation at many, but by no means all, state administrative agencies. Many states have their own version of the federal Administrative Procedure Act quoted above.

Of course, the organized bar has never been happy with this special authorization given to nonattorneys within federal or state administrative agencies. Since there are state statutes on who can practice law (and often criminal penalties for nonattorneys who practice law in violation of these statutes), how can an administrative agency allow a nonattorney to engage in activity that is clearly the practice of law? The answer to this question is somewhat different for federal and state agencies.

If the agency permitting nonattorney representation is a *federal* agency (for example, the United States Patent Office, the Interstate Commerce Commission, the Internal Revenue Service, and the Social Security Administration), its authorization takes precedence over any *state* laws on the practice of law that would prohibit it. This principle was established in the United States Supreme Court case of *Sperry v. State of Florida ex rel the Florida Bar.*[15] The case involved a nonattorney who was authorized to represent clients before the United States Patent Office. The Florida Bar claimed that the nonattorney was violating the state practice-of-law statute. The Supreme Court ruled that the *Supremacy Clause* of the United States Constitution gave federal laws supremacy over conflicting state laws. The Court also said:

> Examination of the development of practice before the Patent Office and its governmental regulation reveals that: (1) nonlawyers have practiced before the Office from its inception, with the express approval of the Patent Office and to the knowledge of Congress; (2) during prolonged congressional study of unethical practices before the Patent Office, the right of nonlawyer agents to practice before the Office went unquestioned, and there was no suggestion that abuses might be curbed by state regulation; (3) despite protests of the bar, Congress in enacting the Administrative Procedure Act refused to limit the right to practice before the administrative agencies to lawyers; and (4) the Patent Office has defended the value of nonlawyer practitioners while taking steps to protect the interests which a State has in prohibiting unauthorized practice of law. We find implicit in this history congressional (and administrative) recognition that registration in the Patent Office confers a right to practice before the Office without regard to whether the State within which the practice is conducted would otherwise prohibit such conduct.
>
> Moreover, the extent to which specialized lay practitioners should be allowed to practice before some 40-odd federal administrative agencies, including the Patent Office, received continuing attention both in and out of Congress during the period prior to 1952. The Attorney General's Committee on Administrative Procedure which, in 1941, studied the need for procedural reform in the administrative agencies, reported that "[e]specially among lawyers' organizations there has been manifest a sentiment in recent years that only members of the bar should be admitted to practice before administrative agencies. The Com-

---

[15]373 U.S. 379, 83 S.Ct. 1322, 10 L.Ed.2d 428 (1963).

mittee doubts that a sweeping interdiction of nonlawyer practitioners would be wise. . . ."

••••••••••••••

Suppose, however, that a *state* agency permits nonattorney representation. Can this be challenged by the bar? The issue may depend on who has the *power* to regulate the practice of law in a particular state. If the state legislature has this power, then the agency authorization of nonattorney representation is valid, since the agency is under the jurisdiction and control of the legislature. So long as the nonattorney representation is based on a statute of the legislature, it is valid. If, however, the state judiciary has the power to control the practice of law in a state, then the courts may be able to invalidate any nonattorney representation that is authorized by the agency.

Nonattorneys who have the authority to provide representation at an administrative agency may do so as independent paralegals, or as full-time employees of attorneys. The following ethical opinion from California involves the latter—a paralegal employee of a law firm. The opinion discusses some of the issues that are involved when the law firm wants its paralegal to use the special authorization for nonattorney representation at a particular administrative agency—the Worker's Compensation Appeals Board. Later in Chapter 2 we will examine some of the ethical issues involved in this opinion in greater depth.

Formal Opinion 1988–103
State Bar Committee on
Professional Responsibility and Conduct
California

Issue

May a law firm, having advised its clients of its intention to do so, delegate authority to a paralegal employee to make appearances at Workers' Compensation Appeals Board hearings and to file petitions, motions, or other material?

Digest

A law firm may delegate such authority, provided that the paralegal employee is adequately supervised.

Authorities Interpreted

Rules 3-101, 3-103 and 6-101 of the Rules of Professional Conduct of the State Bar of California.

* * *

Issue

A client has contracted for the services of a law firm for representation in a matter pending before the Workers' Compensation Appeals Board (hereinafter "WCAB"). The law firm employs and intends to utilize the services of the paralegal in connection with the proceedings pending before the WCAB to make appearances, file petitions and present motions.

The client has consented to the law firm utilizing the services of the paralegal, after being informed as to the potential consequences of representation by a person of presumably lesser qualification and skill than may be reasonably expected of an attorney. In addition, the status of the employee as a paralegal rather than an attorney will be fully disclosed at all proceedings at which the paralegal appears and on all documents which the paralegal prepares.

Discussion

It is unlawful for any person to practice law in this state without active membership in the State Bar of California. (Bus. & Prof. Code, ¶6125) The practice of law includes the performing of services in any matter pending in a court or administrative proceeding throughout its various stages, as well as the rendering of legal advice and counsel in the preparation of legal instruments and contracts by which legal rights are secured. (cf. *Smallberg v. State bar* (1931) 212 Cal. 113.)

It has been held that the representation of claimants before the Industrial Accident Commission (predecessor to the WCAB) constitutes the performance of legal services. (*Bland v. Reed* (1968) 261 Cal.App.2d 445, 448.) However, the representation by a nonattorney of an applicant before the WCAB is expressly authorized by Labor Code 5501 and 5700 as follows:

The application may be filed with the appeals board by any party in interest, his attorney, or other representative authorized in writing . . . . Either party may be present at any hearing, in person, by attorney, or by any other agent, and may present testimony pertinent under the pleading.

Thus, the principal issue is whether an attorney may hire a nonattorney to engage in conduct on behalf of the attorney's client which the employee is authorized to perform independently, but which, if performed by the attorney, would constitute the practice of law.

It is the opinion of the Committee that because the client has been informed about and has consented to the involvement of the paralegal, no violation occurs with respect to dishonesty or deceit. (See Bus. & Prof. Code, ¶6106, 6128, subd.(a).) In addition, if the status of the employee as a paralegal rather than attorney is fully disclosed at all proceedings at which the paralegal appears and on all documents which the paralegal prepares, no violation of the prohibition on an attorney lending his or her name to be used as an attorney by a person not licensed to practice law will occur. (See Bus. & Prof. Code, ¶6105.)

In addition, because Labor Code sections 5501 and 5570 expressly authorize nonattorneys to represent applicants before the WCAB, the proposed arrangements would not constitute a violation of Rule of Professional Conduct 3-101(A), which provides as follows:

A member of the State Bar shall not aid any person, association, or corporation in the *unauthorized* practice of law. (Emphasis added.)

Further, there is no indication that the facts presented that the relationship between the paralegal and the law firm would constitute a partnership in violation of Rule of Professional Conduct 3-103, which provides as follows:

A member of the State Bar shall not form a partnership with a person not licensed to practice law if any of the activities of the partnership consist of the practice of law.

The pivotal consideration is that the client contracted for the services of the law firm, rather than a paralegal, for representation. However, since the safeguards mentioned above have been taken to avoid misleading or deceiving the client or any one else regarding the status of the paralegal, the Committee finds no ethical insufficiency inherent in the participation of paralegals.

A lawyer or law firm contemplating entering into such an arrangement should remember that an attorney stands in a fiduciary relationship with the client. (*Krusesky v. Baugh* (1982) 138 Cal.App.3d 562, 567.) When acting as a fiduciary, the law imposes upon a member the strictest duty of prudent conduct as well as an obligation to perform his or her duties to the best of the attorney's ability. (*Clark v. State Bar* (1952) 39 Cal.2d 161, 167; and cf. Bus. & Prof. Code, ¶6067; Rule of Professional Conduct 6-101(A).) However, an attorney does not have to bear the entire burden of attending to every detail of the practice, but may be justified in relying to some extent on nonattorney employees. (*Moore v. State Bar* (1964) 62 Cal.2d 74, 80; *Vaughn v. State Bar* (1972) 6 Cal.3d 847, 857.)

The attorney who delegates responsibilities to his or her employees must keep in mind that he or she, as the attorney, has the duty to adequately supervise the employee. In fact, the attorney will be subject to discipline if the lawyer fails to adequately supervise the employee. (*Chefsky v. State Bar* (1984) 36 Cal.3d 116, 123; *Palomo v. State bar* (1984) 36 Cal.3d 785; *Gassman v. State Bar* (1976) 18 Cal.3d 125.)

What constitutes adequate supervision will, of course, depend on a number of factors, including, but not limited to, the complexity of the client matter, the level of experience of the paralegal and the facts of the particular case.

It is the opinion of the Committee that, even though the paralegal will be providing substantive legal services to the client, adequate supervision under these unique facts does not require the attorney to ensure that the paralegal performs the services in accordance with the level of competence that would be expected of the attorney under rule 6-101.

So long as the paralegal is adequately supervised and the law firm does not mislead the client that the services will be performed in accordance with the attorney level of competence or that an attorney will be handling the matter, the Committee does not believe the attorney would be in violation of the Rules of Professional Conduct.

This opinion is issued by the Standing Committee on Professional Responsibility and Conduct of the State Bar of California. It is advisory only. It is not binding upon the courts, the State Bar of California, its Board of Governors, or any persons or tribunals charged with regulatory responsibility or any member of the State Bar.

■ ASSIGNMENT 1.3

Make a list of every state and local administrative agency in your state. Have a class discussion in which students identify as many state and local agencies as they can. Then divide the total number of agencies by the number of students in the class so that each student will be assigned the same number of agencies. For your agencies, find out whether nonattorneys can represent citizens. What are the requirements, if any, to provide this representation informally (e.g., calling or writing the agency on behalf of someone else) or formally (e.g., representing someone else at an agency hearing)? Check your state statutes. Check the regulations of the agency. If possible, call the agency to ask what its policy is and whether it can refer you to any statutes or regulations on the policy.

■ ASSIGNMENT 1.4

Paul is a nonattorney who works at the Quaker Draft Counseling Center. One of the clients of the center is Dan Diamond. Paul says the following to Mr. Diamond:

> You don't have anything to worry about. The law says that you cannot be drafted until you have had an administrative hearing on your case. I will represent you at that hearing. If you are drafted before that hearing, I will immediately draft a habeas corpus petition that can be filed at the United States District Court.

Any problems with Paul's conduct?

■ Section C. Licensing of Paralegals

Many occupations (electricians, brokers, nurses, etc.) are licensed by the government. To date, *no* federal, state, or local government has imposed a licensing requirement on traditional paralegals. Proposals for licensing have been made in some legislatures, but none has been enacted into law. For paralegals who work under the supervision of attorneys, licensing is arguably unnecessary, since the public is protected by this supervision. But what about the relatively small number of independent paralegals who work directly with the public without attorney supervision? Many have argued that there *is* a need to license them in order to protect the public. The phrase *limited licensing* refers to a government authorization to perform a designated number of activities that are now part of the attorney monopoly. While no limited licensing proposal has yet been enacted into law, the likelihood of passage is very real in spite of substantial attorney opposition. Before covering limited licensing, let's examine efforts to enact broad-based licensing schemes covering all activities of all paralegals.

Broad-Based Licensing

A number of states have proposed legislation to license all paralegals. Many of these proposals confuse the word *certification* with *licensure*. Certification is usually a statement by a *non*governmental organization that a person has met certain qualifications. Licensure, on the other hand, is a permission or authorization *by a government* to engage in a certain activity.

In 1977, for example, the Michigan legislature gave serious consideration to passing the Legal Assistant Act to "regulate the practice of legal assistants." Under this proposal, a nine-member commission would be created to establish the requirements for the "certification" of legal assistants. Even though the proposal uses the word *certification*, it was a licensure program, since it would establish the qualifications to engage in a particular occupation. If this legislation had been enacted, a person could not be a legal assistant in Michigan without passing a statewide examination and having the educational credentials identified by the commission.

This plan was *not* adopted in Michigan. Such licensing schemes are usually vigorously opposed by paralegal associations as being premature, unnecessary, and unduly restrictive. A commonly voiced fear is that the license might limit what paralegals are now authorized to do without a license, and that some competent paralegals who now work in law offices might not fit within rigid eligibility criteria that might be established for the license. The organized bar is also opposed to broad-based licensing. The following excerpts from bar association reports give some of the reasons why:

North Carolina Bar, *Report of Special Committee on Paralegals* 3 (1980)
Several states have considered the possibility of adopting a licensing statute for paralegals, but none has done so. Licensing itself is subject to great public and legislative concern at present. So long as the work accomplished by non-lawyers for lawyers is properly supervised and reviewed by a licensed and responsible attorney, there would seem to be no need for a further echelon of licensing for the public's protection. Furthermore, licensing might be more dangerous than helpful to the public. The apparent stamp of approval of a license possibly could give the impression to the public that a person having such a license is qualified to deal directly with and give legal advice to the public. Although the Committee would not attempt to close the door on licensing of paralegals in the future if circumstances change and if, for example, the use of independent, non-lawyer employee paralegals were to become widespread, present conditions, at least, do not call for any program of licensing for paralegals.

Illinois State Bar Association, *Report on the Joint Study Committee on Attorney Assistants* 6 (6/21/77)
Our Joint Committee arose because there was a suggestion that attorney assistants be licensed. After due consideration we recommend no program of licensure or certification of attorney assistants or other lay personnel.

We are opposed to licensure because the standards on which licensure are to be based are difficult or impossible to formulate. Furthermore, we have started with a premise that precedes this conclusion; to wit: no delegation of any task to an attorney assistant shall diminish the responsibility of the attorney for the services rendered. We believe that any program which purports to say who is "licensed" and who is "not licensed" creates a standard which will diminish the attorney's responsibility. It furthermore may exclude from useful and desirable employment people who, under the supervision and control of an attorney, may perform useful tasks but who may not meet the standards of licensure involved.

We are further opposed to licensure because of the danger that it poses to the public. If a group of persons appears to be authorized to perform tasks directly for the public, without the intervening control of an attorney, it would be humanly inevitable that many of the licensed persons would try to deal directly with the public. We think these risks would be substantially increased by licensure.

■ ASSIGNMENT 1.5

How would you characterize the opposition to licensure expressed in the above excerpts from the bar reports? Do you think there is a conflict of interest in attorneys making these judgments about paralegal control? Explain.

Limited Licensing

As we saw earlier, some independent, or freelance, paralegals have their own businesses, through which they sell their services to attorneys. A smaller number work directly for the public without attorney supervision. For example, a paralegal might sell divorce forms and type them for clients. This is not the illegal practice of law, so long as no legal advice is given in the process. One of the reasons Rosemary Furman got into trouble was that she gave such advice along with the forms she typed, and hence was charged with the unauthorized practice of law by the Florida bar.

Some have argued that the law that led to the prosecution of people like Rosemary Furman should be changed. Why not grant them a limited license (sometimes called a specialty license) to practice law? Remarkably, a suggestion to this effect was actually made by a Commission of the American Bar Association! The ABA does not favor broad-based licensing of all paralegals. In a 1986 report, however, an ABA Commission on Professionalism cautiously suggested—on page 52 of the report—that there be "limited licensing of paralegals" and "paraprofessionals" to perform certain functions such as handling some real estate closings, drafting simple wills, and performing certain tax work. The report argued that such a proposal could help reduce the cost of legal services:

No doubt, many wills and real estate closings require the services of a lawyer. However, it can no longer be claimed that lawyers have the exclusive possession of the esoteric knowledge required and are therefore the only ones able to advise clients on any matter concerning the law.[16]

This remarkable proposal caused quite a stir. Many refer to the controversy it created as the "page 52 debate." For years, many attorneys were suspicious of paralegalism because of a fear that paralegals might eventually be licensed and compete with attorneys. Then along comes a report of an ABA Commission that recommends licensing! Yet it must be remembered that neither the report nor the Commission speaks for the entire ABA. In fact, the proposal in the report "drew the ire" of other ABA members *and is unlikely to be given serious consideration by the ABA as a whole any time soon.* This will not, however, prevent continued suggestions in favor of some form of licensing—even from within segments of the ABA itself.

Before paralegals had time to recover from the drama of the "page 52 debate," another shock wave arrived. In 1989, the State Bar of California stated that there was "an overwhelming unmet need" for better access to legal services, and created a *Commission on Legal Technicians* to study whether independent paralegals can help meet this need. Its answer was *yes!* The Commission recommended that the California Supreme Court adopt a Rule of Court authorizing nonattorneys to engage in the practice of law in the following three areas: bankruptcy law, family law, and landlord-tenant law. (Other areas might be added later.) As "licensed independent paralegals," they would not be required to have attorney supervision. They could open an office and sell their services directly to the public. In effect, the state's rules on the unauthorized practice of law would be abolished for those services. Court representation, however, would not be included. If a client needed to go to court, an attorney would have to be hired. This "limited license" program would be administered by the California State Department of Consumer Affairs with help from an Advisory Committee consisting of two independent paralegals, one attorney, and four members of the public who are not independent paralegals or attorneys.

Here are some of the other features of the proposal:

- Applicants for the license must be at least 18 years of age.
- Applicants must submit fingerprints.
- Applicants must take and pass a two-part written examination: (1) a general knowledge examination, including an ethics section, and (2) a specialty exam in an area of practice. In order to be licensed, an applicant must take and pass both the general and specialty examinations within a two-year period.
- Applicants must meet minimum levels of education and/or experience, as recommended by the Advisory Committee. However, as of the date of implementation of the enabling legislation, persons who have practiced in the field for two years should have the right to take the examination without additional entry requirements. (The last sentence constitutes the grandfathering provision of the proposal.)

---

[16]*In the Spirit of Public Service: A Blueprint for Rekindling of Lawyer Professionalism*, 52 (ABA, Comm'n on Professionalism, 1986).

- For license renewal, licensees must fulfill annual continuing education requirements.
- Complaints and investigations would be handled by the Department of Consumer Affairs' centralized services.
- A client security fund would be established to provide compensation to victims of independent paralegal thefts. The initial annual fee would be $25.00 per licensee and the Advisory Committee would develop recommended guidelines for disbursement, including an appropriate cap to be placed on each claim paid by the fund.
- Standards for denial of licensure and for discipline would be established.
- The Supreme Court would approve a code of professional conduct for licensed independent paralegals.

The reaction among paralegals to this proposal has been surprisingly mixed. The two national paralegal associations—the National Association of Legal Assistants (NALA) and the National Federation of Paralegal Associations (NFPA)—have taken very different positions. As we will see later, this is not the first time that these two giants have clashed over the issue of regulating paralegals.

The National Association of Legal Assistants is *against* the California proposal for a number of reasons. First, the proposal does not provide guidelines to determine the kinds of bankruptcy, family law, or landlord-tenant cases an independent paralegal is competent to handle. Many of these cases are complex at the outset or become complex as they unfold. Such cases require the attention of an attorney. Independent paralegals are not in the best position to determine

Demonstration in front of the California State Bar Association on the issue of limited licensing.

when a case is beyond their skills. Second, the licensing of independent paralegals could eventually lead to a climate in which traditional paralegals and legal
assistants who work for attorneys would have to become licensed. Third, the
licensing of independent paralegals will lead to open warfare with attorneys and
to public disillusionment with the legal system. "For all practical purposes, . . ."
the independent paralegals covered by the California proposal ". . . will become
direct and fierce competitors of . . . lawyers who will not look kindly upon these
untrained 'mini-lawyers.' It is only a matter of time . . . [until] the inevitable
will occur; the public will have a bad experience working with one of these
untrained, inadequately educated non-lawyers and it will become further disil-
lusioned with the legal system. Thus the results will further blacken the public's
image of lawyers and the law profession." [17] Finally, NALA objects to the use
of the word *paralegal* for anyone who does not work under the supervision of
an attorney.

The National Federation of Paralegal Associations, on the other hand, has
taken a different approach. While not directly endorsing or opposing the California proposal, the NFPA has laid out the conditions under which it will support "regulation of paralegals who deliver legal services directly to the public."
The conditions are as follows:

- the regulation expands the utilization of paralegals to deliver cost-efficient
  legal services,
- there is a demonstrated public need,
- the regulation includes minimum criteria for performing independent paralegal services such as experience under the supervision of an attorney or of a
  licensed paralegal,
- the paralegals pass a performance-based proficiency examination.

Applying these conditions to the California proposal, the NFPA would probably favor the proposal, although, as indicated, no formal position has been
taken on it.

As revolutionary as this proposal is, there is another proposal in California
from *HALT (Help Abolish Legal Tyranny)* that is even more radical. HALT is
a national legal consumer group. It has proposed that nonattorneys be allowed
to practice law in fourteen specialty areas.[18] A Board of Legal Technicians in
the Department of Consumer Affairs would decide which of these specialty
areas require registration (involving little more than providing information
about yourself), and which require licensing (involving passing an
examination).

Other states are also considering proposals for limited licensing. In Illinois,
for example, an Independent Paralegal Licensing Act was introduced in the leg-

---

[17]National Ass'n of Legal Assistants, *Statement to . . . State Bar of California* (1991).

[18]The areas are: immigration law, family law, housing law, public benefits law, litigation support
law, conservatorship and guardianship law, real estate law, liability law, estate administration law,
consumer law, corporate/business law, intellectual property law, estate planning law, bankruptcy
law. (Under the HALT proposal, other specialty areas might be added later.)

islature. The origin of this plan is quite interesting. A paralegal student designed a regulation plan as part of a class assignment. When this student went to work for an Illinois state legislator, the plan eventually became the basis of the licensing plan that was actually introduced in the legislature!

As you might expect, many attorneys have been intensely opposed to any form of limited licensing. A former president of the State Bar of California said, "It's like letting nurses do brain surgery." Here are some other comments from attorneys: "This is the worst thing since the plague!" They think "just about everybody should be able to practice law. I guess they think everybody should be able to slice open a belly and remove an appendix." "I cannot think of anything that would be more injurious to the public." This is an idea "whose time has not yet come." And "this is potentially the most fractious and controversial issue ever confronted" by the bar association. So far, such opposition has been successful since none of the limited license proposals have been enacted into law.

A much more modest form of limited licensing, however, has in fact been enacted into law in the state of Washington. A totally new category of worker has been created in the real estate industry, the *Limited Practice Officer* (LPO), also referred to as a Closing Certified Officer. This individual is a nonattorney with the authority "to select, prepare and complete legal documents incident to the closing of real estate and personal property transactions." [19] The State Supreme Court has created a Limited Practice Board to which applicants apply for "admission" to become an LPO. (See Figure 1.4.) The Board approves the form of the documents that the LPO can "select, prepare, and complete" in a closing, e.g., deeds, promissory notes, guaranties, deeds of trust, reconveyances, mortgages, satisfactions, security agreements, releases, Uniform Commercial Code documents, assignments, contracts, real estate excise tax affidavits, and bills of sale. Like the system for regulating attorneys, an LPO applicant must demonstrate "good moral character" and pass a combined essay and multiple-choice examination on the law. Once certified, LPOs can be disciplined for violating their authority. At present, there are no educational requirements to become an LPO, although such requirements are anticipated. LPOs must provide proof of financial responsibility by such means as purchasing a liability insurance policy ("errors and omissions insurance coverage") or showing that coverage exists under a bond taken out by their employer.

■ ASSIGNMENT 1.6

(a) Compare the LPO program in Washington with the two proposals for limited licensing in California.

(b) Do you agree with NALA's position on limited licensing, or that of NFPA? Why?

What are the chances of a licensing requirement becoming law? Even though proposals for broad-based licensing continue to appear, passage is un-

---

[19]Washington Supreme Court Rule 12(a).

FIGURE 1.4   Application for Admission to Limited Practice as a Limited Practice Officer in the State of Washington under the Admission to Practice Rule 12

To the Washington State Limited Practice Board:

I hereby apply for a limited license to practice law in the State of Washington as a limited practice officer under the Admission to Practice Rule 12.

Applicant's Name in Full
_____
Last   First   Middle

Applicant's Date of Birth
_____
Month   Day   Year

Applicant's Business Address _____
Address

_____
City   State   Zip Code

Applicant's Business Phone   ( )_____
Area Code   Number

Applicant's Home Address   _____
Address

_____
City   State   Zip Code

Applicant's Home Phone   ( )_____
Area Code   Number

Applicant's Social Security Number _____

Please list:
Employers/Supervisors	**From**	**To**	**Telephone Number**
(Past five years) Attach separate sheet if needed.			

---

likely in view of widespread opposition from attorneys and paralegals. Limited licensing, on the other hand, may eventually become a reality, in spite of the position of NALA. The LPO program in Washington represents a small crack in the door. Will current proposals, such as those under serious consideration in California and Illinois, eventually kick the door through?

It is becoming increasingly difficult for attorneys to oppose limited licensing on the basis of the need to protect the public. A system now exists for identifying and punishing unscrupulous and incompetent attorneys; a similar system could be designed to regulate independent paralegals. And, of course, no one is proposing the equivalent of allowing nondoctors to perform brain surgery. The proposals for limited licensing simply try to identify services that do not require all of the skills of an attorney.

Perhaps the most compelling argument for limited licensing is the fact that attorneys have priced themselves out of the market. Recent studies continue to document a vast unmet need for legal services in our society. Attorneys, however, point to the reforms that have made legal services more accessible at a

FIGURE 1.5   Reforms in the Practice of Law

- *Pro bono work.* Many law firms and corporations give their attorneys time off to provide free legal services to the poor.

- *Simplified forms.* Bar associations have helped create legal forms that are relatively easy for the public to use without the assistance of an attorney.

- *Prepaid legal services.* Some companies and unions have developed programs of legal insurance under which participants pay a set amount each month for designated legal services that might be needed while the participant is in the program.

- *Attorney advertising.* Advertising has arguably made the public more aware of legal services and more inclined to use such services.

- *Publicly funded legal services.* The bar associations have consistently supported increased funding by the government for organizations that provide free legal services to the poor.

- *Traditional paralegals.* The increased use of paralegals by attorneys can lead to lower client costs since the billing rate for paralegal time is considerably lower than the billing rate for most attorneys.

lower cost. See Figure 1.5. Yet, in spite of these reforms and in spite of the dramatic increase in the number of attorneys coming out of our law schools, the unmet need for legal services among the poor and middle class continues to grow. Here, for example, are some of the conclusions of legal-needs studies covering two large states:

> Each year in Illinois, by conservative estimates, 300,000 low-income families face approximately 1,000,000 civil legal problems for which they do not receive legal help.[20]

> The poor in New York face nearly 3,000,000 civil legal problems per year without legal help. Not more than 14% of their overall need for legal assistance is being met.[21]

The statistics are even more alarming if the legal needs of the middle class are included. In the light of these numbers, critics are calling for drastic reform.

In areas such as divorce and bankruptcy, an increasingly large underground network of nonattorneys are providing low-cost legal services to citizens. Why not bring these nonattorneys out into the open? Subject them to testing and other license requirements to help ensure competence and honesty. While many attorneys see this cure as worse than the disease, others are more receptive to the idea.

Each state must make its own determination of whether limited licensing should be adopted. It is quite possible that one or two states will take the plunge in the near future and enact limited licensing. Will your state do so? Keep in mind that even if it does, it will probably affect very *few* paralegals in your state. The likelihood is that the requirement will apply only to those paralegals who do not work for attorneys. This means that the vast majority of paralegals in the state who work for attorneys would continue as they are—with no license

---

[20]Illinois State Bar Association and Chicago Bar Association, *Illinois Legal Needs Study* 5 (1989).
[21]New York State Bar Association, *New York Legal Needs Study: Draft Final Report*, 196 (1989).

requirement. It is true that some paralegals favor limited licensing for traditional paralegals who work under the supervision of attorneys in order to expand what they are allowed to do for attorneys. But any movement toward such
expansion is considerably weaker than the current momentum toward licensing
independents.

. . . .

When a licensing proposal—or a proposal for any kind of paralegal regulation—comes before the legislature, here are some of the steps that should be
taken immediately:

What to Do When the Legislature Proposes Legislation to Regulate Paralegals

1. Obtain a copy of the proposed legislation or bill as soon as possible. If you
   know the name of the legislator sponsoring the bill, write or call him or her
   directly. Otherwise contact the office of the Speaker of the House, Speaker
   of the Assembly, President of the Senate, etc. Ask how you can locate the
   proposed bill.

2. Find out the exact technical status of the bill. Has it been formally
   introduced? Has it been assigned to a committee? What is the next
   scheduled formal event on the bill?

3. Immediately inform the sponsoring legislator(s) and the relevant
   committee(s) that you want an opportunity to comment on the bill. Find
   out if hearings are going to be scheduled on the bill. Make known your
   interest in participating in such hearings. Your goal is to slow the process
   down so that the bill is not rushed into enactment. Be particularly alert to
   the possibility that the paralegal bill may be buried in proposed legislation
   on a large number of related or unrelated topics. Again, there is a real
   danger that the bill will get through relatively unnoticed.

4. Determine why the paralegal bill is being proposed. What is the *public*
   reason given for the proposal of the bill? More important, what is the
   underlying *real* reason for the proposal? Perhaps some special interest or
   small group (real estate agents, for instance) is seeking a special privilege in
   a law-related field. Yet the language of the bill they are proposing may be
   so broad that paralegals will be adversely affected.

5. Alert your local paralegal association. It needs to be mobilized in order to
   express an organized position on the bill. Contact the major national
   paralegal associations: NFPA and NALA (see Appendix D). Do they know
   about the proposed legislation? Have they taken a position? They need to
   be activated.

6. If your local bar association has a paralegal committee, seek its support.

7. Launch a letter-writing campaign. Make sure that large numbers of
   paralegals in the area know about the bill and know how to express their
   opinion to the legislature.

8. Ask local paralegal schools to take a position.

. . . .

Keep in mind that we are talking about mandatory *licensing* by the state, not voluntary *certification* by entities such as paralegal associations. The certification debate will be covered later in the chapter.

■ ASSIGNMENT 1.7

(a) Do you favor broad-based licensing for every paralegal? Limited licensing? Will licensing advance or restrict the development of paralegalism?

(b) If all attorneys in the country drastically cut their fees, would there be a need for paralegal licensing?

(c) There are some tasks that even paralegals who work for attorneys cannot perform, such as taking the deposition of a witness. Should there be limited licensing to authorize such tasks?

■ ASSIGNMENT 1.8

Evaluate the following observation: "The emerging professions and the more established professions have frequently sought greater regulation of their occupational group. They are often motivated, despite the obligatory language on protection of the public interest, to do so in efforts to establish their 'territorial imperative' or to establish barriers to entry into the profession and thereby enhance their economic self-interest." Sapadin, *A Comparison of the Growth and Development of the Physician Assistant and the Legal Assistant,* in Journal of the American Association for Paralegal Education: Retrospective 1983, 142 (1983).

■ Section D. Bar Association Control of Paralegal Education

Since the early 1970s, the American Bar Association has been "approving" paralegal training programs after a recommendation is made by its standing Committee on Legal Assistants, all of whose members are attorneys. There is no requirement that a school be ABA-approved in order to train paralegals. In fact, most training programs are not so approved. The approval process is voluntary, and the majority of programs have decided *not* to apply for approval. A program must meet state government accreditation standards, but it does not have to seek the approval of the ABA or of any other bar association.

The ABA approval process has been controversial from its inception. Those who oppose total attorney control of paralegalism feel that the bar associations are inappropriate mechanisms to regulate training institutions. Since a major objective of attorneys is to increase their profits by employing paralegals, critics argue that it is a conflict of interest for attorneys to control the field totally. When regulatory decisions must be made on matters such as the approval of schools, whose interest would the attorneys be protecting in making these decisions? The interest of the paralegals? The interest of the public? Or the profit interest of the attorney-regulators?

The ABA has been somewhat sensitive to this criticism, and, as we will see, at one time considered withdrawing from the approval process. In recent years, challenges have been made to the monopoly that bar associations exercise over the practice of law. In 1975, the United States Supreme Court sent shock waves throughout the legal profession when the Court ruled that attorneys were no longer exempt from the *antitrust* laws, and that some minimum fee schedules are a violation of these laws.[22] In 1979, an antitrust charge was brought against the ABA on the ground that its paralegal-school approval process was designed to eliminate competition from, and restrict entry into, the market for recruitment, training, and placement of paralegals. The ABA won this case.[23] Despite the victory, the ABA remains vulnerable to future challenge.

Note that the ABA uses the word *approval* rather than accreditation in describing its process of exercising control over educational institutions. Yet the process meets the accepted definition of accreditation presented in Figure 1.1 at the beginning of this chapter. The use of the more euphemistic word *approval* may be an indication that the ABA is itself not sure whether it should be in the business of regulating paralegal education. Indeed, in 1981, the House of Delegates of the ABA instructed its Committee on Legal Assistants to terminate ABA involvement in the approval process. However, some schools that had already received approval objected. As a result, the Committee proposed and the House of Delegates accepted an alternative system of approving schools.

The alternative was the creation of an ABA Approval Commission to implement the approval process. The final decision on approval of individual schools is still left in the hands of the ABA. The Commission makes its recommendations on approval to the Committee on Legal Assistants, which in turn makes it recommendations to the House of Delegates of the ABA. The major difference between the Committee and the Commission is that the latter must contain nonattorney members. There are eleven members of the Commission, all of whom are appointed by the president of the ABA on advice from the Committee:

- Three attorneys (one of whom has taught in a paralegal program)
- One attorney who represents the ABA Committee on Legal Assistants
- One paralegal nominated by the National Federation of Paralegal Associations (NFPA)
- One paralegal nominated by the National Association of Legal Assistants (NALA)
- Two representatives nominated by the American Association for Paralegal Education (AAfPE)
- One representative nominated by the Association of Legal Administrators (ALA)
- One nonlegal educator
- One representative of the general public

---

[22]Goldfarb v. Virginia State Bar, 421 U.S. 773 (1975).

[23]*Paralegal Institute, Inc. v. American Bar Association*, 475 F. Supp. 1123 (E.D.N.Y. 1979).

The ABA does not view the Commission as a permanent institution. The plan is to phase it out over a period of years and to replace it with an *independent* accrediting body that is equally broad based. It is unclear, however, whether this replacement is feasible. It depends on the willingness of paralegal schools to submit themselves to this still-voluntary approval process. Furthermore, an independent body would be very expensive to run. Its revenues would come from fees paid by the schools that apply for approval and for renewals of approval. If large numbers of schools continue to bypass a national accrediting or approval entity, the process will lose both the political and financial support it needs. Since there is no realistic hope that an independent accrediting body will be formed, the ABA will probably continue its approval program indefinitely.

■ ASSIGNMENT 1.9

Who should control accreditation? Are there too many attorneys on the ABA Approval Commission? Too few paralegals? Could there be too many paralegals on such a body? Do you favor an independent accrediting entity? Who should run it? Should it be voluntary?

Only one thing is sure: change is on the horizon. The legal profession can no longer feel secure in its privileged position, as the following speech demonstrates.

The Legal Profession:
A Bow to the Past—a Glimpse of the Future
by J. Sims

[Mr. Sims was the Deputy Assistant Attorney General in the Antitrust Division of the United States Department of Justice. The following are excerpts from a speech he delivered on February 11, 1977, before a conference of the Federation of Insurance Counsel in Arizona.]

Today, in Los Angeles, legal services are being advertised on television. That fact alone gives us some idea of how much change has come to the legal profession in the last few years.

That change has not always come easy, but the fact that it has come so far, so fast, tells us quite a bit about what will happen in the future. We lawyers as a group have grumbled and argued, fought and yelled, struggled and been confused—but there are now lawyers advertising on television. Even a casual observer cannot fail to appreciate the significance of this change.

Competition, slowly but surely, is coming to the legal profession. This opening of traditional doors, the breaking of traditional barriers is the result of many forces—the number of new lawyers, the awakening of consumerism, the growing realization that the complexity of our society requires legal assistance in more and more areas. But one contributing factor has been antitrust litigation and the Department of Justice. . . .

[T]he Supreme Court fired the shot heard 'round the bar [o]n June 16, 1975. [I]n a unanimous decision [Goldfarb v. Virginia State Bar, 421 U.S. 773 (1975)], the Court held that the minimum fee schedule challenged by the Goldfarbs violated Section 1 of the Sherman Act. This decision broke the dam and released the flood of change that we see engulfing the profession today. For better or worse, the Goldfarbs had set in motion a series of events that were to change the character of the legal profession forever.

The Court decided several things in *Goldfarb*, but the most important was that the legal profession was subject to the antitrust laws—there was no "professional exemption." The response to *Goldfarb* was fascinating. A large number of private suits were filed challenging various aspects of bar regulation. . . .

[An] area sure to be controversial in the future is unauthorized practice. There is already at least one antitrust challenge, against the Virginia State Bar, seeking to prohibit the bar from promulgating unauthorized practice opinions. This case, which involves title insurance, is a direct challenge to the extraordinary power that the legal profession now has—in most states—to define the limits of its own monopoly. It would be strange indeed for a state to hand over to, say its steel industry, not only the power to regulate entry into the industry and the conduct of those within it, but also the power to define what the industry was. In many states, that is exactly the power the organized bar now has, and that power is being challenged as inconsistent with the antitrust laws.

The heart of this challenge is that lawyers shouldn't be deciding what is the practice of law—defining the scope of the legal monopoly. The papers filed in that case . . . indicate that the objection is not to such a decision being made; the objection is to the State's delegation of that power to the profession.

In fact, of course, the principle behind this lawsuit could be expanded not only to other subject matter areas, but also to arrangements between the organized bar and other professions which have as their basic result the division of commercial responsibilities.

For example, the American Bar Association has entered into "statements of principles" with respect to the practice of law with a variety of other professions and occupations ranging from accountants to claim adjusters, publishers, social workers, and even professional engineers [page 5]. These documents generally set forth the joint views of the professions as to which activities fall within the practice of law and which activities are proper for members of the other profession. They nearly all provide that each profession will advise its clients to seek out members of the other profession in appropriate circumstances.

As a general rule, two competitors may not agree with each other to allocate markets, or bids, or even functions; if they do, they violate the antitrust laws. At the least, this traditional antitrust principle raises some questions about the legal effect of such "statements of principles."

[T]he efforts of the bar to limit the scope of paralegal responsibilities and, in some jurisdictions, to seek a certification requirement for paralegals are seen by many as simply another effort to preserve and protect the legal services monopoly. Many believe that non-lawyers could perform many tasks reserved today for people with law degrees.

ASSIGNMENT 1.10

What are the implications of Mr. Sims' remarks on the role of bar associations in regulating paralegal education?

Section E. Should Paralegals Become Part of Bar Associations?

At present, no paralegals are full members of any bar associations. In 1981, however, the State Bar of Texas created a Legal Assistant Division of the bar. Its unique aspect is that all of its regular members *must* be paralegals. Hence, while paralegals cannot become members of the bar association, they can become members of a Division of the bar association. The Division is not a mere advisory committee of the bar; it is part of the bar association itself, which means that it is under the ultimate control of the Board of Directors of the State Bar of Texas.

The qualifications for membership in the Division are as follows:

- The applicant must *not* be a Texas attorney.
- The applicant must perform "substantial paralegal services in rendering direct assistance to an attorney." (Someone who does occasional paralegal work would not qualify.)
- The applicant's supervising attorney must certify that the applicant performs substantial paralegal services for that attorney.

Members pay annual dues of $25.

The bylaws of the Division state its purpose as follows: "to enhance legal assistants' participation in the administration of justice, professional responsibility and public service in cooperation with the State Bar of Texas." All the officers of the Division are paralegals elected by the membership. The budget of the Division, however, must be approved by the State Bar of Texas.

The Division has been very popular among paralegals in Texas; by the middle of 1990, almost 2,000 paralegals had joined. The State Bar of Michigan recently adopted a similar program by creating a Legal Assistant Section of the bar consisting of legal assistants who are *affiliate members* of the bar. Other bar associations have also created special membership categories. There are, for example, *associate members* of the Columbus Bar Association (Ohio), associate members of the Bar Association of San Francisco, paralegal affiliate members of the Association of Trial Lawyers of America, and associate members of the American Immigration Lawyers Association.[24] Not all bar associations, however, have moved in this direction. The Louisiana State Bar Association, for example, voted in 1989 *not* to offer associate membership to paralegals because "the occupation of paralegals has not been sufficiently defined so as to provide guidance as to who is a trained and qualified paralegal, and who is not."[25]

■ ASSIGNMENT 1.11

Does the state, city, or county bar association where you live have a membership category for paralegals? If so, what are the eligibility requirements for membership and what are the benefits of membership?

What about the major national bar association—the American Bar Association (ABA)? For a long time, many argued that paralegals should become af-

---

[24]As of 1991, associate membership status existed or was under serious consideration in the following states either in the bar itself or in one of its committees or sections: Alaska, Arizona, Colorado, Connecticut (pending), District of Columbia, Florida, Illinois, Massachusetts, Michigan, Missouri (St. Louis County Bar only), New Jersey, New Mexico, North Dakota, Ohio (pending), Pennsylvania (pending), Texas, Wisconsin (pending), and West Virginia. Maze, *Bar Associate Membership Status for Legal Assistants,* 17 Facts & Findings 6 (NALA, March 1991).

[25]Landers, *Louisiana State Bar Association Decides Against Associate Membership for Paralegals,* 4 The Advocate (Louisiana State Paralegal Ass'n, August 1989).

filiated with the ABA in some way. In 1982 the ABA Committee on Legal Assistants proposed that the ABA create a new category of membership for paralegals. The National Association of Legal Assistants (NALA) warmly endorsed the proposal, while the National Federation of Paralegal Associations (NFPA) opposed it. Initially the House of Delegates of the ABA rejected the proposal of the Committee on the ground that the addition of this nonattorney membership category would further "dilute" the primary attorney category. Eventually, however, this objection was overcome. The House of Delegates agreed to accept a *legal assistant associate* category of membership. (For an application form, see Figure 1.6.) An ABA member who supervises the legal assistant must sign the latter's application for associate membership. As of 1991, there were 1,200 Legal Assistant Associates in the ABA.

As indicated, not all paralegals endorsed the concept of associate or affiliate membership in bar associations when the idea was first proposed. Here are some typical comments in opposition:

> I haven't been able to understand why paralegals would want to become second class members of an organization that represents the interests of another profession. [Some paralegals view associate membership] as a positive development, while the very idea is enough to raise the blood pressure of other paralegals.[26]

> [It is] in the public interest that the allied legal professions remain autonomous. [It is] necessary and advisable that paralegals retain primary control in the development of the paralegal profession.[27]

> It is a recognized and uncontested fact that the purpose of any bar association is to promote and protect attorneys and their practice of law, rather than legal assistants. Further, associate members do not participate in the administrative and substantial legal decisions which are made by the Bar Association, e.g., no vote on dues, by-laws, budget or substantive issues of membership requirements. [A separate identity may] eliminate possible conflicts of interest on issues where attorneys and legal assistants hold differing perspectives and opinions regarding the future of legal practice.[28]

Those who viewed paralegals as an autonomous, self-directed profession tended to disagree with the effort to join bar associations in any form. Yet this point of view is *not* shared by the majority of paralegals today. The momentum is toward more and more bar associations creating membership categories for paralegals. The reasons are best summed up by the following comment made before the ABA created the associate membership category:

> It is time our profession stopped being paranoid about ABA Associate Membership and open our eyes to opportunities presented to us. [We should not be spending time] dreaming up reasons to reject a chance for growth and improved

---

[26]Whelen, *An Opinion: Bar Association's Paralegal Non-Voting Membership*, 15 At Issue 9 (San Francisco Ass'n of Legal Assistants, May 1987).

[27]*NFPA Findings*, 8 The Journal 3 (Sacramento Ass'n of Legal Assistants, January 1986).

[28]Heller, *Legal Assistant Associate Membership in the ABA*, 14 On Point 1, 14 (Nat'l Capital Area Paralegal Ass'n, August 1988).

FIGURE 1.6 ABA Associate Membership Application

Membership Department • American Bar Association • 750 North Lake Shore Drive, Chicago, Illinois 60611, (312) 988-5522 FAX: (312) 988-6281

ADDRESS

Please print the way you wish your name and address to appear in the ABA records and on your Associate card and certificate. All materials will be sent to this address.

Name _____

Firm/Agency/Organization _____

Address _____

_____

City _____ State _____ Zip Code _____

Country _____

This address is my ☐ Home   ☐ Business   ☐ Both

Home Phone ( )_____ Business Phone ( ) _____

Birth Date _____/_____/_____ Gender ☐ Male ☐ Female

EMPLOYMENT

Employer _____

Your Title _____

Number of Years in this position _____

For Judicial Associate applicants only, please indicate:
☐ Judge   ☐ Court administrator   ☐ Federal court executive

Employment Setting (Check one):
① Law Firm   ② Corporate Law Dept.   ③ Gov't.   ④ Judiciary
⑤ Law School   ⑥ Legal Service/Public Defense Agency   ⑦ Military
⑨ Other _____

Number of attorneys at this office:
Ⓐ Solo   Ⓑ 2-5   Ⓒ 6-9   Ⓓ 10-19   Ⓔ 20-99   Ⓕ 100+

EDUCATION

Institution _____

Type of Degree or Certificate _____

ANNUAL ASSOCIATE DUES ARE $75

The ABA year runs from Sept. 1 to Aug. 31. Associates who join after October 1st receive a pro-rated credit toward next year's dues. Section dues are not pro-rated. *Some Associate categories REQUIRE you to join an ABA section. They are indicated by an *. These required section dues are reflected in the total annual dues.*

Check your selection(s):	Total Annual Dues
☐ Administrative Law Associate Administrative Law and Regulatory Practice Section* ($25.00)	$100.00
☐ Bar Executive Associate	$ 75.00
☐ Criminal Justice Associate Criminal Justice Section* ($25.00)	$100.00
☐ Educational Associate Legal Education and Admissions to the Bar Section* ($25.00)	$100.00
☐ Governmental Business Associate	$ 75.00
☐ Industrial Organization Economist Associate	$ 75.00
☐ International Associate	$ 75.00

Jurisdiction(s) in which admitted to practice _____

_____ Admission year(s): _____

Bar associations or legal organizations of which applicant is a member, and any offices held in them _____

☐ Judicial Associate Judicial Administrative Division* ($25.00)	$100.00
☐ Law Librarian Associate	$ 75.00
☐ Law Office Administrative Associate Law Practice Management Section* ($27.50)	$102.50
☐ Legal Assistant Associate	$ 75.00 *

Supervising Attorney Verification: I, _____,
ABA Membership I.D. Number: _____
a member of the Bar of the State of _____ verify that the above applicant for Legal Assistant Associate does or has performed for me in a capacity which meets the requirements described on page 2.

Attorney
Signature _____
(required)

Subtotal (from above) $ _____

Subtotal for additional sections (from page 4) $ _____

Total $ _____

AMERICAN BAR ASSOCIATION ASSOCIATE AFFILIATION

Article Three of the ABA Constitution and Bylaws provides for the establishment of classes of Associates, composed of non-members with whom affiliation is considered to be in the interest of the Association. Associates are not members of the Association and do not, as a group, constitute a membership classification. Associates of the American Bar Association, except for International Associates, are non-lawyers who are not eligible for membership within the Association, but serve within the legal profession. Pursuant to Article 21.12 of the Association Bylaws, persons who are ineligible to be members of the Association may qualify for election by the Board of Governors as Associates if they are in one of the classifications listed above, and satisfy such further eligibility requirements as may be approved by the Board.

PRIVILEGES OF ASSOCIATES

1. To attend meetings of the Association, including sessions of the House of Delegates and the Assembly, and to enjoy any floor privileges extended to non-members.

2. To receive Association publications that are regularly provided to all members of the Association.

3. To be appointed to any Committee or Commission of the Association for which non-members are eligible for appointment.

4. To participate in the economic benefit programs available to ABA members, with the exception of the insurance programs of the American Bar Endowment.

5. To affiliate with one or more of the sections of their choice, upon application and payment of the annual section dues then in effect. All Associates under the age of 36 shall automatically become Associates of the Young Lawyers Division (see page 4).

Legal Assistant Associate: Persons who, although not members of the legal profession, are qualified through education, training, or work experience, are employed or retained by a lawyer, law office, governmental agency, or other entity in a capacity or function which involves the performance, under the direction and supervision of an attorney, of specifically-delegated substantive legal work, which work, for the most part, requires a sufficient knowledge of legal concepts such that, absent that legal assistant, the attorney would perform the task.

relations within the established legal community. No guarantees have been given to assure us that associate membership would be beneficial, but why close *any* doors opened to us? If just a few paralegals would like to take advantage of this opportunity, why slam the door in their faces? The spirit of cooperation and teamwork within the legal community are the key reasons to encourage associate membership.[29]

■ ASSIGNMENT 1.12

(a) Should paralegals become a formal part of bar associations? What effect do you think associate membership would have on existing paralegal associations? Strengthen them? Destroy them? Is it healthy or unhealthy for paralegals to organize themselves as independent entities? Is it healthy or unhealthy for them to be able to challenge the organized bar? What is the conflict-of-interest argument against associate membership? Do you agree with this argument?

(b) Should a paralegal association allow *attorneys* to become associate members of the *paralegal* association? Why or why not?

(c) Under the ABA associate membership category, what kinds of paralegals are excluded from membership? Is such exclusion a good idea?

(d) To become an associate or affiliate member of a bar association, the applicant usually must obtain the signed statement of an attorney-employer asserting or attesting certain facts about the applicant—for instance, that he or she is a paralegal who works for the attorney. The statement is called an attorney attestation. For example, to obtain affiliate membership in the State Bar of Michigan, the attorney must "hereby attest" that the applicant "is employed by me and is recognized as a legal assistant (paralegal) and that he/she, under the supervision and direction of a lawyer, performs the services" specified elsewhere on the application. Some *paralegal* associations require the same kind of attorney attestation as a condition of allowing paralegals to join the paralegal association. Do you think attorney attestation is a good idea for associate/affiliate membership in a bar association? For full membership in a paralegal association?

(e) As indicated elsewhere in this book, there are a fairly large number of paralegals who have moved on to management positions as paralegal coordinators or legal assistant managers. Should these individuals become members of traditional paralegal associations?

■ Section F. Self-Regulation by Paralegals: The Certification Debate

As we have seen, there are two major national associations of paralegals:

■ National Federation of Paralegal Associations (NFPA): An association of associations; its membership consists of state and local paralegal associations

---

[29]Anderson, *ABA Associate Membership: A Different Perspective,* 3 Findings and Conclusions 7 (Washington Ass'n of Legal Assistants, August 1987).

■ National Association of Legal Assistants (NALA): an association of individuals, plus a number of state and local paralegal associations, and several student paralegal associations

In Appendix A, there is a list of state and local paralegal associations, with a notation of whether they are part of NFPA, part of NALA, or unaffiliated.

NALA is *not* a member of NFPA, and vice versa. In fact, the two groups take very different positions on a number of issues, two of the most important of which are limited licensing of independent paralegals and certification of all paralegals. Earlier in this chapter we examined the clash of views on limited licensing. We turn now to the older and perhaps more bitter debate over certification. NALA has created two major certification programs for paralegals—the Certified Legal Assistant (CLA) program and the Certified Legal Assistant Specialist (CLAS) program. The major opponent of the very existence of these programs has been NFPA. The following two excerpts present a detailed description of the position of both associations on certification. At the end of the descriptions, you will be asked which side is correct.

The Case for Certification[30]
by Jane H. Terhune

[Jane H. Terhune is a past president of the National Association of Legal Assistants. She is employed as a legal assistant for the firm of Hall, Estill, Hardwick, Gable, Collingsworth & Nelson, Tulsa, Oklahoma.]

Professional competence of an *individual* can be assessed by two recognized mechanisms: licensing or certification. Accreditation or approval, on the other hand, examines educational *programs* to determine whether they meet established standards of quality. Although the ABA has an institutional approval process, this paper is concerned only with the assessment of *individual* competence and therefore will not deal with the issue of institutional accreditation or approval.

Since the early 1970s legal assistants have obtained employment by means of formal training, in-house training, or other law office experience. While each method of training has certain advantages, no one method has proven superior to the others. Thus the dilemma: how can prospective employers or clients assess or legal assistants demonstrate paralegal skills and knowledge when there is no standard for performance?

Is licensing the appropriate mechanism to assure professional competence of legal assistants at this time? Several states have recently considered it, but none has yet adopted it. It is generally agreed that requirements for licensing would either severely limit the growth and development of the still new paralegal field or be so weak as to be meaningless. Licensing, by definition, is a mandatory requirement and is usually administered and controlled by government entities or well-established and strong professional associations. It is doubtful that state legislatures can define the legal assistant profession well enough to regulate it effectively at this time. Therefore, licensing appears to be impractical as well as premature.

Certification, on the other hand, is a voluntary professional commitment that appears to be a practical alternative, and the National Association of Legal Assistants believes that one national certification program is preferable to a multitude of possible state programs. Certification is not new or unique. Many professions and paraprofessions have developed and supported certification as an alternative to licensing or other forms of regulation. Certification recognizes expertise and proven ability without limiting entrance into or employment in the field, and the same standards are applied regardless of the individual's background or training. Furthermore, a certification program can help guide educational institutions in developing and evaluating their legal assistant curricula. It is argued

30. American Bar Association, Standing Committee on Legal Assistants, *Legal Assistant Update '80* 5–16 (1980). This article has been updated to reflect current positions of NALA and NFPA.

that certification would limit the development of the paralegal field, but the PLS (Professional Legal Secretary) certification of legal secretaries has in no way interfered with their employment. To the contrary, secretaries with the Certified PLS title are regarded as professionals in their respective fields.

In 1974, as part of an effort to set high professional standards for legal assistants while the field was in its early development, the NALA Certifying Board for Legal Assistants was created. It was composed of nine members—five legal assistants (working in different areas of the law), two paralegal educators, and two attorneys. The composition of the Board has remained the same to date, and in number is similar to many certification boards or committees in other fields. During the first year of its existence the Certifying Board acted mainly as a feasibility study group. All known national professional associations with certification programs were contacted for advice and guidance. Paralegal

educators were contacted for information about their programs as well as entrance and graduation requirements. Legal assistant duties and responsibilities in various areas of the law were surveyed, and correspondence with the Institute of Legal Executives in England began. Our English counterparts were anxious to share their ten years of experience with NALA. After several months of gathering information, replies were tabulated and summarized and the NALA Certifying Board for Legal Assistants was ready to embark on its task. Its first task was to create an examination. Passing this examination would enable a legal assistant to become a CLA—Certified Legal Assistant.

Although many legal assistants work in special areas of law rather than as generalists, there are general skills and knowledge which apply to all legal fields and, for this reason, general subjects or topics were selected for inclusion in the examination.

The CLA Examination—Outline

The two-day CLA examination contains objective questions, such as multiple choice, true/false, and matching. There are also essay questions and short answer questions. The examination covers the follow areas:

Communications. This section of the CLA examination contains questions on:

word usage	capitalization	grammar
number usage	vocabulary	correspondence
punctuation	word division	nonverbal communication
sentence structure	concise writing	

Ethics. This section deals with ethics in the legal assistant's contacts with employers, clients, co-workers, and the general public. Unauthorized practice, ethical rules, practice rules, and confidentiality are among the topics tested by this section. Knowledge of the American Bar Association Rules of Professional Conduct and the National Association of Legal Assistants, Inc., Code of Ethics and Professional Responsibility is required for this examination.

Human Relations and Interviewing Techniques. The Human Relations portion encompasses professional and social contacts with the employer, clients, and other office visitors, co-workers, including subordinates, and the public outside of the law office. For this reason, the legal assistant should be familiar with authorized practice, ethical rules, practice rules, delegation of authority, consequences of delegation, and confidentiality.

Interviewing techniques cover basic principles, as agreed upon by most authors on the subject, definitions of terms of basic principles, and handling of specialized interviews. Subject areas included in this section of the examination are:

General considerations for the interviewing situation: courtesy, empathy, and physical setting

Initial Roadblocks—lapse of time, prejudice, etc.

Manner of questions

Use of checklists for specific matters

Special-handling situations: the elderly, the very young

The test covers initial and subsequent interviews as well as both client and witness interviews.

Judgment and Analytical Ability. The sections of this part deal with (1) analyzing and categorizing facts and evidence; (2) the legal assistant's relationship with the lawyer, the legal secretary, the client, the courts, and other law firms; (3) the legal assistant's reactions to specific situations; (4) handling telephone situations; and (5) reading comprehension and data interpretation.

Legal Research. It is extremely important for the legal assistant to be able to use the most important tool of the legal profession—the law library. The purpose of the legal research section of the CLA Examination is to test your knowledge of the use of state and federal codes, the statutes, the digests, case reports, various legal encyclopedias, court reports, shepardizing, and research procedure.

Legal Terminology. The sections of this part deal with (1) Latin phrases; (2) legal phrases or terms in general; and (3) utilization and understanding of common legal terms. The questions involve legal terminology and procedures used in general practice.

Substantive Law. The substantive law section of the CLA examination is divided into nine parts: (1) general (which includes American Legal System); (2) bankruptcy; (3) corporate; (4) estate planning and probate; (5) contract; (6) litigation; (7) real estate; (8) criminal; and (9) administrative law. Each examinee will be required to take the first part and must select four out of the remaining eight parts.

After passing the examination, a legal assistant may use the *CLA (Certified Legal Assistant)* designation, which signifies certification by the National Association of Legal Assistants, Inc. CLA is a service mark duly registered with the U.S. Patent and Trademark Office (No. 1131999). Any unauthorized use is strictly forbidden.

Based on the premise that education, a commitment of all professionals, is a never ending process, Certified Legal Assistants are required periodically to submit evidence of continuing education in order to maintain certified status. The CLA designation is for a period of five years, and if the CLA submits proof of continuing education in accordance with the stated requirements, the certificate is renewed for another five years. Lifetime certification is not permitted.

Continuing education units are awarded for attending seminars, workshops or conferences in areas of substantive law or a closely related area. The seminars, etc., do not have to be sponsored by NALA, although all NALA seminars and workshops qualify.

The development of the specific test items was a time-consuming and difficult project. Rather than employ professional testing companies unfamiliar with the legal assistant field, it was decided that the Certifying Board, composed of legal assistants, attorneys, and educators from the legal assistant field, was best qualified to prepare the exams. Then followed a series of meetings to review, refine, and evaluate the proposed exams. The exams were pilot-tested, testing times were noted, results were systematically analyzed, and problems were identified. Every question in each section was carefully scrutinized for "national scope," and questions which did not apply to all states were removed from the exam.

Eligibility Requirements for CLA Examination

Applicants for the Certified Legal Assistant examination must meet one of the following three requirements at the time of filing the application.

1. Graduation from a legal assistant program that is:

   a) Approved by the American Bar Association; or

   b) An associate degree program; or

   c) A post-baccalaureate certificate program in legal assistant studies; or

   d) A bachelor's degree program in legal assistant studies; or

   e) A legal assistant program which consists of a minimum of sixty semester hours (or equivalent quarter hours) of which at least fifteen semester hours (or equivalent quarter hours) are substantive legal courses.

2. A bachelor's degree in any field plus one (1) year's experience as a legal assistant.

3. A high school diploma or equivalent plus seven (7) years' experience as a legal assistant under the supervision of a member of the Bar plus evidence of a minimum of twenty (20) hours of continuing legal education credit to have been completed within a two (2) year period prior to the application date.

Applicants meeting any one of these criteria may take the exam. They need not be members of the National Association of Legal Assistants to apply for or receive the CLA (Certified Legal Assistant) certification.

The CLA examination was first offered in November, 1976, at regional testing centers. Approximately 50% of the first group of applicants passed the entire exam, and the board was particularly pleased that the passing percentage was uniform throughout the country, a fact which seemed to indicate that the test was free of state or regional bias. Although the passing rate has fluctuated slightly in subsequent testing, the uniformity has been maintained. In the March 1990 exam, there was a 51.5% pass rate, as 504 of 977 legal assistants passed the test. As of April 1991, there were 4,265 CLAs in the country. The following states have the most CLAs:

Florida:	1120	Colorado:	122
Texas:	967	Kansas:	106
Arizona:	316	Iowa:	77
Oklahoma:	202	Louisiana	73
California:	157	New Mexico:	63

Certification is an ambitious and expensive project for a young professional association. Over $20,000 and thousands of hours were initially invested in the CLA program, but the National Association of Legal Assistants believes it has been a wise investment. Traditionally, where new professions do not set their own standards, related professions or governments have done so for them. NALA felt a responsibility to develop a quality national certification program for legal assistants desiring professional recognition. The CLA exam has been in use for a number of years, but work on the project continues. The question bank is continually expanded so that an indefinite number of exam versions can be created, and questions are being reviewed and updated constantly.

Specialty Certification

Recently NALA launched a major new component of its CLA program. It is now possible for someone who has already achieved CLA status to take additional examinations in order to receive *Specialty Certification* in one or more of the following areas:

- **Civil Litigation** covers Federal Rules of Civil Procedure, Federal Rules of Evidence, and Federal Rules of Appellate Procedure; document control; drafting pleadings; abstracting information; and general litigation procedures.

- **Probate and Estate Planning** covers general probate and trust law, federal estate tax, fiduciary income tax, drafting wills and trusts, and estate planning concepts.

- **Corporate and Business Law** covers the knowledge and applications of those principles of contract, tort, property, agency, employment, administrative, corporate, and partnership law which commonly constitute the subject matter known as business law. Examinees must be thoroughly familiar with the Uniform Commercial Code, Uniform Partnership Act, Uniform Limited Partnership Act, Model Business Corporate Act, as well as with the regulatory authority of those federal agencies which affect the business relationship such as the SEC, FTC, OSHA, and EPA.

- **Criminal Law and Procedure** covers an applicant's knowledge in the area of criminal procedure and law from arrest through trial. The examination covers components of substantive criminal law, procedural matters, and constitutional rights guaranteed to defendants. Applicants must be thoroughly familiar with the Federal Rules of Criminal Procedure, Federal Rules of Evidence, the Model Penal Code, and major United States Supreme Court cases.

- **Real Estate** covers the applicant's knowledge in the area of real estate purchases, sales, terminology, actions affecting title, landlord-tenant relations, oil and gas, easements, abstracts, title insurance, liens, cluster developments, types of conveyances, methods of passing title included in conveyances, legal remedies associated with real estate, and legal descriptions of real estate.

Each of these specialty examinations takes four hours to complete. Upon passing one of them, the legal assistant becomes a *CLAS—a Certified Legal Assistant Specialist.* The CLA examination tests broad *general* skills required of *all* legal assistants. Specialty certification, on the other hand, recognizes significant competence in a *particular* field. Yet both the CLA exam and the CLAS exam are similar in that they do not test the law of any particular state. They are national in scope, since NALA believes that standard national examinations will ensure uniformity of professional standards as well as permit legal assistants to move from one state to another without loss of certified status.

From the inception of the CLAS program in 1982 up to 1990, 298 legal assistants have achieved CLAS status in the country.

The Case Against Certification
by Judith Current

[Judith Current is a past president of the National Federation of Paralegal Associations. She is employed as a legal assistant in the firm of Holme, Roberts & Owen, Denver, Colorado.]

The National Federation of Paralegal Associations (NFPA) is a professional organization composed of fifty-two state and local paralegal associations representing over

17,000 paralegals across the country. NFPA was founded in 1974 and adopted the following purposes in 1975:

- to constitute a unified national voice of the paralegal profession
- to advance, foster, and promote the paralegal concept
- to monitor and participate in developments in the paralegal profession
- to maintain a nationwide communications network among paralegal associations and other members of the legal community

NFPA has continued to foster these goals through its established policies and activities. In 1977 NFPA adopted its Affirmation of Responsibility (p. 116).

NFPA recognizes that certification of paralegals is of national concern, but it feels that there has been insufficient study as to the impact of certification and the means by which certification should be administered. NFPA will only support a certification program which is coordinated by a national, broadly based, autonomous body in which paralegals have at least equal participation with attorneys and other members.

The topic of certification of legal assistants has been of concern to NFPA since its inception. It has found every certificate proposal advanced to date to be seriously lacking in the understanding of the true nature of the profession, particularly its diversity, and the proposals have offered a structure that provides little or no representation to the persons most affected, the legal assistants themselves.

Specifically, its reservations fall within the following areas:

Need/Prematurity

Since there is tremendous diversity in the functions and classifications of paralegals, it is extremely difficult to create generalized standards that can be fairly applied. This problem may eventually find an acceptable solution; but it will require much study and considerable input from all affected sectors.

No studies have been conducted that have demonstrated a need for certification. A study conducted by the American Bar Association in 1975 concluded that certification was premature. The California State Bar in 1978 rejected a proposal for certification and accreditation after nearly two years of study. Other states have similarly rejected certifica-

tion. Until a need for certification is clearly demonstrated, certification will be premature.

Premature regulation runs a risk of foreclosing yet unseen avenues of development, as well as creating yet another layer of costly bureaucracy when, in fact, none may be needed. NFPA sees nothing to prevent, and everything to encourage, an extremely cautious approach to the enactment of any program of certification. Meanwhile, the normal mechanisms of the marketplace, the existing unauthorized practice laws and ethical guidelines, the increasing numbers of legal assistants with demonstrable experience, and the ever-growing reputations of various training programs can serve as guidelines for those who seek the sorts of yardsticks that certification might provide.

Impact of Certification

No studies have been conducted that satisfactorily assess the potential impact of certification on the delivery of legal services. Some of the possible negative effects include:

1. *The growth, development, and diversity of the paralegal profession could be diminished by certification.* The paralegal profession has been developing steadily without a demonstrated need for such regulation. Regulating the profession could curtail development into new areas, stifling the potential growth of the field and unnecessarily limiting the role of the paralegals in the delivery of legal services.

2. *Certification could result in a decrease of the availability of legal services to the poor.* Legal aid offices are economically dependent upon paralegals who represent clients at various administrative hearings. Most of these paralegals are in-house trained specialists who are paid lower salaries than private sector paralegals. If certification is implemented, it is conceivable that administrative agencies may initiate a system in which only certified paralegals, or attorneys, would be allowed to represent clients at the hearings. Many paralegals successfully working in this area might not meet the educational or testing requirements imposed by certification, and the legal aid offices would not be able to meet the salary demands that would be made by certified paralegals.

3. *Innovation in paralegal education programs could diminish as a result of certi-*

fication. Schools would be forced by necessity to gear their courses to a certification examination rather than to the needs of the legal community and the marketplace. While some standardization of training programs might be desirable in the future, it would be premature at this time because the training programs have not been in existence long enough to determine which types of programs are most effective and because the paralegal profession is still in a dynamic stage of development. Experimentation and variety are currently essential to the field of paralegal education.

4. *Entry into the profession could be curtailed by certification.* At the present time, a paralegal can enter the profession in a variety of ways, including formal education, in-house training, promotion from legal secretary, or a combination thereof. Certification could limit these entry paths by establishing prescribed educational requirements.

No Acceptable Model for Certification

In the opinion of NFPA, no acceptable model or program of certification has yet been devised. Oregon is the only state to have adopted a certification program, but it was discontinued shortly after it began because of a lack of interest from paralegals and attorneys in the state. NFPA questions the propriety of the Oregon State Bar controlling the certification of paralegals, and deplores the fact that the paralegals were denied equal representation on the certifying board. The Oregon program failed adequately to recognize specialization and failed to make any distinctions between the tasks which may be performed by a certified paralegal and those which may be performed by an uncertified paralegal. Thus, certification did not enhance the position of paralegals in Oregon.

NFPA feels that the certification program conducted by the National Association of Legal Assistants (NALA) is unacceptable. The criteria for eligibility to take the certification examination is not based on objective data. The examination, in the Federation's opinion, contains questions irrelevant to a practicing paralegal and is not an effective measure of a person's ability to work successfully as a paralegal. The NALA certification program is not officially recognized by a governmental body, and a person certified under this program is not allowed to perform any tasks other than those which may also be performed by uncertified paralegals.

Control and Representation

No certification program will be acceptable to NFPA unless it is developed, implemented, and controlled by an autonomous group which is composed of an equal number of attorneys, paralegals, paralegal educators, and members of the public. Self-regulation is unacceptable to NFPA since self-regulation can become self-interest, and self-interest can conflict with the public interest. NFPA strongly believes that bar control of paralegals is inappropriate in that such regulation may meet the interests of the organized bar and lawyers but not necessarily the interests of the public or the paralegal profession. NFPA also questions the propriety of the organized bar attempting to regulate another profession.

National Coordination

NFPA believes that any program of certification will be most efficient and equitable if it is developed as a national program rather than on a state-by-state basis. A national program would eliminate duplication of effort on the part of each individual state. It would allow for mobility and would avoid a conflict of standards between states.

NFPA recommends that the need for and possible methods of certification be studied in much greater depth, and that this study be conducted by an autonomous group which provides equal representation to paralegals, attorneys, paralegal educators, and members of the public. NFPA also recommends that bar associations work with paralegals and educators to educate lawyers in the proper and effective utilization of paralegals and that paralegals work to promote the growth and the development of the profession through support of and participation in the local and national paralegal associations.

▓ ASSIGNMENT 1.13

(a) Which side is correct? Conduct a debate in your class on the advantages and disadvantages of certification.

(b) Do you agree with NFPA that self-regulation is unacceptable?

Certification in Florida

Florida Legal Assistants (FLA) is a statewide paralegal association that is affiliated with the National Association of Legal Assistants. Florida is a big NALA state; over 25% of all CLAs in the country live in Florida. Several years ago, FLA began its own exam on Florida law for those legal assistants who had passed the CLA exam of NALA. In 1984, FLA launched the Certified Florida Legal Assistant Examination. A person who is a CLA and passes this exam on Florida law can become a *CFLA—a Certified Florida Legal Assistant*. Like the CLA exam, the CFLA exam is voluntary; no one is required to take it. The program is not endorsed by any of the bar associations in Florida. It is run exclusively by FLA. "Some legal assistants view the CFLA designation as a step up from NALA's CLA designation."[31]

Certification in Texas?

The Florida certification program was inaugurated with relative calm. The exact opposite occurred when certification proposals emerged in Texas. As we saw earlier, there is a *Legal Assistant Division* within the State Bar of Texas. A survey of the members of the Division revealed very high interest in adopting a voluntary certification program specifically for Texas. Over 76% of the members indicated that they would take a certification exam if it were offered. Consequently, the Division drafted two certification proposals and conducted a series of hearings on them in 1986. The proposals were as follows:

Proposal 1. The Division would develop and administer its own two-day exam on generic topics (such as legal analysis and communications) and on Texas law. Only legal assistants with at least two years working experience as a legal assistant would be eligible to take the exam.

Proposal 2. The Division would join forces with NALA and give two exams. NALA would administer its two-day Certified Legal Assistant (CLA) exam. Then the Division would administer its half-day exam designed with a focus on Texas law. Anyone who had previously passed the CLA exam would be required to have worked as a legal assistant in Texas for one year before taking the Division's Texas exam.

These two proposals stirred great controversy in Texas and throughout the country. The National Federation of Paralegal Associations (NFPA) vigorously opposed both proposals, raising many of the same arguments against certification discussed earlier. But the Dallas Association of Legal Assistants (which is a member of NFPA) criticized NFPA for its opposition. The National Association

---

[31]Morris, *State Certifying Test for Legal Assistants in Florida: Is Arizona Next?*, The Digest, p. 1 (Arizona Paralegal Ass'n, October 1989).

of Legal Assistants (NALA) endorsed the Texas move toward certification. Of course, this is not surprising in view of NALA's history of supporting certification. And NALA would play a major role if the second proposal were adopted.

The debate was not limited to NFPA and NALA. Eight public hearings were held throughout Texas, and 187 persons submitted written comments. *But no clear consensus emerged from the hearings on the two proposals.* There was considerable confusion about the nature, purpose, and scope of the two proposals, and indeed, about the value of certification itself.

In spite of these difficulties, there is continued interest in developing a state-specific certification program in Texas within the structure of the state bar association. The most recent proposal under consideration is the establishment of a series of voluntary specialty examinations on Texas law to recognize "advanced professional competency" within a particular specialty. The likelihood of enacting such a proposal is very high. The bar's Legal Assistants Committee has appointed a Certification Committee to study it.

Position of the American Bar Association on Certification

The ABA has taken the following positions on paralegal certification:

1. Certification of *minimal,* or *entry-level,* paralegal competence is *not* appropriate.
2. Voluntary certification of *advanced* paralegal competence or proficiency in specialty areas of the law *might* be appropriate *if* it were administered by the appropriate body.
3. The ABA is *not* the appropriate body to undertake a program of certifying paralegals in advanced competence or proficiency in specialty areas of the law.
4. A voluntary program of certifying advanced paralegal competence or proficiency in specialty areas of the law, if undertaken at all, should be undertaken on a national basis by a board that includes attorneys, paralegals, educators, and members of the general public.
5. Since such a board does not presently exist, there should not be any certification at this time.

According to the ABA, certification of minimal competence does not have the benefits that would justify the time, expense, and effort to implement it. Furthermore, any of the benefits would be outweighed by potential detriment from it. A major danger the ABA sees is that such certification could evolve into licensure, which the ABA opposes.

But the ABA does see benefit in certifying paralegals in areas of specialization *after* they have been on the job. This kind of advanced certification would be a way of recognizing professional advancement. "Such certification would be a measure of quality of work and experience. Its function would be to demonstrate to employers or prospective employers a high degree of legal assistant competence in a particular area of practice that has already been obtained, rather than just the potential for such competence." [32]

The ABA feels, however, that advanced certification must be administered by the appropriate body. This body should be broad based, including attorneys, paralegals, educators, and members of the public. The ABA recognizes that it is *not* such a body. Neither is the National Association of Legal Assistants nor the National Federation of Paralegal Associations. In fact, such a body simply does not exist. It would take a great deal of money, energy, and political skill to create one. Beyond a lot of rhetoric, no one is even trying.

Hence, as a practical consequence, it can be said that the ABA is opposed to *any* certification at this time.

■ ASSIGNMENT 1.14

When a new local paralegal association is formed, it is often lobbied by NALA and by NFPA to become a part of one of these national organizations. The local association will usually make one of three decisions: affiliate with NALA, affiliate with NFPA, or remain unaffiliated. If you were a member of a local association faced with the decision of whether to join NALA, NFPA, or stay unaffiliated, what would your vote be? Why?

■ ASSIGNMENT 1.15

Is it a good idea to have two national associations? Why or why not?

Throughout this book the importance of paralegal associations has been stressed. They have had a major impact on the development of paralegalism. Many state and local bar associations as well as the ABA have felt the effect of organized paralegal advocacy through the associations.

As soon as possible, you should join a paralegal association. Find out if the association allows students to become members. (See Appendix D.) If an association does not exist in your area, you should form one and decide whether you want to become part of the National Federation of Paralegal Associations or the National Association of Legal Assistants. The paralegal association is your main voice in the continued development of the field. Join one now and become an active member. In addition to the educational benefits of membership and the job placement services that many associations provide, you will experience the satisfaction of helping shape your career in the years to come. Attorneys and the bar associations should not be the sole mechanism for controlling paralegals.

---

[32]ABA Standing Committee on Legal Assistants, *Position Paper on the Question of Legal Assistant Licensure or Certification,* 5 Legal Assistant Today 167 (1986).

G. Fair Labor Standards Act

Yes, I am paid overtime. I am paid at time and a half rate. I agree with being paid overtime. If the attorney asks me to work additional long hours and weekends, then yes I do believe I should be compensated for yielding my free time for work. This does not make me any less of a professional. My professionalism will show through my work product.[33]

My firm doesn't pay paralegals overtime, and I don't want to be classified as a person eligible for overtime. For one thing, people paid overtime are non-professionals, and I don't think of myself as a non-professional. I feel that my salary, salary increases, and bonuses reflect a degree of compensation for the extra hours I work.[34]

One of the hot topics in the field is GOD: the Great Overtime Debate. "The mere mention of the subject of overtime in any group of working legal assistants is guaranteed to spark a prolonged session of horror-story telling." [35] The topic is so controversial that one paralegal association recently established a hotline to answer questions confidentially. Some paralegals have filed—and won—lawsuits against their employers for failure to pay *overtime compensation* for hours worked beyond forty hours in a week.

There is a definite body of law that determines whether overtime compensation must be paid; the issue is not dependent on the preferences of individual paralegals. The governing law is the federal *Fair Labor Standards Act*,[36] which is enforced by the Wage and Hour Division of the U.S. Department of Labor. Under the Act, overtime compensation must be paid to employees unless they fall within one of the three "white collar" exemptions. Exempt employees are those who work in a professional, administrative, or executive capacity.[37] The

---

[33]*The Member Connection*, 14 Facts & Findings 7 (NALA, June 1988).
[34]*The Membership Responds*, 9 The ParaGraph (Georgia Ass'n of Legal Assistants, September/October 1987).
[35]Acosta, *Let's Talk About Overtime!*, 10 Ka Leo O' H.A.L.A. 6 (Hawaii Ass'n of Legal Assistants, August/September 1987).
[36]29 U.S.C.A. §§ 201 *et seq.* (1976).
[37]The Professional Employee Exemption:

- Primary duty consists of work requiring knowledge of an advanced type in a field customarily acquired by a prolonged course of specialized intellectual instruction and study. (Such course of study means at least a baccalaureate degree or equivalent.)
- Work requires the consistent exercise of judgment and discretion.
- Work is predominantly intellectual and varied in character, as opposed to routine, mental or physical work.

The Administrative Employee Exemption:

- The employee's primary duty consists of work related to management policies or general business operations.
- The employee regularly exercises discretion and independent judgment.

The Executive Employee Exemption:

- The employee's primary duty consists of the management of the enterprise.
- The employee regularly supervises two or more other employees. 29 C.F.R. part 541 (1983).

vast majority of traditional paralegals do *not* fit within any of these exemptions. Since they are nonexempt, they *are* entitled to the protection of the Act. Phrased another way, they are not considered professionals, administrators, or executives under the Act and must therefore be paid overtime compensation. If, however, the paralegal is a supervisor with extensive management responsibilities over other employees, an exemption may apply. But this would cover only a small segment of the paralegal population. The following opinion letter explains the position of the government on this issue. As you will see, the criteria used to distinguish exempt from nonexempt employees are the actual job responsibilities of the employee, not the job title or compensation policy of the office.

Wage and Hour Division
United States Department of Labor
September 27, 1979

This is in further reply to your letter of July 12, 1979, . . . concerning the exempt status under section 13(a)(1) of the Fair Labor Standards Act of paralegal employees employed by your organization. . . .

The specific duties of the paralegal employees (all of which occur under an attorney's supervision) are interviewing clients; identifying and refining problems; opening, maintaining, and closing case files; acting as the liaison person between client and attorney; drafting pleadings and petitions, and answering petition, and interrogatories; filing pleadings and petitions; acting as general litigation assistant during court proceedings; digesting depositions, and preparing file profiles; conducting formal and informal hearings and negotiations; preparing and editing newsletters and leaflets for community development and public relations purposes; performing outreach services; coordinating general activities with relevant local, State, and Federal agencies; assisting in establishing and implementing community legal education programs; and working as a team with other employees to deliver quality legal services. You state that the job requires at least two years of college and/or equivalent experience.

[The Fair Labor Standards] Act provides a complete minimum wage and overtime pay exemption for any employee employed in a bona fide executive, administrative, or professional capacity . . . . An employee will qualify for exemption if all the pertinent tests relating to duties, responsibilities, and salary . . . are met. In response to your first question, the

paralegal employees you have in mind would not qualify for exemption as bona fide professional employees as discussed in section 541.3 of the regulations, since it is clear that their primary duty does not consist of work requiring knowledge of an advanced type in a field of science or learning customarily acquired by a prolonged course of specialized intellectual instruction and study, as distinguished from a general academic education and from an apprenticeship and from training in the performance of routine mental, manual, or physical processes.

With regard to the status of the paralegal employees as bona fide administrative employees, it is our opinion that their duties do not involve the exercise of discretion and independent judgment of the type required by section 541.2(b) of the regulations. The outline of their duties which you submit actually describes the use of skills rather than discretion and independent judgment. Under section 541.207 of the regulations, this requirement is interpreted as involving the comparison and evaluation of possible courses of conduct and acting or making a decision after the various possibilities have been considered. Furthermore, the term is interpreted to mean that the person has the authority or power to make an independent choice, free from immediate direction or supervision with respect to matters of significance.

The general facts presented about the employees here tend to indicate that they do not meet these criteria. Rather, as indicated above, they would appear to fit more appropriately into that category of employees who apply particular skills and knowledge in preparing assignments. Employees who merely apply knowledge in following prescribed procedures or determining whether specified standards have been met are not deemed to be exercising independent judgment, even if they have some leeway in reaching a conclusion. In addition, it should be noted that most jurisdictions have strict prohibitions against the unauthorized practice of law by lay persons. Under the American Bar Association's Code of Professional Responsibility, a delegation of legal tasks to a lay person is proper only if the lawyer maintains a direct relationship with the client, supervises the delegated work, and has complete professional responsibility for the work produced. The implication of such strictures is that the paralegal employees you describe would probably not have the amount of authority to exercise independent judgment with regard to legal matters necessary to bring them within the administrative exemption. . . .

With regard to your [other] questions, all nonexempt employees, regardless of the amount of their wages, must be paid overtime premium pay of not less than one and one-half times their regular rates of pay for all hours worked in excess of forty in a workweek. The fact that an employee did not obtain advanced approval to work the overtime does not relieve the employer from complying with the overtime provisions of the Act.

We hope this satisfactorily responds to your inquiry. However, if you have any further questions concerning the application of the Fair Labor Standards Act to the situation you have in mind, please do not hesitate to let us know.

Sincerely,

C. Lamar Johnson
Deputy Administrator

■ ASSIGNMENT 1.16

(a) If you had a choice, would you want to receive overtime compensation as an entry-level paralegal?

(b) Surveys have shown that between 20–40% of nonexempt paralegals today do *not* receive overtime compensation. Can you explain this startling fact?

■ Section H. Tort Liability of Paralegals

Thus far we have discussed a number of ways that paralegal activities are or could be regulated:

■ Criminal liability for violating the statutes on the unauthorized practice of law

■ Special authorization rules on practice before administrative agencies and other tribunals

■ Licensing

■ Bar rules on paralegal education

■ Self-regulation

■ Labor laws

Finally, we come to *tort liability,* which is another method by which society defines what is and is not permissible. A tort is a private wrong or injury other than a breach of contract or the commission of a crime, although some breaches of contract and crimes can also constitute torts.

Two questions need to be kept in mind. First, when are paralegal employees *personally liable* for their torts? Second, when are employers *vicariously liable* for the torts of their paralegal employees? (As we will see, vicarious liability simply means being liable because of what someone else has done or failed to do.) The short answer to the first question is: *always.* The short answer to the second question is: *when the wrongdoing by the paralegal was within the scope of employment.* After covering both questions, we will then examine the separate question of when malpractice insurance will pay for such liability.

Several different kinds of wrongdoing are possible. The paralegal might commit:

- The tort of negligence
- An intentional tort, such as battery.
- An act which is both a crime (such as embezzlement) *and* an intentional tort (such as conversion).

A client who is injured by any of these torts can sue the paralegal in the same manner that a patient in a hospital can sue a nurse. Paralegals are not relieved of liability simply because they work for, and function under the supervision of, an attorney. Every citizen is *personally* liable for the torts he or she commits. The same is true of criminal liability.

Next we turn to the employers of paralegals. Are they *also* liable for wrongdoing committed by their paralegals? Assume that the supervising attorneys did nothing wrong themselves. For example, the attorney did not commit the tort or crime as an active participant with the paralegal, or the attorney was not careless in selecting and training the paralegal. Our question is: Can an attorney be liable to a client solely because of the wrongdoing of a paralegal? When such liability applies, it is called *vicarious liability,* which exists when one person is liable solely because of what someone else has done or failed to do. The answer to our question is found in the doctrine of *respondeat superior,* which makes employers responsible for the torts of their employees or agents when the wrongdoing occurs within the scope of employment.[38]

Hence, if a tort is committed by a paralegal within the scope of employment, the client can sue the paralegal or the attorney, or both. This does not mean that the client recovers twice; there can be only one recovery for a tort. The client is simply given a choice in bringing the suit. In most cases, the primary target of the client will be the employer, who is the so-called *deep pocket,* meaning the one who has resources from which a judgment can be satisfied.

Finally we need to examine what is meant by *scope of employment.* Not every wrongdoing of a paralegal is within the scope of employment simply because it is employment related. The test is as follows: Paralegals act within the scope of employment when they are furthering the business of their employer, which for our purposes is the practice of law. Slandering a client for failure to

---

[38]We are talking here of vicarious *civil* liability, or more specifically, the tort liability of employers because of the torts committed by their employees. Employers are not subject to vicarious *criminal* liability. If a paralegal commits a crime on the job, only the paralegal goes to jail (unless the employer actually participated in the crime).

pay a law firm bill certainly furthers the business of the law firm. But the opposite is probably true when a paralegal has an argument with a client over a football game and punches the client during their accidental evening meeting at a bar. In the latter example, the client could not sue the paralegal's employer for the intentional tort of battery under the doctrine of *respondeat superior,* because the battery was not committed while furthering the business of the employer. Only the paralegal would be liable for the tort under such circumstances.

The most common tort committed by attorneys is negligence. This tort occurs when a client is injured because of a failure to use the ordinary skill, knowledge, and diligence normally possessed and used, under similar circumstances, by a member of the profession in good standing. In short, the tort is committed by failure to exercise the reasonable care expected of an attorney. An attorney is not, however, an insurer. Every mistake will not lead to negligence liability even if it causes harm to the client. The harm must be due to an unreasonable mistake, such as forgetting to file an action in court before the statute of limitations runs out.

When a paralegal commits negligence for which the attorney becomes liable under *respondeat superior,* the same standard applies. Since the work product of the paralegal blends into the work product of the supervising attorney, the attorney becomes as fully responsible for what the paralegal did as if the attorney had committed the negligence. Unreasonableness is measured by what a reasonable attorney would have done, not what a reasonable paralegal would have done.

There have not been many tort cases in which paralegals have been sued for wrongdoing in a law office. Yet as paralegals become more prominent in the practice of law, more are expected to be named as defendants. The most common kinds of cases involving paralegals have occurred when the paralegal was a notary and improperly notarized signatures under pressure from the supervising attorney.

■ ASSIGNMENT 1.17

Mary Smith is a paralegal at the XYZ law firm. One of her tasks is to file a document in court. She negligently forgets to do so. As a result, the client has a default judgment entered against her. What options are available to the client?

■ ASSIGNMENT 1.18

Go to the *American Digest System.* Give citations to and brief summaries of court cases on the topics listed in (a) and (b) below. Start with the Descriptive Word Index volumes of the most recent Decennial. After you check the appropriate key numbers in that Decennial, check those key numbers in all the General Digest volumes that follow the most recent Decennial. Then check for case law in at least three other recent Decennials. Once you obtain citations to case law in the digest paragraphs, you do not have to go to the reporters to read the full text of the opinions. Simply give the citations you find and brief summaries of the cases as they are printed in the digest paragraphs.

(a) Cases, if any, dealing with the negligence of attorneys in the hiring and supervision of legal secretaries, law clerks, investigators, and paralegals. (If there are many, select any five cases.)

(b) Cases, if any, dealing with the negligence of doctors and/or hospitals in the hiring and supervision of nurses, paramedics, and other medical technicians. (If there are many, select any five cases.)

▨ Section I. Malpractice Insurance

Legal *malpractice* generally refers to wrongful conduct by an attorney for which an injured party (the attorney's client) can receive damages. Just as doctors purchase malpractice insurance against suits by their patients, so too attorneys can buy such insurance to cover suits against them by their clients for alleged errors and omissions. We need to examine how paralegals fit into this picture.

Until the 1940s, not many attorneys bought malpractice insurance because suits by clients were relatively rare. Today, the picture has changed radically; cautious attorneys do not practice law without such insurance against their own malpractice. "Statistically, the new attorney will be subjected to three claims before finishing a legal career." [39] Hence, very few attorneys are willing to *go bare,* that is, practice without insurance. This change has been due to a number of factors. As the practice of law becomes more complex, the likelihood of error increases. Furthermore, the public is becoming more aware of its right to sue. In spite of disclaimers by attorneys that they are not guaranteeing any results, client expectations tend to be high, and hence clients are more likely to blame their attorney for an unfavorable result. And attorneys are increasingly willing to sue each other. In fact, some attorneys have developed a legal malpractice specialty in which they take clients who want to sue other attorneys. As malpractice awards against attorneys continue to rise (see Figure 1.7), the market for malpractice insurance has dramatically increased. And so has the cost. In some cities, the premium for insurance is over $6,000 per year per attorney.

There are two kinds of professional liability insurance policies covering attorney malpractice: occurrence policies and claims-made policies. An *occurrence policy* covers all occurrences (such as negligent error or omission) during the period the policy is in effect, even if the claim on such an occurrence is not actually filed until after the policy expires. Insurance companies are reluctant to write such policies because of the length of time it sometimes takes to uncover the existence of the negligent error or omission. Here's an example: An attorney makes a careless mistake in drafting a will that is not discovered until the person who hired the attorney dies many years later. Under an occurrence policy, the attorney is protected if the mistake occurred while the policy was in effect, even if the actual claim was not filed in court until after the policy terminated. The most common kind of policy sold by insurance companies today is the *claims-*

---

[39] R. Mallen & J. Smith, *Legal Malpractice,* 3rd ed., 2 (1989).

FIGURE 1.7 Malpractice Liability Claims Against Attorneys

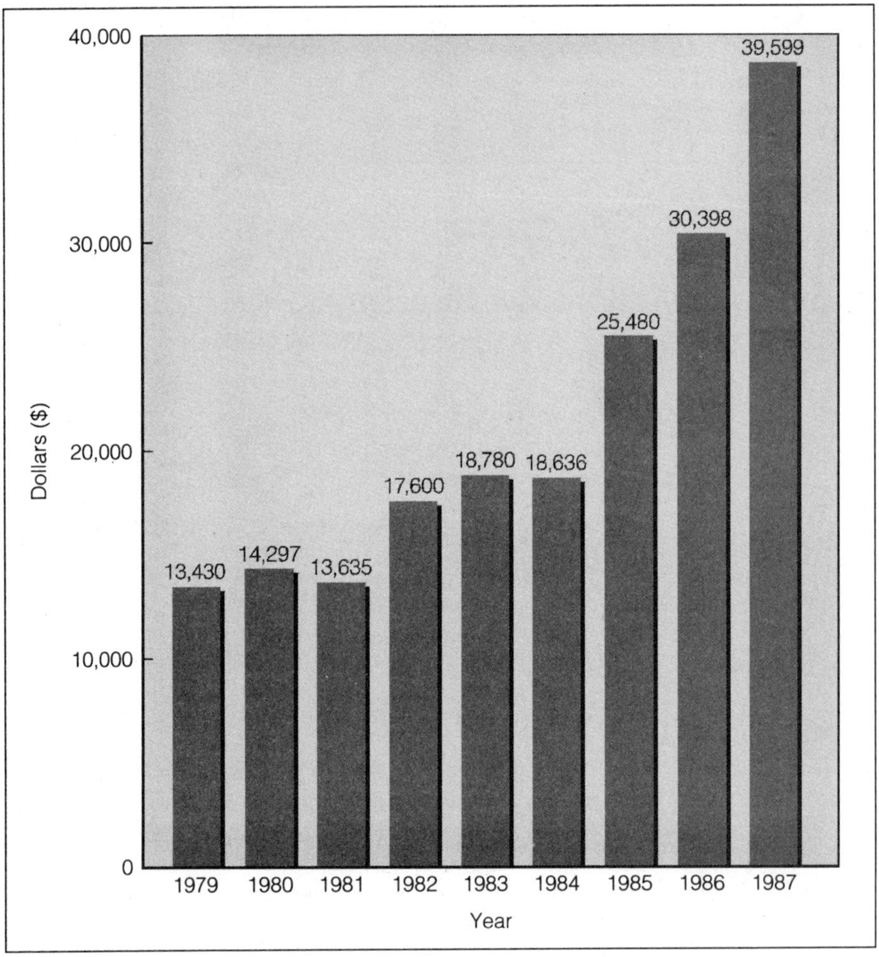

In 1979 the average claim paid, including all expenses, was $13,430. By 1987 this amount rose 295% to a new average of $39,599.

Source: St. Paul Fire & Marine Insurance Company

made policy under which coverage is limited to claims actually filed (made) during the period in which the policy is in effect.[40]

Malpractice policies usually cover all the attorneys *and* the nonattorney employees of the law office. One policy, for example, defines the individuals covered—"the insured"—as follows:

> The insured includes the firm, all lawyers within the firm, and all non-lawyer employees, as well as former partners, officers, directors and employees solely while they acted on behalf of the insured firm.[41]

---

[40]It is possible for a claims-made policy to cover a negligent error or omission that took place *before* the effective date of the policy, but most companies exclude coverage for prepolicy claims that the attorney knows about or could have reasonably foreseen at the time the policy is applied for.

[41]Home Insurance Companies, Professional Liability Insurance.

Such inclusion of employees is not always automatic, however. The policies of some insurance companies do not include paralegals or secretaries unless the law firm specifically requests coverage for them and pays an additional premium for their inclusion. Paralegals should therefore ask their employers if their malpractice policy explicitly covers paralegals.

What about freelance or independent paralegals who sell their services to attorneys? Although they may not be considered employees of the firm, they will usually be covered under the firm's policy in the same manner as full-time, in-house paralegal employees. So long as the employing attorney supervises and is responsible for the conduct of the paralegal, the malpractice policy usually provides coverage. In the language of one widely used policy, coverage is provided for "any other person for whose acts, errors or omissions the insured is legally responsible," [42] which would include freelance paralegals.

Nevertheless, some freelance paralegals have explored the possibility of obtaining their own malpractice insurance policies. To date, most traditional insurance companies have not made such policies available, although there are exceptions. Complete Equity Markets, Inc., for example, offers "Paralegals Professional Indemnity Insurance" as a claims-made policy. For approximately $1,800 a year, a paralegal can purchase $250,000 worth of malpractice insurance. Since most paralegals work for an attorney and are already covered under the attorney's policy, few paralegals have purchased their own policy. Yet if paralegals are eventually granted a form of limited license that authorizes them to sell their services directly to the public, separate paralegal malpractice policies will become common and may even be mandated as a condition of receiving the license. [43]

☐ Chapter Summary

Criminal prosecution may result from violating statutes on the unauthorized practice of law. In general, they prohibit nonattorneys from appearing for another in a representative capacity, drafting legal documents, and giving legal advice. Nonattorneys can sell forms and other legal materials but cannot give individual help in using them.

There are some major exceptions to the prohibitions on nonattorney conduct. In a limited number of circumstances, nonattorneys are authorized to do what would otherwise constitute the unauthorized practice of law. For example:

- In most states, a real estate broker can draft sales contracts.

- Several specialized courts allow nonattorneys to represent clients in court, although this is rare.

- A few states allow paralegals to "appear" in court to request a continuance or a new date for the next hearing in a case.

Continued

---

[42] American Home Assurance Company, Lawyers Professional Liability Policy.

[43] As we saw earlier, most Enrolled Agents are nonlawyers who are authorized to provide certain tax services to the public. The National Association of Enrolled Agents offers a "Professional Liability Insurance Plan" through the St. Paul Fire and Marine Insurance Company. The Association's brochure says, "You can now secure protection against an unexpected lawsuit or penalty for damages arising from services you provide as an Enrolled Agent." Attorneys are not eligible to purchase this insurance.

☐ Chapter Summary—*Continued*

- An inmate can "practice law" in prison—for example, he or she can draft court documents for and give legal advice to another inmate if the prison does not offer adequate alternative methods of providing legal services.

- Many administrative agencies, particularly at the federal level, allow nonattorneys to represent clients before the agencies.

A number of states have considered broad-based licensing (which would cover all activities of all paralegals) and limited licensing (which would cover specified activities of those paralegals, often called legal technicians, who are not supervised by attorneys). To date, neither kind of licensing has been enacted. Relatively soon, however, a limited-license requirement will probably be enacted in one or two states. While this would be a dramatic event, it would affect very few paralegals, since limited licensing would not apply to paralegals who work for attorneys.

All paralegal schools in the country must be licensed by their state. There is no requirement that they be accredited by the bar association. The American Bar Association, however, has an "approval" process whereby a school can be approved by the ABA.

A number of bar associations allow paralegals to become associate or affiliate members. For example, the American Bar Association has a membership category called Legal Assistant Associate.

Certification has been a major point of disagreement between the National Association of Legal Assistants (NALA) and the National Federation of Paralegal Associations (NFPA). NALA has instituted a national test that leads to certification as a Certified Legal Assistant (CLA). Even though this is a voluntary program, NFPA opposes its very existence.

The Fair Labor Standards Act requires employers to pay overtime compensation to employees unless they function in an executive, administrative, or professional capacity. Paralegal managers with major responsibility for the supervision of other paralegals would fall within one of the exceptions, and hence would not be entitled to overtime compensation. All other paralegals, however, do not fall within an exception and therefore must be paid overtime compensation.

If a paralegal commits a tort, such as negligence, he or she is personally liable to the defendant. Under the theory of *respondeat superior*, the supervising attorney is also liable for the wrong committed by the paralegal if it occurred within the scope of employment. Most attorneys have a claims-made malpractice insurance policy that covers their employees.

Key Terms

accreditation	practice of law	*Johnson v. Avery*
approval	unauthorized practice of	Administrative Procedure
certification	law	Act
certified	authorized practice of	registered agent
certificated	law	agency practitioner
ethics	statement of principles	enrolled agent
guideline	treaties	supremacy clause
licensure	certified domestic	page 52 debate
limited licensure	violence advocate	legal technician
specialty licensure	ex parte order	licensed independent
registration	jailhouse lawyer	paralegal
regulation	writ writer	HALT

limited practice officer
pro bono
prepaid legal services
legal insurance
approval commission
antitrust
monopoly
associate members
affiliate members
attorney attestation
CLA

CLAS
CFLA
specialty certification
legal assistant division
entry-level certification
advanced certification
GOD
Fair Labor Standards
    Act
overtime compensation
Wage and Hour Division

exempt paralegal
nonexempt paralegal
tort liability
personal liability
vicarious liability
respondeat superior
deep pocket
malpractice
go bare
occurrence policy
claims-made policy

CHAPTER

2

Attorney Ethics and Paralegal Ethics

■ Chapter Outline

■ Section A. The Ten Commandments of an Ethical Conservative

When it comes to ethics, *a paralegal must be conservative.* To an ethical conservative, the question is not, "What can I get away with?" but rather, "What is the right thing to do?" With this guideline in mind, we will examine many ethical principles in this chapter. Some of the most important are presented in Figure 2.1.

■ Section B. Enforcing Ethics

Ethics and Sanctions

Ethics are rules that embody standards of behavior to which members of an organization must conform. The organization is often an association of in-

FIGURE 2.1   Paralegal Ethics: The Ten Commandments of
a Conservative

1. Know the ethical rules governing attorneys. If you understand when attorneys are vulnerable to charges of unprofessional conduct, you will be better able to help them avoid such charges.

2. Know the ethical rules governing paralegals. At the start of your paralegal career, promise yourself that you will adhere to rigorous standards of professional ethics, even if these standards are higher than those followed by people around you.

3. Never tell anyone who is not working on a case anything about that case. This includes your best friend, your spouse, and your relatives.

4. Assume that people outside your office do not have a clear understanding of what a paralegal or legal assistant is. Make sure that everyone with whom you come in contact (clients, attorneys, court officials, agency officials, the public) understand that you are not an attorney.

5. Know what legal advice is and refuse to be coaxed into giving it, no matter how innocent the question asked of you appears to be.

6. Never make contact with an opposing party in a legal dispute, or with anyone closely associated with that party, unless you have the permission of your supervising attorney and of the attorney for the opposing party, if the latter has one.

7. Don't sign your name to anything if you are not certain that what you are signing is 100% accurate and that the law allows a paralegal to sign it.

8. Never pad your time sheets. Insist that what you submit is 100% accurate.

9. Know the common rationalizations for misrepresentation and other unethical conduct:

   ■ it's always done

   ■ the other side does it

   ■ the cause of our client is just

   ■ if I don't do it, I will jeopardize my job

   Promise yourself that you will not allow any of these rationalizations to entice you to participate in misrepresentation or other unethical conduct.

10. If what you are asked to do doesn't feel right, don't proceed until it does.

dividuals in the same occupation—for example, attorneys, paralegals, stockbrokers, or accountants. The ethical rules of some organizations are enforced by *sanctions*. A sanction is any penalty or punishment imposed for unacceptable conduct.[1] Other organizations, however, have ethical rules that are not tied to any system of enforcement.

All of the major national paralegal associations have adopted ethical rules, as we shall see later in the chapter, but none are enforced by sanctions. No paralegal, for example, has ever been thrown out of a paralegal association for unethical conduct. It could happen, but it is unlikely since it is very expensive to establish and operate an enforcement system. Paralegal associations simply do not have the resources that would be required.

Attorneys, on the other hand, *are* subject to enforceable ethical rules. These rules attempt to govern everything an attorney does in the practice of law. Of

---

[1]Another meaning of the word *sanction* is to authorize or to give formal approval. Example: the court *sanctioned* the payment of attorney fees.

course, one of the things an attorney does is employ paralegals. Hence, as we will see, there are rules on how an attorney can use paralegals ethically. Unethical use of paralegals can subject the attorney to sanctions.

Paralegals and Attorney Ethics

Can a paralegal *also* be sanctioned for violating these ethical rules? No. The rules govern attorney conduct only.[2] Since paralegals cannot join a bar association as full members, they cannot be sanctioned by a bar association or by any other agency set up to monitor attorney conduct. Serious wrongdoing by paralegals may result in their being fired and might subject them to negligence suits or to criminal prosecution (as we saw in Chapter 1,) but they cannot be punished for unethical conduct by the entity that regulates attorneys.

This does not mean, however, that paralegals can ignore the ethical rules governing attorneys. Quite the contrary. *One of the paralegal's primary responsibilities is to help an attorney avoid being charged with unethical conduct.* (A recent seminar conducted by the Los Angeles Paralegal Association was entitled "Law Firm Ethics: How to Keep Your Attorneys off '60 Minutes' "!) Hence, the paralegal must be intimately familiar with ethical rules. Our goal in this chapter is to provide you with that familiarity.

Courts, Legislatures, and Bar Associations

In most states, the regulation of attorneys is primarily under the control of the highest court in the state (often called the Supreme Court), which determines when an attorney can be granted a license to practice law and under what conditions the license will be taken away or suspended because of unethical conduct. Since the state legislature may also exert some regulatory authority over attorneys, a dispute occasionally arises over which branch of government can control a particular aspect of the practice of law. The judiciary often wins this dispute and becomes the final authority. In practice, however, the judicial branch and the legislative branch usually share regulatory jurisdiction over the practice of law, with the dominant branch being the judiciary. The day-to-day functions of regulation are delegated to an entity such as a state bar association and a disciplinary board or grievance commission.

There are three kinds of bar associations:

■ National (for example, American Bar Association, Association of Trial Lawyers of America, Hispanic National Bar Association)

■ State (for example, Illinois State Bar Association, State Bar of Montana)

■ Local (for example, Boston Bar Association, San Diego County Bar Association)

---

[2]Remarkably, there is one jurisdiction—the District of Columbia—that allows a nonattorney to become a full owner/partner of a law firm! This individual must agree to abide by the ethical code that governs attorneys. In D.C., therefore, the ethical rules governing attorneys *do* apply to nonattorneys. (The first nonattorney to become a partner of a law firm was an accountant.)

All national and local bar associations are voluntary; no attorney is required to be a member. The majority of state bar associations in the country are *integrated,* which simply means that membership is required as a condition of practicing law in the state. (Integrated bar associations are also referred to as *mandatory* or *unified* bar associations. See Figure 2.2.) There is a state bar association in every state. Most, but not all, are mandatory.

Under the general supervision of the state's highest court, the state bar association has a large role in regulating most aspects of the practice of law. For example, dues charged by integrated bar associations are used to fund the state's system of enforcing ethical rules. States that do not have integrated bar associations often have a *registration* requirement. Each attorney in the state registers to practice law and pays a registration fee that is used to fund that state's system of enforcing the ethical rules. Even in these states, the state bar association has a great influence over the regulation of attorneys. Given this dominant role of bar associations, the method of regulating attorneys in America is essentially that of self-regulation: attorneys regulating attorneys.[3]

There is no national set of ethical rules that applies to every state. Each state can adopt its own rules to regulate the attorneys licensed in that state. The rules are found in documents with various names, such as code of ethics, canons of ethics, code of professional responsibility, model rules. In fact, however, there is considerable similarity in the rules that the states have adopted. The reason for this similarity is the influence of the American Bar Association.

As indicated, the American Bar Association is a voluntary national bar association; no attorney must belong to it. Yet approximately 55% of the attorneys in America do belong to the ABA. It publishes ethical rules but does *not* discipline attorneys for unethical conduct. The role of the ABA in this area is to write ethical rules and to *propose* to the individual states that they be accepted. A state is free to adopt, modify, or reject them. The current recommendation of the ABA is found in a document called the *Model Rules of Professional Conduct.*[4] This document has been very influential throughout the country. Many states adopted it with relatively minor changes.

Accusation of Unethical Conduct

When an attorney is charged with unethical conduct, the case is investigated by a disciplinary body appointed by the state's highest court. The name for this body differs from state to state, e.g., the Grievance Commission, the Attorney Registration and Disciplinary Commission, the Committee on Professional Conduct, the Board of Professional Responsibility.

---

[3]This is so even in states that allow nonattorneys to serve on boards or commissions that regulate an aspect of the legal profession.

[4]The *Model Rules of Professional Conduct* is a 1983 revision of the ABA's *Model Code of Professional Responsibility.* The latter document consists of three main parts. First, there are nine *canons,* which are general statements of norms that express the standards of professional conduct expected of attorneys. Second, and more important, there are *disciplinary rules* (abbreviated DR), which are mandatory statements of the minimum conduct below which no attorney can fall without being subject to disciplinary action. Third, there are *ethical considerations* (abbreviated EC) which represent the objectives toward which each member of the profession should strive.

FIGURE 2.2   States with Unified Bar Associations (1991)

Alabama	Idaho	Montana	North Dakota	Utah
Alaska	Kentucky	Nebraska	Oklahoma	Virginia
Arizona	Louisiana	Nevada	Oregon	Washington
California	Michigan	New Hampshire	South Carolina	West Virginia
Florida	Mississippi	New Mexico	South Dakota	Wisconsin
Georgia	Missouri	North Carolina	Texas	Wyoming

A hearing is held to determine whether unethical conduct was committed by the accused attorney. The commission, committee, or board then makes its recommendation to the state's highest court which makes the final determination of whether to accept this recommendation. A number of sanctions can be imposed by the court. See Figure 2.3.

Section C. The Ethical Rules

We turn now to an overview of specific ethical rules that apply to attorneys. Where appropriate, a paralegal perspective on the rules will be presented. At the end of the overview, there will be a more concentrated focus on paralegals, particularly on ethical issues not covered earlier in the chapter. The overview is based on the ABA *Model Rules of Professional Conduct.* The rule numbers used in the discussion (such as Model Rule 1.5) refer to these *Model Rules,* which will either be quoted or summarized.

1. Competence

An attorney shall provide competent representation to a client. Model Rule 1.1

FIGURE 2.3 Attorney Sanctions for Unethical Conduct

DISBARMENT:	The termination of the right to practice law. The disbarment can be permanent or temporary. If it's temporary, the attorney will be allowed to apply for readmission after a designated period.
SUSPENSION:	The removal of an attorney from the practice of law for a specified minimum period, after which the attorney can apply for reinstatement. An *interim suspension* is a temporary suspension pending the imposition of final discipline.
REPRIMAND:	A public declaration that the attorney's conduct was improper. This does not affect his or her right to practice. Reprimand is also called *censure* or *public censure.*
ADMONITION:	A nonpublic declaration that the attorney's conduct was improper. The mildest form of punishment that can be imposed, it does not affect his or her right to practice. An admonition is also known as a *private reprimand.*
PROBATION:	Allowing the attorney to continue to practice but under specified conditions, such as submitting to periodic audits of client funds controlled by the attorney or making restitution to a client whose funds were wrongly taken by the attorney.

A *competent* attorney uses the *knowledge* and *skill* that are reasonably necessary to represent a particular client. What is reasonably necessary depends on the complexity of the case. A great deal of knowledge and skill, for example, may be needed when representing a corporate client accused of complicated antitrust violations.

How do attorneys obtain this knowledge and skill? They draw on the general principles of legal analysis and legal research learned in law school. But more importantly, they take the time needed to *prepare* themselves. They spend time in the law library. They talk with their colleagues. In some instances, they formally associate themselves with more experienced attorneys in the area. Attorneys who fail to take these steps are acting unethically if their failure means that they do not have the knowledge and skill reasonably necessary to represent a particular client.

Some attorneys have so many clients that they could not possibly give proper attention to each. Always looking for more lucrative work, they run the risk of neglecting the clients they already have. As a consequence, they might miss court dates or other filing deadlines, lose documents, fail to determine what law governs a client's case, etc. Such an attorney is practicing law "from the hip"—incompetently and unethically.

> Example: Mary Henderson, Esq. has a large criminal law practice. She agrees to probate the estate of a client's deceased son. She has never handled such a case before. Five years go by. No progress is made in determining who is entitled to receive the estate. If some minimal legal research had been done, Henderson would have been able to close the case within six months of taking it.

Henderson has probably acted unethically. The failure to do basic research on a case is a sign of incompetence. The need for such research is clear in view of the fact that she has never handled a probate case before. Either she must take the time to find out how to probate the estate, or she must contact another attorney with probate experience and arrange to work with this attorney on the case. Not doing either is unethical.

The vast majority of graduates of law schools need a good deal of on-the-job study and guidance before they are ready to handle cases of any complexity. A law school education does little more than help ensure that the attorney is equipped to go out and *continue* learning through experience and legal research. A good attorney is always learning the law—long after law school is over. The first day on the job for new attorneys is often a very nerve-wracking event because they are acutely aware of how much they do *not* know.

In addition to sanctions for unethical conduct, an attorney's incompetence may have other consequences as well. The client might try to sue the attorney for negligence in a legal malpractice case. (Such suits were discussed in Chapter 1.) If the client is a criminal defendant who was convicted, he or she may try to appeal the conviction on the ground that the attorney's incompetence amounted to a denial of the effective "Assistance of Counsel" guaranteed by the 6th Amendment of the U.S. Constitution.

Paralegal Perspective:

■ "An attorney who utilizes a legal assistant's services is responsible for determining that the legal assistant is competent to perform the tasks assigned, based on the legal assistant's education, training, and experience . . . ." [5] While the attorney has this supervisory responsibility, paralegals also have a responsibility to maintain their own competence.

■ If you are given assignments that are beyond your knowledge and skill, let your supervisor know. Either you must be given training with close supervision, or you must be given other assignments. A "lawyer should explain to the legal assistant that the legal assistant has a duty to inform the lawyer of any assignment which the assistant regards as beyond his capability." [6]

■ After you complete an assignment, look for an opportunity to ask your supervisor how you could have improved your performance on the assignment. Do not wait for a year-end evaluation to learn what you can do to become a more competent paralegal.

■ Find out which attorneys, administrators, paralegals, and secretaries in the office have a reputation for explaining things well. Spend time with such individuals even if you do not work with them on a daily basis. Take them to lunch. Find time to sit with them on a coffee break. Ask lots of questions. Let them know you respect high-quality work and appreciate anything they can tell you to help you increase your competence.

■ Take the initiative in continuing your formal paralegal education after you are employed. Do not wait for someone to suggest further training. Find out

---

[5] ABA Standing Committee on Legal Assistants, *Model Guidelines for the Utilization of Legal Assistant Services,* Draft, Comment to Guideline 1 (March 1991). (Hereinafter cited as ABA *Model Guidelines.*)
[6] Section 20–110, Committee Commentary, *New Mexico Rules Governing the Practice of Law* (Judicial Pamphlet 16).

what seminars and conferences are being conducted by paralegal associations and bar associations in your area. Attend those that are relevant to your job even if you must pay for them yourself.

2. Diligence/Unwarranted Delay

An attorney shall act with reasonable diligence and promptness in representing a client. Model Rule 1.3

An attorney must make reasonable efforts to expedite litigation. Model Rule 3.2

Angry clients often complain that attorneys take forever to complete a case, and keep clients in the dark about what is happening. "He never answers my calls." "It took months to file the case in court." "He keeps telling me that everything is fine, but nothing ever gets done." Such complaints do not necessarily indicate unethical behavior by the attorney. Events may be beyond the control of the attorney. For example, the court calendar is crowded, the other side is not responding. Yet this does not excuse a lack of regular communication with clients to keep them reasonably informed about the status of their case.

Other explanations for a lack of diligence and promptness, however, are more serious:

■ The attorney is disorganized. The law office has not developed adequate systems to process cases. The delays are due to careless mistakes and a lack of skill.

■ The attorney is taking many more cases than the office can handle. Additional personnel should be hired to do the needed work, or new cases should not be accepted.

Often, the failure to use reasonable diligence and promptness causes harm to the client. For example, the attorney neglects to file a suit before the statute of limitations has run against the client. Unreasonable procrastination, however, can be unethical even if such harm does not result.

Another problem is the attorney who intentionally seeks numerous delays in an effort to try to wear the other side down. It is unethical to engage in such dilatory practices. Attorneys must use reasonable efforts to expedite litigation, consistent with protecting the interests of their clients.

Paralegal Perspective:

■ An overloaded attorney probably works with an overloaded paralegal. Successful paralegals often take the initiative by asking for additional work. But reason must prevail. If you have more work than you can handle, you must let your supervisor know. Otherwise, you might be contributing to the problem of undue procrastination.

■ Learn everything you can about office systems. Find out how they are created. After you have gained some experience in the office, you should start designing systems on your own initiative.

■ When a busy attorney is in court or cannot be disturbed because of pressing work on another case, someone in the office should be available to communicate with clients who want to know the status of their case. In many offices, the paralegal is in a position to provide this information. The role is delicate, however, since in addition to asking about the status of their case, clients often asks questions that call for legal advice. Giving such advice may constitute the unauthorized practice of law. Later we will examine in greater depth the temptations and pressures on a paralegal to give legal advice.

3. Fees

An attorney's fee shall be reasonable. Model Rule 1.5(a)

There is no absolute standard to determine when a fee is excessive and therefore unreasonable. A number of factors must be considered: the amount of time and labor involved, the complexity of the case, the experience and reputation of the attorney, the customary fee in the locality for the same kind of case, etc.

Examples: In 1979, a court ruled that $500 an hour was excessive in a simple battery case involving a guilty plea and no unusual issues. In 1984, a court ruled that a fee of $22,500 was excessive in an uncomplicated real estate case involving very little time. The case was settled through the efforts of someone other than the attorney.

The basis of the fee should be communicated to the client before or soon after the attorney starts to work on the case. This is often done in the contract of employment called a *retainer.*[7]

At one time, bar associations published a list of "recommended fees" that should be charged for designated kinds of services. These *minimum-fee schedules* have now been prohibited by the United States Supreme Court. They constitute illegal price fixing by the bar in violation of the antitrust laws.

Contingent fees can sometimes present ethical problems. A contingent fee is a fee that is dependent on the outcome of the case.

Example: An attorney signs a retainer to represent a client in an automobile negligence case. If the jury awards the client damages, the attorney will receive 30% of the award. If the client loses the case, the attorney receives no fee.

This is a contingent fee since it is dependent on the outcome of the negligence case.

The benefit of a contingent fee is that it provides an incentive for an attorney to take the case of a client who does not have funds to pay an attorney while the case is pending. But contingent fees are not ethical in every case, even if the amount to be received by the successful attorney is otherwise reasonable. A contingent fee in a criminal case, and in most divorce cases, for example, is unethical.

---

[7]Another meaning of the word *retainer* is the amount of money or other assets that will serve as an advance payment for services. Depending on the agreement reached, the retainer may or may not be refundable in the event that the attorney-client relationship ends before all the legal services are performed.

> Example: Gabe Farrell is a client of Sam Grondon, Esq. in a criminal case where Gabe is charged with murder. Gabe agrees to pay Grondon $100,000 if he is found innocent. Grondon will receive nothing if Gabe is convicted of any crime.

This fee agreement is unethical. Contingent fees are not allowed in criminal cases. Note the pressures on Grondon. He arguably has no incentive to try to negotiate a guilty plea to a lesser charge, since such a plea would mean a conviction and, hence, no fee. In such a situation, the attorney's own personal interest (obtaining the $100,000) could conflict with the interest of the client (receiving a lesser penalty through a negotiated plea). Similar pressures can arise in family-law cases.

> Example: To obtain a divorce from his wife, a client hires an attorney. The fee is $25,000 if the divorce is granted.

As the case develops, suppose there is a glimmer of hope that the husband and wife might reconcile. Hence, the attorney's interest (obtaining the $25,000) could conflict with the interest of the client (reconciling). This might lead the attorney to discourage the reconciliation or to set up roadblocks to it. Reconciliation obviously removes the possibility of the contingency—obtaining the divorce—from occurring. In family law cases, therefore, contingent fees are unethical if the fee is dependent on securing a divorce, on the amount of alimony obtained, on the amount of support obtained, or on the amount of a property settlement in lieu of alimony or support. Model Rule 1.5(d). This is so even if the terms of the contingent fee are otherwise reasonable.

One final theme should be covered: *fee splitting*. The splitting or division of a fee refers to a single client bill covering the fee of two or more attorneys who are not in the same firm.

> Example: John Jones, Esq. is hired by a singer who is charging her record company with copyright infringement and breach of contract. Jones calls in Randy Smith, Esq., a specialist in copyright law from another firm. Both work on the case. The singer receives one bill for the work of both attorneys even though they work for different law firms.

The attorneys are splitting or dividing the fee between them.[8] This arrangement is proper under certain conditions. For example, the total fee must be reasonable, and the client must be told about the participation of all the attorneys and not object.

Suppose, however, that the attorney splits the fee with a nonattorney.

> Example: Frank Martin is a freelance investigator. He refers accident victims to a law firm. For every client he refers to the firm, he receives 25% of the fee collected by the firm.

> Example: Helen Gregson is a chiropractor. She refers medical malpractice cases to a law firm which compensates her for each referral.

These are improper divisions of fees with nonattorneys—even if the amount of the division is reasonable and the clients brought in by Martin or Gregson con-

---

[8]The attorney who refers a case to another attorney receives what is called a *referral fee* or *forwarding fee* from the latter.

sent to their receiving a part of the fee. An attorney cannot share with a nonattorney a portion of a fee paid by particular clients. The rationale behind this prohibition is that the nonattorney might exercise some control over the attorney and thereby jeopardize the attorney's independent judgment.

For the same reason, an attorney cannot form a partnership with a nonattorney if any of the activities of the partnership consist of the practice of law. If the office practices law as a corporation, a nonattorney cannot own any interest in the company or be a director or officer.[9]

Paralegal Perspective:

■ An attorney or law firm may include paralegals and other nonattorney employees in a compensation or retirement plan, even though the plan is based in whole or in part on a profit-sharing arrangement. Model Rule 5.4(a)(3).

> Example: Frank is a paralegal at a law firm. The firm has a retirement plan under which the firm contributes a portion of its profits into the plan. Frank is a member of this retirement plan.

The firm is not acting unethically. In most states, paralegals can receive compensation and retirement benefits that are based on the fees received by the firm so long as they are not receiving all or part of *particular* legal fees. "The linchpin of the prohibition [against splitting fees with a legal assistant] seems to be the advance agreement of the lawyer to 'split' a fee based on a preexisting contingent arrangement. There is no general prohibition against a lawyer who enjoys a particularly profitable period recognizing the contribution of the legal assistant to that profitability with a discretionary bonus. Likewise, a lawyer engaged in a particularly profitable specialty of legal practice is not prohibited from compensating the legal assistant who aids materially in that practice more handsomely than the compensation generally awarded to legal assistants in that geographic area who work in law practices that are less lucrative. Indeed, any effort to fix a compensation level for legal assistants and prohibit greater compensation would appear to violate the federal antitrust laws." [10]

■ A related restriction in many states is that an attorney cannot give a paralegal any compensation for referring business to the attorney. "It appears clear that a legal assistant may not be compensated on a contingent basis for a particular case or paid for 'signing up' clients for a legal practice." [11]

■ Attorneys must not allow their paralegals to accept cases, to reject cases, or to "set fees." The responsibility "for establishing the amount of a fee to be charged for a legal service" may not be delegated to a paralegal.[12]

---

[9]Wolfram, C., *Modern Legal Ethics*, § 9.2.4 (1986). In the District of Columbia, however, where nonattorneys are allowed to be owner-partners in law firms, nonattorneys can obviously share legal fees with attorneys. See footnote 2.

[10]ABA *Model Guidelines*, Comment to Guideline 9, see footnote 5.

[11]Ibid.

[12]ABA *Model Guidelines*, Guideline 3(b), see footnote 5.

- "A lawyer may include a charge for the work performed by a legal assistant in setting a charge for legal services."[13] Most attorneys bill clients for paralegal time. Paralegals record their time on time sheets that become the basis of bills sent to clients. The amount that an attorney bills for paralegal time must be reasonable. Reasonableness is determined by a number of factors, such as the experience of the paralegal, the nature of the tasks the paralegal undertakes, and the market rate for paralegals in the area.

- *Double billing* must be avoided. The paralegal's time should not have already been figured into the attorney's hourly rate. Some states ask the attorney to submit an affidavit to support the amount claimed for the paralegal's time. The affidavit must give a detailed statement of the time spent and services rendered by the paralegal, a summary of the paralegal's qualifications, etc. In New Mexico, the attorney must disclose to the client the amount to be charged for the services of the paralegals in the office.

- As a paralegal, your time records should be contemporaneous, that is, made at approximately the same time as the events you are recording. Try to avoid recording time long after you perform tasks that require time records.

- Time sheets must also be accurate; padding is clearly unethical. Padding occurs when someone records time that was not in fact spent. When a client is billed on the basis of time sheets that have been padded, fraud has been committed. Padding is a serious problem in the practice of law:

  [It] occurs most typically when attorneys are under the gun to bill a large number of hours. Everyone knows of lawyers who begin work at 8:00, leave the office at 6:00 and yet bill 10 hours a day—a feat that utterly amazes me. Whether it be eating lunch, talking to a spouse, working with support staff, reading advance sheets or just taking a break, some portion of every day is spent on non-billable matters. [A young Midwestern associate at a medium-sized firm says] padding or fabrication of entries is encouraged, or at the very least tolerated, at his firm, and many others, to judge from his friends' experiences. The pressure to pad is intense.[14]

  Unfortunately, paralegals can find themselves under a similar pressure, which, of course, should be resisted.

  One of the most common temptations that can corrupt a paralegal's ethics is to inflate billable hours, since there is often immense pressure in law firms to bill high hours for job security and upward mobility. Such "creative billing" is not humorous; it's both morally wrong and illegal. It's also fraudulent and a plain and simple case of theft.[15]

4. Crime or Fraud by an Attorney

An attorney must not engage in criminal or fraudulent conduct. Model Rule 8.4

Sadly, it is not uncommon for an attorney to be charged with criminal conduct, such as theft of client funds, *insider trading* and securities fraud, falsifying

---

[13]ABA *Model Guidelines*, Guideline 8, see footnote 5.
[14]Doe, *Billing: Is "Padding" Widespread?*, 76 American Bar Ass'n Journal 42 (December 1990).
[15]Smith, *AAfPE National Conference Highlights*, 8 Legal Assistant Today 103 (Jan./Feb. 1991).

official documents, or tax fraud. Since such conduct obviously affects the attorney's fitness to practice law, sanctions for unethical conduct can be imposed in addition to prosecution in a criminal court. Once an attorney is convicted of a serious crime in court, a separate disciplinary proceeding is often instituted to suspend or disbar the attorney for unethical conduct growing out of the same incident.

Paralegal Perspective:

▪ Value your integrity above all else. A paralegal in Oklahoma offers the following advice: "Insist on the highest standards for yourself and for your employer. One small ethical breach can lead to a series of compromises with enormous" disciplinary and "legal malpractice consequences." [16]

▪ If your supervisor is charged with criminal conduct, the chances are good that you will be questioned by prosecutors, and you might become a suspect yourself.

▪ In the highly charged, competitive environment of a law office, there are attorneys who are willing to violate the law in the interest of winning. Be sensitive to the overt and subtle pressures on you to participate in such violations. Talk with other paralegals who have encountered this problem. Don't sit in silence. If there is no one in the office with whom you can frankly discuss the elimination of these pressures, you must consider quitting. (See Section F of this chapter.)

▪ Paralegals who are also notaries are sometimes asked by their supervisors to notarize documents that should *not* be notarized. In fact, paralegals "are most often named as defendants for false notarization of a signature." [17] Such acts may not be covered in malpractice liability insurance policies since they are intentional acts. Be extremely cautious of what you are asked to sign.

▪ At some law firms, employees have succumbed to the temptation of using a "hot tip" that crosses their path in a corporate takeover case.[18] Assume that Company X is planning to merge with Company Y. The news is not yet public. When it does become public, the value of the stock in Company X is expected to rise dramatically. You work at a law firm that represents Company X and you find out about the planned merger while at work. If you buy stock in Company X before the announcement of the merger, you would benefit from the increased value of the stock that would result after the announcement. This might be an illegal use of inside information. In a dramatic recent case, a paralegal who worked at a securities law firm in Boston was charged with insider trading by the Securities and Exchange Commission (SEC). While working on a case involving a proposed merger, she learned certain information which she gave to outside investors who used it

---

[16]Tulsa Ass'n of Legal Assistants, *Hints for Helping Your Attorney Avoid Legal Malpractice*, TALA Times (August 1989).

[17]Race, *Malpractice Maladies*, Paradigm 12 (Baltimore Ass'n of Legal Assistants, July/Aug. 1989).

[18]Milford, *Law Firms Expected to Take Steps to Avert Insider Trading Scandals*, The News Journal D3 (October 16, 1989).

to make illegal profits in the stock market. The story made national news. One headline read, "SEC Says Boston Paralegal Gave Tip Worth $823,471." Soon after the incident, she was fired. All employees of law firms must be extremely careful. Innocently buying stock as a personal investment could turn into a nightmare. One attorney "recommends that any paralegal who would like to buy or sell securities should check first with a corporate attorney in the firm to see if the firm represents the issuer or a company negotiating with the issuer. If it does, an accusation of 'insider trading' might later be made." [19] The same caution applies when a member of the paralegal's immediate family buys or sells such securities.

■ Another problem area is the use of so-called *pirated software*. Many businesses buy one copy of computer software and then copy it so that other employees in the office can use it on other terminals. This is illegal, and can subject violators to fines and other criminal penalties.

■ In all aspects of your career as a paralegal, adopt the motto, "If it doesn't feel right, it probably isn't."

5. Crime or Fraud by a Client

An attorney shall not counsel a client to engage in conduct the attorney knows is criminal or fraudulent. Model Rule 1.2(d)

The client hires the attorney and controls the purpose of the attorney-client relationship. Furthermore, the client is entitled to know the legal consequences of any action he or she is contemplating. This does not mean, however, that the attorney must do whatever the client wants.

Example: The president of a corporation hires Leo Richards, Esq. to advise the company on how to dump toxic waste into a local river.

Note that the president has not asked Richards *if* the dumping is legal. It would be perfectly ethical for Richards to answer such a question. In the example, the president asks *how* to dump. If Richards feels that the dumping can legally take place, he can so advise the president. Suppose, however, that it is clear to Richards that the dumping would violate the federal or state criminal code. Under such circumstances, it would be unethical for Richards to advise the president on how to proceed with the dumping. The same would be true if the president wanted help in filing an environmental statement that misrepresented the intentions of the company. Such an application would be fraudulent, and an attorney must not help someone commit what the attorney knows is fraudulent conduct.

When attorneys are later charged with unethical conduct in such cases, their defense is often that they did not know the conduct proposed by the client was criminal or fraudulent. If the law applicable to the client's case is unclear, an attorney can make a good faith effort to find a legal way for the client to achieve his or her objective. The point at which the attorney crosses the ethical

---

[19]Shays, *Ethics for the Paralegal*, Postscript 15 (Manhattan Paralegal Ass'n, August/September 1989).

line is when he or she *knows* the client is trying to accomplish something criminal or fraudulent.

Paralegal Perspective:

- An attorney will rarely tell paralegals or other staff members that he or she knows the office is helping a client do something criminal or fraudulent. But you might learn that this is so, particularly if there is a close, trusting relationship between you and your supervising attorney. You must let this attorney or some other authority in the office know you do not feel comfortable working on such a case.

6. Frivolous Legal Positions

An attorney must not bring a frivolous claim or assert a frivolous defense. Model Rule 3.1

A client has a right to an attorney who is a vigorous advocate. But there are limits on what this can entail. It is unethical, for example, for an attorney to assert *frivolous positions* as claims or defenses. There are two major tests for determining when a legal position is frivolous: the good-faith test and the intentional-injury test. First, a position is frivolous if the attorney is unable to make a good-faith argument that existing law supports the position, or the attorney is unable to make a good-faith argument that existing law should be changed or reversed to support the position. A position is not necessarily frivolous simply because the attorney happens to think that the client will ultimately lose. The key is whether there is a good-faith argument to support the position. If the attorney can think of absolutely no rational support for the position, it is frivolous. Since the law is often unclear, it is difficult to establish that an attorney is acting unethically under the test of good faith. Second, a position is frivolous if the client's primary purpose in having the position asserted is to harass or maliciously injure someone.

Paralegal Perspective:

- In the heat of controversy, tempers can run high. Attorneys do not always exhibit the detachment expected of professionals. They may so thoroughly identify with the interests of their clients that they lose perspective. Paralegals working for such attorneys may get caught up in the same fever, particularly if there is a close attorney-paralegal working relationship on a high-stakes case that has lasted a considerable time. The momentum is to do whatever it takes to win. While this atmosphere can be exhilarating, it can also create an environment where less and less attention is paid to the niceties of ethics.

7. Safekeeping Property

An attorney shall hold client property separate from the attorney's own property. Model Rule 1.15

A law office often receives client funds or funds of others connected with the client's case—for example, attorneys receive money as trustees of a will or trust, as escrow agents in closing a business deal, or as settlement of a case. Such funds should be held in separate accounts, with complete records kept on each. The attorney should not *commingle* (i.e., mix) law firm funds with client funds. It is unethical to place everything in one account. This is so even if the firm maintains accurate records on what amounts in the single account belong to which clients and what amounts belong to the firm. In a commingled account, the danger is too great that client funds will be used for nonclient purposes.

Paralegal Perspective:

■ Use great care whenever your responsibility involves client funds, such as receiving funds from clients, opening bank accounts, depositing funds in the proper account at a bank, and making entries in law firm records on such funds. It should be fairly obvious to you whether an attorney is violating the rule on commingling funds. It may be less clear whether the attorney is improperly using client funds for unauthorized purposes. Attorneys have been known to "borrow" money from client accounts and then return the money before anyone discovers what was done. They may even arrange to pay the account interest while using the money. Elaborate bookkeeping and accounting gimmicks might be used to disguise what is going on. Such conduct is unethical even if the attorney pays interest and eventually returns all the funds. In addition, the attorney may eventually be charged with theft or criminal fraud. Of course, anyone who knowingly assists the attorney could be subject to the same consequences.

8. False Statements and Failure to Disclose

An attorney shall not knowingly:
(1) make a false statement of material fact or law to a tribunal,
(2) fail to disclose a material fact to a tribunal when disclosure is necessary to avoid assisting a client to commit a criminal or fraudulent act,
(3) fail to tell a tribunal about laws or other authority directly against the position of the attorney's client if this law or authority is not disclosed by opposing counsel, or
(4) offer evidence that the attorney knows is false. Model Rule 3.3(a)

One of the reasons the general public holds the legal profession in low esteem is their perception that attorneys seldom comply with the above rules. Our legal system is *adversarial,* which means that legal disputes are resolved by neutral judges after listening to fiercely partisan opponents. In effect, the parties do battle through their attorneys. This environment does not always encourage the participants to cooperate in court proceedings. In fact, quite the opposite is often true. In extreme cases, attorneys have been known to lie to the court, to offer knowingly false evidence, etc. Under Model Rule 3.3(a), such conduct is unethical.

Subsection (3) of Model Rule 3.3(a) is particularly startling.

Example: Karen Singer and Bill Carew are attorneys who are opposing each other in a bitter case involving a large sum of money. Singer is smarter than Carew. Singer knows about a very damaging but obscure case that goes against her client. But because of sloppy research, Carew does not know about it. Singer never mentions the case and it never comes up during the litigation.

Singer must pay a price for her silence. She is subject to sanctions for a violation of her ethical obligation of disclosure under Model Rule 3.3(a)(3).

Another controversial part of Model Rule 3.3(a) is subsection (2) requiring disclosures that involve criminal or fraudulent acts. Since this raises issues of confidentiality, we will discuss such disclosures later when we cover confidentiality.

Paralegal Perspective:

- Be aware that an attorney who justifies the use of deception in one case will probably repeat such deceptions in the future on other cases. To excuse the deception, the attorney will often refer to the necessity of protecting the client or to the alleged evilness of the other side. Deceptions are unethical despite such justifications.

- Chances are also good that employees of such an attorney will be pressured into participating in deception—for example, give a false date to a court clerk, help a client lie (commit perjury) on the witness stand, help an attorney alter a document to be introduced into evidence, or improperly notarize a document.

- Do not compromise your integrity no matter how much you believe in the cause of the client, no matter how much you detest the tactics of the opposing side, no matter how much you like the attorney for whom you work, and no matter how important this job is to you.

9. Withdrawal

An attorney must withdraw from a case: if continuing would result in a violation of ethical rules or other laws; if the client discharges the attorney, or if the attorney's physical or mental condition materially impairs his or her ability to represent the client. Model Rule 1.16(a)

Attorneys are not required to take every case. Furthermore, once they begin a case, they are not obligated to stay with the client until the case is over. If, however, the case has already begun in court after the attorney has filed a notice of appearance, *withdrawal* is usually improper without the permission of the court.

There are circumstances in which an attorney *must* withdraw from a case that has begun:

- Representation of the client would violate ethical rules—for example, the attorney discovers that he or she has a conflict of interest with the client which cannot be cured (i.e., corrected or overcome) by the consent of the client.

- Representation of the client would violate the law—for example, the client insists that the attorney provide advice on how to defraud the Internal Revenue Service.

- The client fires the attorney. (An attorney is an agent of the client. Clients are always free to dismiss their agents.)
- The attorney's physical or mental condition has deteriorated (through problems with alcohol, depression due to marital problems, etc.) to the point where the attorney's ability to represent the client has been materially impaired.

An attorney has the option of withdrawing if the client insists on an objective that the attorney considers repugnant (such as pursuing litigation solely to harass someone), or imprudent (such as refiling a motion the attorney feels is an obvious waste of time and likely to incur the anger of the court). Model Rule 1.16(b)(3).

Paralegal Perspective:

- When you have a close working relationship with an attorney, you become aware of his or her professional strengths and personal weaknesses, particularly in a small law office. Bar associations around the country are becoming increasingly concerned about the *impaired attorney*, someone who's not functioning properly due to alcohol, drugs, or related problems. A paralegal with such an attorney for a supervisor is obviously in a predicament. Seemingly small problems have the potential of turning into a crisis. If it is not practical to discuss the situation directly with the attorney involved, you need to seek the advice of others in the firm.

10. Confidentiality of Information

An attorney must not reveal information relating to the representation of a client unless (a) the client consents to the disclosure or (b) the attorney reasonably believes the disclosure is necessary to prevent a client from committing a criminal act that is likely to result in imminent death or substantial bodily harm. Model Rule 1.6

Information is confidential if others do not have a right to receive it. When access to information is restricted in this way, the information is considered *privileged*. While our primary focus in this section is on the ethical dimensions of confidentiality, we also need to examine confidentiality in the related contexts of the attorney-client privilege and the attorney work-product rule.

Ethics and Confidentiality

The ethical obligation to maintain *confidentiality* applies to *all* information that relates to the representation of a client, whatever its source. Note that the obligation is broader than so-called secrets or matters explicitly communicated in confidence. Confidentiality has been breached in each of the following examples:

At a party, an attorney tells an acquaintance from another town that the law firm is representing Jacob Anderson, whose employer is trying to force him to retire.

At a bar association conference, an attorney tells an old law school classmate that a client named Brenda Steck is considering a suit against her brother over the ownership of property left by their deceased mother.

A legal secretary carelessly leaves a client's file open on his desk where a stranger (e.g., another client) can and does read parts of it.

The rule on confidentiality is designed to encourage clients to discuss their case fully and frankly with their attorney, including embarrassing and legally damaging information. Arguably, a client would be reluctant to be open with an attorney if he or she had to worry about whether the attorney might reveal the information to others. The rule on confidentiality makes it unethical for attorneys to do so.

Of course, a client can always consent to an attorney's disclosure about the client—*if* the client is properly consulted about the proposed disclosure in advance. Furthermore, sometimes the client implicitly authorizes disclosures because of the nature of his or her case. In a dispute over alimony, for example, the attorney would obviously have to disclose certain financial information about the client to a court or to opposing counsel during the settlement negotiations.

Disclosure can also be ethically permissible in cases involving future criminal conduct.

Example: An attorney represents a husband in a bitter divorce action against his wife. During a meeting at the law firm, the husband shows the attorney a gun which he says he is going to use to kill his wife later the same day.

Can the attorney tell the police what the husband said? Yes. It is not unethical for an attorney to reveal information about a crime if the attorney reasonably believes that disclosure is necessary to prevent the client from committing a criminal act that could lead to someone's imminent death or substantial bodily harm.

Finally, some disclosures can be proper in suits between attorney and client. Suppose, for example, that the attorney later sues the client for nonpayment of a fee, or the client sues the attorney for malpractice. In such proceedings, an attorney can reveal information about the client if the attorney reasonably believes disclosure is necessary to present a claim against the client or to defend against the client's claim.

Attorney-Client Privilege

The *attorney-client privilege* serves a similar function as the ethical rule on confidentiality. The two doctrines overlap. The attorney-client privilege is an *evidentiary* rule that applies to judicial and other proceedings in which an attorney may be called as a witness or otherwise required to produce evidence concerning a client. Under the attorney-client privilege, the attorney can refuse to disclose communications with his or her client whose purpose was to facilitate the provision of legal services for the client. The privilege also applies to employees of an attorney with respect to the same kind of communication—those whose purpose was to facilitate legal services.

Who May Not Testify Without Consent
Colorado Revised Statutes
(1984 Cum. Supp.)
13-90-107 (1)(b)

An attorney shall not be examined without the consent of his client as to any communication made by the client to him or his advice given thereon in the course of professional employment; nor shall an attorney's secretary, paralegal, legal assistant, stenographer, or clerk be examined without the consent of his employer concerning any fact, the knowledge of which he has acquired in such capacity.

The *ethical* rule on confidentiality tells us when sanctions can be imposed on attorneys for disclosing confidential client information to anyone outside the law office. The *attorney-client privilege* tells us when attorneys (and their employees) can refuse to answers questions pertaining to confidential client information.

Attorney Work-Product Rule

Suppose that, while working on a client's case, an attorney prepares a memorandum or other in-house document that does *not* contain any confidential communications. The memorandum or document, therefore, is *not* protected by the attorney-client privilege. Can the other side force the attorney to provide a copy of the memorandum or document? Are they *discoverable,* meaning that an opposing party can obtain information about it during discovery? This question leads us to the work-product rule.

Under this rule, the *work product* of an attorney is considered confidential. Work product consists of any notes, working papers, memoranda, or similar documents and tangible things prepared by the attorney in anticipation of litigation. An example is a memorandum the attorney writes to the file indicating his or her strategy in litigating a case. Attorneys do not have to disclose their work product to the other side. It is not discoverable.[20] To the extent that such documents are not discoverable, they are privileged. (The work-product rule is sometimes referred to as the work-product privilege.)

Inadvertent Disclosure of Confidential Material

The great fear of law office personnel is that the wrong person will obtain material that should be protected by ethics, by the attorney-client privilege, or by the work-product rule. This can have devastating consequences. For example, if a stranger overhears a confidential communication by a client to the attorney or to the attorney's paralegal, a court might rule that the attorney-client privilege has been waived. At a recent paralegal conference, a speaker told a stunned audience that a paralegal in her firm accidentally faxed a strategy memo on a current case to the opposing attorney! The paralegal punched in the wrong phone number on the fax machine!

[20]An exception exists if the "party seeking discovery has substantial need of the materials in the preparation of his case" and is unable to obtain them without undue hardship by other means. This test is rarely met. Federal Rule of Civil Procedure 26(b)(3).

Paralegal Perspective:

■ Attorneys must instruct their paralegals and other nonattorney assistants on the obligation not to disclose information relating to the representation of a client. "It is the responsibility of a lawyer to take reasonable measures to ensure that all client confidences are preserved by a legal assistant." [21]

■ As we shall see later, the two major national paralegal associations also stress the ethical obligation of confidentiality in their own ethical codes:

- "A legal assistant must protect the confidences of a client, and it shall be unethical for a legal assistant to violate any statute . . . controlling privileged communications." Canon 7. National Association of Legal Assistants, Code of Ethics and Professional Responsibility (page 117).

- "A paralegal shall preserve client confidences and privileged communications. Confidential information and privileged communications are a vital part of the attorney, paralegal, and client relationship. The importance of preserving confidential and privileged information is understood to be an uncompromising obligation of every paralegal." IV. National Federation of Paralegal Associations, Affirmation of Professional Responsibility (page 116).

■ There are *many* temptations on paralegals to violate confidentiality. For example, a paralegal inadvertently reveals confidential information:

- while networking with other paralegals at a paralegal-association meeting;

- during animated conversation with another paralegal at a restaurant or on an elevator;

- after returning home from work during casual discussions with a relative, spouse, or roommate about interesting cases at the office.

Recall the scope of the rule: *all* information relating to the representation of a client must not be revealed. Some paralegals make the mistake of thinking that the rule applies only to damaging or embarrassing information or that the rule simply means you should not reveal things to the other side in the dispute. Not so. The rule is much broader. *All* information relating to the representation of a client must not be revealed to *anyone* who is not working on the case in the office.

■ In Missouri, the obligation of silence is even broader. The paralegal must not disclose information—"confidential or otherwise"—relating to the representation of the client.[22] In Texas, confidential information includes both privileged information and unprivileged client information. An attorney must "instruct the legal assistant that all information concerning representation of a client (indeed even the fact of representation, if not a matter of public record) must be kept strictly confidential."[23] In Philadelphia, paralegals are

---

[21]ABA *Model Guidelines,* Guideline 6, see footnote 5.
[22]*Guidelines for Practicing with Paralegals,* Missouri Bar Ass'n (1987).
[23]State Bar of Texas, *General Guidelines for the Utilization of the Services of Legal Assistants by Attorneys* (1981). Rule 1.01, Texas Disciplinary Rules of Professional Conduct (1990).

warned that it is "not always easy to recognize what information about your firm's clients or office is confidential. Moreover, a client of your office might be offended to learn that a . . . firm employee has discussed the client's business in public, even if the information mentioned is public knowledge. The easiest rule is to consider *all* work of the office to be confidential: do not discuss the business of your office or your firm's clients with any outsider, no matter how close a friend, at any time, unless you are specifically authorized by a lawyer to do so." [24] Under guidelines such as these, there is very little that paralegals can tell someone about their work!

- During the war, sailors were told that "loose lips sink ships." The same applies to law firms. One law firm makes the following statement to all its paralegals, "Throughout your employment, you will have access to information that must at all times be held in strictest confidence. Even the seemingly insignificant fact that the firm is involved in a particular matter falls within the orbit of confidential information. Unless you have attorney permission, do not disclose documents or contents of documents to anyone, including firm employees who do not need this information to do their work." [25]

- If you attend a meeting on a case outside the office, ask your supervisor if you should take notes or prepare a follow-up memo on the meeting. Let the supervisor decide whether your notes or the memo might be discoverable.[26]

- Be *very* careful when you talk with clients in the presence of third persons. Overheard conservations might constitute a waiver of the attorney-client privilege.

- Use a stamp marked *privileged* on protected documents.

- During a job interview, be very careful about submitting writing samples that contain confidential information, such as privileged communications or the identity of clients at law offices where you may have worked or volunteered in the past.[27] Your lack of professionalism in carelessly referring to confidential information during an interview will probably destroy your chances of getting the job.

11. Conflict of Interest

An attorney should avoid a conflict of interest with his or her client.

"Like obscenity, *conflicts of interest* are difficult to define, but easy to recognize." [28] A conflict of interest is divided loyalty that actually or potentially

---

[24]*Professional Responsibility for Nonlawyers,* Professional Responsibility Committee of the Philadelphia Bar Ass'n (1989) (emphasis added).

[25]*Orientation Handbook for Paralegals* 2 (Lane, Powell, Moses & Miller, 1984).

[26]Daniels, *Privileged Information for Paralegals,* 17 At Issue 15 (San Francisco Ass'n of Legal Assistants, November 1990).

[27]As we will see later, you may have to disclose the names of cases and clients in order to help the office decide whether you are "tainted" with a conflict of interest and hence could cause the disqualification of the office if you are hired. But this disclosure should occur only when the employment discussions are getting serious *and* with the knowledge of your former employers.

[28]Holtzman, *Conflicts of Interest,* 14 Legal Economics 55 (October 1988).

places one of the participants to whom undivided loyalty is owed at a disadvantage. Such conflicts can exist in many settings.

> Example: Bill Davenport is a salesman who does part-time work selling the same type of product manufactured by two competing companies.

Davenport has a conflict of interest. How can he serve two masters with the same loyalty? Normally, a company expects the undivided loyalty of people who work for it. How can Davenport apportion his customers between the two companies? There is an obvious danger that he will favor one over the other. The fact that he may try to be fair in his treatment of both companies does not eliminate the conflict of interest. A *potential* certainly exists that one of the companies will be disadvantaged. It may be that the two companies are aware of the problem and are not worried. This does not mean that there is no conflict of interest; it simply means that the affected parties have consented to take the risks involved in the conflict.

The same kind of conflict can exist in other settings.

> Example: Frank Jones is the head of the personnel department of a large company. Ten people apply for a job, one of whom is Frank's cousin.

Frank has a conflict of interest. He has loyalty to his company (pressuring him to hire the best person for the job) and a loyalty to his cousin (pressuring him to help a relative). There is a potential that the company will be disadvantaged, since Frank's cousin may not be the best qualified for the job.

The conflict exists even if the cousin *is* the best qualified, and even if Frank does *not* hire his cousin for the job, and even if the company *knows* about the relationship but still wants Frank to make the hiring decision. For conflict of interest to exist, all you need is the potential for disadvantage due to *divided loyalties;* you do not have to show that disadvantage actually resulted.

In a law office, a number of conflict-of-interest issues can arise:

(a) Business transactions with a client

(b) Loans to a client

(c) Gifts from a client

(d) Multiple representation

(e) Former client/present adversary

(f) Law firm disqualification

(g) Switching jobs and "the Chinese wall"

Our concern is whether the independence of the attorneys' professional judgment is compromised in any way because of conflicting interests.

(a) Business Transactions with a Client

Attorneys sell professional legal advice and representation. When they go beyond such services and enter a business transaction with the client, a conflict of interest can arise.

> Example: Janet Bruno, Esq. is Len Oliver's attorney in a real estate case. Oliver owns an auto repair business for which Bruno has done legal work. Oliver sells

Bruno a 30% interest in the repair business. Bruno continues as Oliver's attorney.

Serious conflict-of-interest problems may exist here. Assume that the business runs into difficulties and Oliver considers bankruptcy. He goes to Bruno for legal advice on bankruptcy law. Bruno has dual concerns: to give Oliver competent legal advice and to protect *her own* 30% interest in the business. Bankruptcy may be good for Oliver but disastrous for Bruno's investment. How can an attorney give a client independent professional advice when the advice may go against the attorney's own interest? Bruno's concern for her investment creates the potential that Oliver will be placed at a disadvantage. Divided loyalties exist.

This is not to say, however, that it is always unethical for an attorney to enter a business transaction with a client. If certain strict conditions are met, it can be proper.

> *An attorney shall not enter a business transaction with a client, unless*
> *(i) the terms of the business transaction are fair and reasonable to the client and are fully disclosed to the client in understandable language in writing, and*
> *(ii) the client is given reasonable opportunity to seek advice on the transaction from another attorney who is not involved with the transaction or the parties, and*
> *(iii) the client consents to the business transaction in writing.*
> Model Rule 1.8(a)

In our example, Oliver must be given the chance to consult with an attorney other than Bruno on letting Bruno buy a 30% interest in the business. Bruno would have to give Oliver a clear, written explanation of their business relationship. And the relationship must be fair and reasonable to Oliver.

(b) *Loans to a Client*

An attorney, like all service providers, wants to be paid. Often a client does not have the resources to pay until *after* the case is over.

> Example: Harry Maxell, Esq. is Bob Stock's attorney in a negligence action in which Stock is seeking damages for serious injuries caused by the defendant. Since the accident, Stock has been out of work and on welfare. While the case is pending, Maxell agrees to lend Stock living expenses and court-filing fees.

The loan covering *living expenses* creates a conflict-of-interest problem. Suppose that the defendant in the negligence case makes an offer to settle the case with Stock. Should he accept the offer? There is a danger that Maxell's advice on this will be colored by the fact that he has a financial interest in Stone—he wants to have his loan repaid. The amount of the offer to settle may not be enough to cover the loan. Should he advise Stock to accept the offer? It may be in Stock's interest to accept the offer but not in Maxell's own interest. Such divided loyalty is an unethical conflict of interest. Model Rule 1.8(e).

The loan covering *litigation expenses,* such as filing fees and other court costs, is treated differently. The amount of such a loan is usually relatively small, and hence unlikely to interfere with the independence of the attorney's judgment. In our example, Maxell's loan to cover the cost of the filing fees is proper.

(c) Gifts from a Client

Clients sometimes make gifts to their attorneys or to the spouse or relative of their attorneys. Such gifts rarely create ethical problems except when a document must be prepared to complete the gift.

> Example: William Stanton, Esq. has been the family attorney of the Tarkinton family for years. At Christmas, Mrs. Tarkinton gives Stanton a television set and tells him to change her will so that Stanton's ten-year-old daughter would receive funds for a free college education.

If a document is needed to carry out the gift, it is unethical for the attorney to prepare that document. Its preparation would create a conflict of interest. In our example, the gift of money for college involves a document—Mrs. Tarkinton's will. Note the conflict. It would be in Mrs. Tarkinton's interest to have the will written so that she, and the executor of her will, retained considerable flexibility when questions arise on how much to pay for the college education. (For example, is there to be a maximum amount? Is room and board included?) And they need flexibility on the effect of contingencies, such as a delay or an interruption in going to college. (What happens if the daughter does not go to college until after she marries and raises her own children?) Other questions could arise as well. Stanton, of course, would want the will drafted so that his daughter received the most money possible; he does not want any contingencies in the will that might threaten receipt of the funds. It is in his interest to prepare the will so that Mrs. Tarkinton and her executor have very little flexibility.

Because of this conflict, an attorney cannot prepare a document such as a will, trust, or contract that results in any substantial gift from a client to the attorney or to the attorney's children, spouse, parents, or siblings. If a client wants to make such a gift, *another* attorney must prepare the document.[29] There is, however, one exception. If the client is *related* to the person receiving the gift, the attorney can prepare the document. Model Rule 1.8(c).

There does not appear to be any ethical problem in taking the gift of the television set from Mrs. Tarkinton. No documents are involved.

(d) Multiple Representation

A client is entitled to the independent professional judgment and vigorous representation of an attorney. Rarely can this occur in a case of *multiple representation* (also referred to as *common representation*), where the same attorney represents both sides in a legal dispute.

> Example: Tom and Henry have an automobile accident. Tom wants to sue Henry for negligence. Both Tom and Henry ask Mary Franklin, Esq. to represent them in the dispute.

---

[29]This other attorney should not be a member of the same law firm. See the related discussion (later) on imputed disqualification.

Franklin has a conflict of interest. How can she give her undivided loyalty to both sides? Tom needs to prove that Henry was negligent; Henry needs to prove that he was not negligent, and perhaps that Tom was negligent himself. How can Franklin vigorously argue that Henry was negligent and at the same time vigorously argue that Henry was not negligent? How can she act independently for two different people who are at odds with each other? Since Tom and Henry have *adverse interests,* she cannot give each her independent professional judgment. (Adverse interests are simply opposing purposes or claims.) The difficulty is not solved by Franklin's commitment to be fair and objective in giving her advice to the parties. Her role as attorney is to be a *partisan advocate* for the client. It is impossible for Franklin to play this role for two clients engaged in a dispute where they have adverse interests. An obvious conflict of interest would exist. In every state, it would be unethical for Franklin to represent Tom and Henry in this case.

Furthermore, this is a case in which consent is *not* a defense. Even if Tom and Henry agree to allow Franklin to represent both of them, it would be unethical for her to do so. The presence of adverse interests between the parties makes it unethical for an attorney to represent both sides.

Suppose, however, that the two sides do not have adverse interests. There are cases that must go before a court even though the parties are in agreement about everything.

> Example: Jim and Mary Smith are separated, and both want a divorce. They have been married only a few months. There are no children and no marital assets to divide. George Davidson, Esq. is an attorney that Jim and Mary know and trust. They decide to ask Davidson to represent both of them in the divorce.

Can Davidson ethically represent both sides here? Some states *will* allow him to do so, on the theory that there is not much of a conflict between the parties. Jim and Mary want the divorce, there is no custody battle, and there is no property to fight over. All they need is a court to decree that their marriage is legally over. Hence the potential for harm caused by multiple representation in such a case is almost nonexistent. Other states, however, disagree. They frown on multiple representation in so-called "friendly divorces" of this kind.

There is no absolute ban on all multiple representation in the Model Rules, although such representation is certainly discouraged.

> *An attorney shall not represent a client if the representation of that client will be directly adverse to another client, unless*
> *(i) the attorney reasonably believes the representation will not adversely affect the relationship with the other client, and*
> *(ii) both clients consent after consultation about the risks of the multiple representation.* Model Rule 1.7

In the Smith example, both conditions can probably be met. Such a divorce is little more than a paper procedure since there is no real dispute between the parties. Hence Davidson would be reasonable in believing that his representation of Jim would not adversely affect Mary, and vice versa. Davidson can represent both sides so long as Jim and Mary consent to the multiple representation after Davidson explains whatever risks might be involved.

Nevertheless, attorneys are urged *not* to engage in multiple representation even if it is ethically proper to do so under the standards listed above. The case may have been "friendly" at the outset, but years later when everything turns sour, one of the parties inevitably attacks the attorney for having had a conflict of interest. Cautious attorneys always avoid multiple representation.

(e) Former Client/Present Adversary

As indicated earlier, clients are encouraged to be very open with their attorney since the latter needs to know favorable and unfavorable information about the client in order to evaluate the legal implications of the case. The more trust that exists between them, the more frank the client will usually be. Assume that such a relationship exists and that the case is eventually resolved. Months later, another legal dispute arises between the same parties, but this time the attorney represents the other side!

> Example: Helen Kline, Esq. represented Paul Andrews in his breach-of-contract suit against Richard Morelli, a truck distributor. Andrews claimed that Morelli failed to deliver five trucks that Andrews ordered. A court ruled in favor of Morelli. Now, a year later, Andrews wants to sue Morelli for slander. After accidentally meeting at a conference, they started discussing the truck suit. Morelli allegedly called Andrews a liar and a thief. In the slander suit, Andrews hires Michael Manna, Esq. to represent him. Morelli hires Helen Kline, Esq.

A former client is now an adversary. Kline once represented Andrews; she is now representing a client (Morelli) who is an adversary of Andrews. Without the consent of the former client (Andrews), it is unethical for Kline to *switch sides* and represent Morelli against him. Model Rule 1.9(a). Consent is needed *when the second case is the same as the first one or when the two are substantially related.* The slander suit is substantially related to the breach-of-contract suit, since they both grew out of the original truck incident.

If the cases are the same or are substantially related, the likelihood is strong that the attorney will use information learned in the first case to the detriment of the former client in the second case. Kline undoubtedly found out a good deal about Andrews when she represented him in the breach-of-contract case. She would now be in a position to use that information *against* him while representing Morelli in the slander case.

Kline had a duty of loyalty when she represented Andrews. This duty does not end once the case is over and all fees are paid. It continues if the same case arises again or if a substantially related case arises later—even if the attorney no longer represents the client. A conflict of interest exists when Kline subsequently acquires a new client who goes against Andrews in the same case or in a substantially related case. This, of course, is what happened in our example. Her duty of undivided loyalty to the second client clashes with her *continuing* duty of undivided loyalty to the former client in the original case.

Suppose, however, that an attorney *can* take the second case against a former client because the second case is totally unrelated to the first. There is still an ethical obligation to refrain from using any information relating to the representation in the first case to the disadvantage of the former client in the second case. There is no ethical ban on taking the case, but if there is any information in the office relating to the first case, that information cannot be used against the former client in the second case.[30]

(f) Law Firm Disqualification

If an attorney is disqualified from representing a client because of a conflict of interest, every attorney in the *same law firm* is also disqualified unless the client being protected by this rule consents to the representation.

> Example: Two years ago, John Farrell, Esq. of the law firm of Smith & Smith represented the stepfather in a custody dispute with the child's grandmother. The stepfather won the case, but the grandmother was awarded limited visitation rights. The grandmother now wants to sue the stepfather for failure to abide by the visitation order. John Farrell no longer represents the stepfather. The grandmother asks John Farrell to represent her. He declines because of a conflict of interest, but sends her to his law partner, Diane Williams, Esq., down the corridor at Smith & Smith.

The *stepfather* would have to consent to the representation of the grandmother by Williams. There would certainly be a conflict of interest if John Farrell tried to represent the grandmother against the stepfather. The custody dispute and the visitation dispute are substantially related. Once one attorney in a firm is disqualified because of a conflict of interest, every other attorney in that firm is also disqualified. (This is known as *imputed disqualification* or *vicarious disqualification*.) The entire firm is treated as one attorney. The disqualification of any one "tainted" attorney in the firm contaminates the entire firm. In our example, Farrell's partner (Williams) is disqualified because Farrell would be disqualified. Model Rule 1.10.

(g) Switching Jobs and "the Chinese Wall"

Finally we need to consider the conflict-of-interest problems that can arise from changing jobs. We just saw that there can be an imputed disqualification of an entire law firm because one of the attorneys in the firm has a conflict of interest with a client. If that attorney now goes to work for a *new* firm, can there be an imputed disqualification of the new firm because of the same conflict of interest?

> Example: Kevin Carlson, Esq. works at Darby & Darby. He represents Ajax, Inc. in its contract suit against World Systems, Inc. The latter is represented by Polk, Young & West. Carlson quits his job at Darby & Darby and takes a job at Polk, Young & West.

While Carlson was at Darby and Darby, he obviously acquired confidential information about Ajax. Clearly, he cannot now represent World Systems in the contract litigation against Ajax. Blatant side-switching of this kind is highly unethical. But what about other attorneys at Polk, Young & West? Is the *entire* firm contaminated and hence disqualified from continuing to represent World

---

[30]While this duty might exist, it is not easy to enforce. Think of how difficult it might be to prove that the attorney in the second case used information obtained in the first case.

Systems because of the hiring of Carlson? If other attorneys at Polk, Young & West are allowed to continue representing World Systems against Ajax, there would be pressures on Carlson to tell these attorneys what he knows about Ajax. Must Polk, Young & West therefore withdraw from the case? The states do not all answer this question in the same way.

In many states, the answer is *yes,* because the tainted attorney[31]—Carlson—possesses confidential information about Ajax, and the case at the new firm involves the same or substantially the same matter as at the prior firm. The confidential information learned at the prior firm would be material to the matter being handled by the new firm. In these states, the only way to avoid disqualification is if Ajax waives its right to object. Ajax must be told that Carlson now works at Polk, Young & West, which represents World Systems, and must consent to allowing an attorney at Polk, Young & West (other than Carlson) to continue to represent World Systems in the case. It is unlikely, however, that Ajax will give this consent. Why would it want to take the chance that Carlson will reveal confidential communications to his new colleagues at Polk, Young & West?

To avoid the drastic penalty of imputed disqualification, law firms often promise to build a *Chinese wall* (sometimes called an *ethical wall* or *cone of silence*) around the attorney who created the conflict of interest—the *tainted* or *contaminated* attorney. The goal of the wall is to screen the tainted attorney from any contact with a case where earlier confidentiality could be compromised. In many states, however, this promise is *ineffective* to avoid the disqualification. Yet there are states that are more sympathetic to a firm that wants to avoid the disqualification, depending on how involved the tainted attorney was in the case while at the previous firm and on the quality of the wall at the new firm.

The screening of the Chinese Wall should take several forms. For example:

■ The tainted attorney promises not to discuss what he or she knows with anyone in the new firm.

■ Those working on the case in the new firm promise not to discuss it with the tainted attorney.

■ The tainted attorney works in an area that is physically segregated from work on the case in the new firm.

■ The files in the case are locked so that the tainted attorney will have no access to the files. In addition, colored labels or "restricted flags" are placed on each of these files to indicate that they are off limits to the tainted attorney.

■ All employees in the new firm are formally told that if they learn anything about the case, they must not discuss it with the tainted attorney.[32]

A tainted employee around whom a Chinese Wall is built is called a *quarantined* employee.

---

[31]Also called the *contaminated* attorney or *infected* attorney.

[32]Another dimension of the Chinese Wall is to forbid the tainted attorney from earning any profit or financial gain from the case in question.

As indicated, there are states where a Chinese Wall will *not* be successful in preventing the imputed disqualification of the new firm.[33] There is skepticism that the tainted attorney will be able to resist the pressure to disclose what he or she knows in spite of these screening mechanisms. "Whether the screen is breached will be virtually impossible to ascertain from outside the firm."[34]

Yet again, not all states take this position. There are states that will not order a disqualification if the court can be convinced that harm to the former client can be avoided. This is most likely to happen if the Wall was in place at the new firm at the outset of the employment transfer, if the new firm built the Wall before the other side raised the conflict-of-interest issue, and, most important, if the tainted attorney's involvement in the case at the old firm was relatively minor. This, of course, was not true for Kevin Carlson, Esq. in our example, since he actually represented Ajax while at Darby & Darby.

Imputed disqualification is a drastic consequence of job switching. In the Carlson example, somebody at Polk, Young & West made a major blunder in hiring Carlson. Before hiring him, a *conflicts check* should have been performed in order to determine whether he might taint the new firm and, if so, whether a Chinese Wall could prevent disqualification. This is done by obtaining the names of the clients Carlson and his old law firm (Darby & Darby) worked for and by determining whether the new firm (Polk, Young & West) ever worked *against* any of them.[35] Unfortunately, law firms often perform such conflicts checks carelessly or not at all.

Some large firms assign paralegals to perform the check under the supervision of an attorney. This paralegal will enter data on parties into a "conflicts index system" and compare it with data already in the system to identify potential conflicts. Computer programs (such as the one shown in Figure 2.4.) have been developed to assist in the task.

Insurance companies that issue malpractice policies to attorneys are very concerned about conflicts of interests that can arise from a *lateral hire*, in which a law firm hires an attorney from another law firm. The same concerns exist when one law firm buys or merges with another law firm. In Figure 2.5, you will find a series of questions one insurance company asks of all law firms applying for malpractice insurance.

Paralegal Perspective:

■ "A lawyer should take reasonable measures to prevent conflicts of interest resulting from a legal assistant's other employment or interests insofar as such other employment or interests would present a conflict of interest if it were that of the lawyer." [36] Many paralegals change jobs one or more times

---

[33]The Model Rules explicitly recognize a Chinese Wall to prevent imputed disqualification only where the attorney has moved from a government position to private employment. Model Rule 1.11.

[34]C. Wolfram, *Modern Legal Ethics* § 7.6.4 (1986).

[35]For each client that is a corporation, the firm should also cross-check the names of the parent corporation, all subsidiary corporations, and the names of chief executive officers. If the client is a partnership, the same kind of check is needed for the names of all general partners.

[36]ABA *Model Guidelines*, Guideline 7, see footnote 5.

FIGURE 2.4   Computer Software Used for Conflicts Checks

```
              LEGALMASTER Conflicts Found
Conflicts checked for case: SAMUE—(10 matches on 3 names)
Rubin (2 matches)
    CSP-        CLNT Rubin Phillip
    FFIC-5      JUDGE Rubin Laurie
Samuel* (6 matches)
    GREGS-1     OPATT Samuels Fritz
    SCOTT-1     EXPRT Samuels Phillip J.
    SMITH-PI    JUDGE Samuels Norman I.
    IBM-        OPATT Samuels Jacob
    CSP-        OPATT Samuels Jacob
    ISIS-2      EXPRT Samuelson Juan
Savag* (2 matches)
    IBM-        CLNT Savage Norm
    GRUPE-7     CLNT Savage Emily
              Press any key to exit.
```

Legalmaster's Conflicts Module. Computer Software for Professionals, Inc.

in the course of their careers. Such changes can create the same kind of conflicts problems that result when attorneys change jobs:

> Example: Paul Benton is a paralegal who works for Sands, Leonard & Wiley. One of the cases Paul works on is Mary Richardson v. Jane Quigly. Sands, Leonard & Wiley represents Richardson. The law firm of Neeley & Neeley represents Quigly. Before the case is resolved, Paul quits in order to take a job as a paralegal with Neeley & Neeley.

Neeley & Neeley is now in a position to determine what Paul found out about Richardson while he worked for Sands, Leonard & Wiley. The latter firm will probably ask a court to force Neeley & Neeley to withdraw from the case because it hired a tainted paralegal—Paul. The courts in some states will do just that. In these courts, imputed disqualification can result from tainted paralegals as well as from tainted attorneys. Yet other states say that paralegals should not be treated the same as attorneys. Under this view, a court is more likely to accept a Chinese Wall built around a tainted paralegal (who becomes a quarantined paralegal) as an alternative to disqualifying the law firm this paralegal recently joined. This view is represented in the ethics opinion of the American Bar Association (Informal Opinion 88-1526) printed below. It must be emphasized, however, that not all states follow this opinion.

■ In a recent, dramatic case, a San Francisco law firm was disqualified from representing nine clients in asbestos litigation involving millions of dollars. The sole reason for the disqualification was that the firm hired a paralegal who had once worked for a law firm that represented the opponents in the asbestos litigation. Soon after the controversy arose, the disqualified firm laid off the tainted paralegal who brought this conflict to the firm. He was devastated when he found out that he was being let go. "I was flabbergasted,

FIGURE 2.5 Questions on Malpractice Insurance Application about Conflict-of-Interest Avoidance

ADMINISTRATIVE SYSTEMS AND PROCEDURES—CONFLICT OF INTEREST	YES	NO
22. Do you have a written internal control system for maintaining client lists and identifying actual or potential conflicts of interest?	☐	☐
23. How does the firm maintain its conflict of interest avoidance system? ☐ Oral/Memory ☐ SIngle Index Files ☐ Multiple Index Files ☐ Computer		
24. Have the firm members disclosed in writing, all actual conflicts of interest and conflicts they reasonably believe may exist as a result of their role as director, officer, partner, employee, or fiduciary of an entity or individual other than the applicant firm?	☐	☐
25. Do firm members disclose to their clients, in writing, all actual conflicts of interest and conflicts they reasonably believe may exist?	☐	☐
26. Upon disclosure of actual or potential conflicts, do firm members always obtain written consent to perform ongoing legal services?	☐	☐
27. Has the firm acquired, merged with, or terminated a formal business relationship with another firm within the last three years?	☐	☐
28. Does the firm's conflict of interest avoidance system include attorney-client relationships established by predecessor firms, merged firms, and acquired firms?	☐	☐

Source: The St. Paul Companies, Professional Liability Application for Lawyers.

totally flabbergasted." He has not been able to find work since.[37] The case was widely reported throughout the legal community. A front-page story in the *Los Angeles Daily Journal* said that it "could force firms to conduct lengthy investigations of paralegals and other staffers before hiring them." [38]

■ One law firm makes the following statement to all its paralegals, "If you or a temporary legal assistant working under your supervision were formerly employed by opposing counsel, this could be the basis for a motion to disqualify [this law firm.] So also could personal relationships such as kinship with the opposing party or attorney or dating an attorney from another firm. Make your attorney aware of such connections." [39]

■ If you have worked (or volunteered) for an attorney in the past in *any* capacity (as a paralegal, as an investigator, as a secretary, etc.), you should make a list of all the clients and cases with which you were involved. When you apply for a new job, your list may be relevant to whether the law firm will be sub-

---

[37]Motamedi, *Landmark Ethics Case Takes Toll on Paralegal's Career, Family,* 7 Legal Assistant Today 39 (May/June 1990). *In re Complex Asbestos Litigation,* 232 Cal.App.3d 572, 283 Cal.Rptr. 732 (Cal.Ct.App. 1991).

[38]M. Hall, *S.F. Decision on Paralegal Conflict May Plague Firms,* 102 Los Angeles Daily Journal 1, col. 2 (September 25, 1989).

[39]Orientation Handbook for Paralegals 3 (Lane, Powell, Moses & Miller, 1984).

ject to disqualification if you are hired. You must be careful, however, with the list. Do not attach it to your resume and randomly send it around town! Until employment discussions have become serious, do not show it to the prospective employer. Furthermore, try to notify prior attorneys with whom you have worked that you are applying for a position at a law firm where its "conflicts check" on you must include knowing what cases you worked on with previous attorneys. Giving them this notice is not always practical, and may not be required. Yet it is a safe procedure to follow whenever possible.

■ Freelance paralegals who work for more than one attorney on a part-time basis are particularly vulnerable to conflict-of-interest charges. For example, in a large litigation involving many parties, two opposing attorneys might unknowingly use the same freelance paralegal to work on different aspects of the same case, or might use two different employees of this freelance paralegal. Another example is the freelance paralegal who worked on an earlier case for a client and now works on a different but similar case in which that client is the opponent. The California Association of Freelance Paralegals has attempted to address this problem in Article 11 of its proposed Code of Ethics: "A freelance paralegal shall avoid conflicts of interest relating to client matters. The freelance paralegal shall not accept any case adverse to the client of [an attorney who hires the paralegal] if the latter case bears a substantial connection to the earlier one or if there is a possibility that the two cases are substantially related, regardless of whether confidences were in fact imparted to the freelance paralegal by the attorney or the attorney's client in the earlier case." [40] There are practical problems with such rules. It is not always easy to determine whether two cases are "adverse" or bear a "substantial connection" with each other. If there is doubt, it is in the economic self-interest of the freelance paralegal *not* to tell the attorney since he or she will most likely refuse to hire the paralegal rather than take the risk of later disqualification because of contamination injected into the case by this paralegal. Finally, conducting a conflicts check could be somewhat difficult for a busy, experienced freelance paralegal who has worked for scores of attorneys and hundreds of clients over the years.

Standing Committee on Ethics and Professional Responsibility of the American Bar Association
Informal Opinion 88-1526

A law firm that employs a nonlawyer who formerly was employed by another firm may continue representing clients whose interests conflict with the interests of clients of the former employer on whose matters the nonlawyer has worked, as long as the employing firm screens the nonlawyer from information about or participating in matters involving those clients and strictly adheres to the screening process described in this opinion and as long as no information relating to the representation of the clients of the former employer is revealed by the nonlawyer to any person in the employing firm. In addition, the nonlawyer's former employer must admonish the nonlawyer against revelation of information relating to the representation of clients of the former employer.

The Committee is asked whether, under the ABA Model Rules of Professional Conduct (1983, amended 1987), a law firm that hires

---

[40]California Ass'n of Freelance Paralegals, "CAFP's Proposed Code of Ethics," Article 11, *Freelancer* 9 (July/August 1991).

a paralegal formerly employed by another lawyer must withdraw from representation of a client under the following circumstances. The paralegal has worked for more than a year with a sole practitioner on litigation matters. One of those matters is a lawsuit which the sole practitioner instituted against a client of the law firm that is about to hire the paralegal and wishes to continue to defend the client. The paralegal has gained substantial information relating to the representation of the sole practitioner's client, the plaintiff in the lawsuit. The employing firm will screen the paralegal from receiving information about or working on the lawsuit and will direct the paralegal not to reveal any information relating to the representation of the sole practitioner's client gained by the paralegal during the former employment. The Committee also is asked whether the paralegal's former employer must take any actions in order to comply with the Model Rules.

Responsibilities of Employing Firm

The Committee concludes that the law firm employing the paralegal should not be disqualified from continuing to defend its client in the lawsuit, as long as the law firm and the paralegal strictly adhere to the screening process described in this Opinion, and as long as no information relating to the representation of the sole practitioner's client is revealed by the paralegal to any person in the employing firm.

The Model Rules require that a lawyer make reasonable efforts to ensure that each of the lawyer's nonlawyer employees maintains conduct compatible with the professional obligations of the lawyer, including the nondisclosure of information relating to the representation of clients. This requires maintaining procedures designed to protect client information from disclosure by the lawyer's employees and agents. . . .

It is important that nonlawyer employees have as much mobility in employment opportunity as possible consistent with the protection of clients' interests. To so limit employment opportunities that some nonlawyers trained to work with law firms might be required to leave the careers for which they are trained would disserve clients as well as the legal profession. Accordingly, any restrictions on the nonlawyer's employment should be held to the minimum necessary to protect confidentiality of client information.

Model Rule 5.3 imposes general supervisory obligations on lawyers with respect to nonlawyer employees and agents. The obligations include the obligation to make reasonable efforts to ensure there are measures in effect to assure that the nonlawyer's conduct is compatible with the professional obligations of the lawyer. With respect to new employees who formerly worked for other lawyers, these measures should involve admonitions to be alert to all legal matters, including lawsuits, in which any client of the former employer has an interest. The nonlawyer should be cautioned: (1) not to disclose any information relating to the representation of a client of the former employer; and (2) that the employee should not work on any matter on which the employee worked for the prior employer or respecting which the employee has information relating to the representation of the client of the former employer. When the new firm becomes aware of such matters, the employing firm must also take reasonable steps to ensure that the employee takes no action and does no work in relation to matters on which the nonlawyer worked in the prior employment, absent client consent after consultation.

Circumstances sometimes require that a firm be disqualified or withdraw from representing a client when the firm employs a nonlawyer who formerly was employed by another firm. These circumstances are present either: (1) where information relating to the representation of an adverse party gained by the nonlawyer while employed in another firm has been revealed to lawyers or other personnel in the new firm . . .; or (2) where screening would be ineffective or the nonlawyer necessarily would be required to work on the other side of the same or a substantially related matter on which the nonlawyer worked or respecting which the nonlawyer has gained information relating to the representation of the opponent while in the former employment. If the employing firm employs the nonlawyer under those circumstances, the firm must withdraw from representing the client, unless the client of the former employer consents to the continued representation of the person with conflicting interests after being apprised of all the relevant factors.

Responsibilities of Former Employer

Under Model Rule 5.3, lawyers have a duty to make reasonable efforts to ensure that nonlawyers do not disclose information relating to the representation of the lawyers' clients while in the lawyer's employ and afterwards. On the facts presented to the Committee here, once the lawyer learns that the paralegal has joined the opposing law firm, the lawyer should consider advising the employing firm that the paralegal must be isolated from participating in the matter and from revealing any information relating to the representation of the lawyer's client. If not satisfied that the employing firm has taken adequate measures to prevent participation and disclosures, the lawyer should consider filing a motion in the lawsuit to disqualify the employing law firm from continuing to represent the opponent. . . .

Therefore, the lawyer who hires the paralegal, under the circumstances before the Committee, must screen the paralegal from participating in the lawsuit with the employing law firm. Both the employing firm and the sole practitioner should admonish the paralegal not to disclose information relating to the representation of the plaintiff in the lawsuit and also of any other client of the sole practitioner for whom the paralegal formerly worked while with the former employer.

The standards expressed in this Opinion apply to all matters where the interests of the clients are in conflict and not solely to matters in litigation. The Committee also notes that these standards apply equally to all nonlawyer personnel in a law firm who have access to material information relating to the representation of clients and extends also to agents who technically may be independent contractors, such as investigators.

12. Communication with the Other Side

In representing a client, an attorney shall not communicate with a party on the other side about the subject of the case if the attorney knows that the party is represented by another attorney. The latter attorney must consent to such a communication. Model Rule 4.2

If the other side is not represented, an attorney must not give him or her the impression that the attorney is uninvolved. The attorney should not give this person advice other than the advice to obtain his or her own attorney. Model Rule 4.3

The ethical concern here is that an attorney will take an unfair advantage of the other side.

Example: Dan and Theresa Kline have just separated and are thinking about a divorce. Each claims the marital home. Theresa hires Thomas Farlington, Esq. to represent her. Farlington calls Dan to ask him if he is interested in settling the case.

It is unethical for Farlington to contact Dan about the case if Farlington knows that Dan has his own attorney. Farlington must talk with Dan's attorney. Only the latter can give Farlington permission to communicate with Dan. If Dan does not have an attorney, Farlington can talk with Dan, but he must not allow Dan to be misled about Farlington's role. Farlington works for the other side; he is not disinterested. Dan must be made to understand this fact. The only advice Farlington can give Dan in such a situation is to seek his own attorney.

Paralegal Perspective:

■ The ethical restrictions on communicating with the other side apply to the employees of an attorney as well as to the attorney. "The lawyer's obligation is to ensure that the legal assistants do not communicate directly with parties known to be represented by an attorney, without that attorney's consent, on the subject of such representation."[41] You must avoid improper communication with the other side. If the other side is a business or some other large organization, do not talk with anyone there unless your supervisor tells you that it is ethical to do so. Never call the other side and pretend you are someone else in order to obtain information.

■ If your office allows you to interview someone who is not represented by an attorney, you cannot give this person any advice other than the advice to secure his or her own attorney.

13. Solicitation

In person, an attorney may not solicit employment from a prospective client with whom the attorney has no family or prior professional relationship when a significant motive for doing so is the attorney's monetary gain.[42] Model Rule 7.3

People in distress are sometimes so distraught that they are not in a position to evaluate their need for legal services. They should not be subjected to pressures from an attorney who shows up wanting to be hired, particularly if the attorney is not a relative or has never represented them in the past.[43] Such in-person solicitation is unethical.

Example: Rachael Winters, Esq. stands outside the police station and gives a business card to any individual being arrested. The card says that Winters is an attorney specializing in criminal cases.

Winters is obviously looking for prospective clients. Doing so in this manner is referred to as *ambulance chasing,* which is a pejorative term for aggressively tracking down anyone who probably has a legal problem in order to drum up business. There is no indication either that Winters is related to any of the people going into the police station or that she has any prior professional relationship with them (for example, they are *not* former clients). Winters appears to have one goal: finding a source of fees. Hence her conduct is unethical. Such direct, in-person, one-on-one solicitation of clients in this way is not allowed. The concern is that an attorney who approaches strangers in trouble may exert undue influence on them. This is less likely to occur if the solicitation comes in the mail, even if it is sent to individuals known to need legal services.

Example: An attorney obtains the names of homeowners facing foreclosure and sends them the following letter: "It has come to my attention that your home is being foreclosed on. Federal law may allow you to stop your creditors and give you more time to pay. Call my office for legal help."

---

[41]Section 20-104, Committee Commentary, *New Mexico Rules Governing the Practice of Law* (Judicial Pamphlet 16).

[42]This prohibition also applies to *live* telephone conversations in which the attorney seeks to be hired.

[43]Furthermore, the improper solicitation of clients and promotion of litigation constitutes the crime of *barratry* in some states. For example, in 1990 three attorneys and an employee of a law firm were indicted in Texas on charges that they illegally sought clients at hospitals and funeral homes after twenty-one students were killed and sixty-nine were injured in a school bus accident. *4 Said to Have Used Bus Crash to Get Business for Law Firm,* New York Times 8, col. 5 (April 7, 1990).

While critics claim that such solicitation constitutes "ambulance chasing by mail," the technique is ethical in most states so long as it is truthful and not misleading.[44] *In-person* solicitation, however, is treated differently because of the obvious pressure that it imposes. It is "easier to throw out unwanted mail than an uninvited guest." [45]

Paralegal Perspective:

- An unscrupulous attorney may try to use a paralegal to solicit clients for the office.

  Example: Bill Hill is a senior citizen who lives at a home for senior citizens. Andrew Vickers, Esq. hires Bill as his "paralegal." His sole job is to contact other seniors with legal problems and to refer them to Vickers.

  Andrew Vickers is engaging in unethical solicitation through Bill Hill. Attorneys cannot hire a paralegal to try to accomplish what they cannot do themselves. Nor can they use a *runner*[46]—an employee or independent contractor who contacts personal-injury victims or other potential clients in order to solicit business for an attorney.

- See also the related discussion above on splitting fees with nonattorneys.

14. Advertising

An attorney may advertise services on radio, on TV, in the newspaper, or through other public media as long as the ad is neither false nor misleading and does not constitute improper in-person solicitation. Model Rule 7.2

There was a time when almost all forms of advertising by attorneys were prohibited. Traditional attorneys considered advertising to be highly offensive to the dignity of the profession. In 1977, however, the United States Supreme Court stunned the legal profession by holding that truthful advertising cannot be completely banned.[47] The First Amendment protects such advertising. Furthermore, advertising does not pose the same danger as in-person solicitation by an attorney. A recipient of advertising is generally under very little pressure to buy the advertised product—in this case, an attorney's services. Hence, attorneys can ethically use truthful, nonmisleading advertising to the general public in order to generate business.

Studies have shown that over one-third of all attorneys in the country engage in some form of advertising. Most of it consists of listings in the Yellow Pages. The use of other marketing tools is also on the rise. Revenue for television advertising, for example, was more than $89 million in 1989.[48] Former Chief Justice Warren Burger commented that some attorney ads "would make

---

[44]*Shapero v. Kentucky Bar Ass'n,* 486 U.S. 466, 108 S.Ct. 1916, 100 L.Ed.2d 475 (1988). Some states impose additional requirements on mail solicitations—for example, the phrase "Advertising Material" must be printed on the outside of the envelope, and the word "advertisement" must be printed at the top of each page of the letter.

[45]Metzner, *Strategies That Break the Rules,* National Law Journal, 16 (July 15, 1991).

[46]Also called a *capper* if the person uses fraud or deception in the solicitation.

[47]*Bates v. State Bar of Arizona,* 433 U.S. 350, 97 S.Ct. 2691, 53 L.Ed.2d 810 (1977).

[48]Hornsby, *The Complex Evolution of Attorney Ad Regs,* Nat'l Law Journal S4 (August 6, 1990).

a used-car dealer blush with shame." Proponents of attorney advertising, however, claim that it has made legal services more accessible to the public and has provided the public with a better basis for choosing among available attorneys.

15. Reporting Professional Misconduct

Attorneys with knowledge that another attorney has committed a serious violation of the ethical rules must report this attorney to the appropriate disciplinary body. Model Rule 8.3

Attorneys may pay a price for remaining silent when they become aware of unethical conduct. The failure of an attorney to report another attorney may mean that both attorneys can be disciplined for unethical behavior. Not every ethical violation, however, must be reported. The ethical violation must raise a substantial question of the attorney's honesty, trustworthiness, or fitness to practice law.

Paralegal Perspective:

■ If a paralegal is aware of unethical conduct of his or her own attorney supervisor, is it unethical for the paralegal to fail to report the attorney to the bar association? No. As indicated earlier, the ethical rules under consideration here apply only to attorneys. Yet the paralegal is still in a predicament. If there is no one to talk to at the firm, he or she must decide whether to remain at this job. Sooner or later, unethical attorneys will probably ask or pressure their paralegal to participate in unethical conduct.

16. Appearance of Impropriety

How would you feel if you were told that, even though you have not violated any rule, you are still going to be punished because what you did *appeared* to be improper? That would be the effect of an obligation to avoid even the appearance of impropriety. In some states, however, it *is* unethical for attorneys to engage in such appearances.[49] The ABA Model Rules, however, does not list appearance of impropriety as an independent basis of determining unethical conduct. To be disciplined in states that have adopted the Model Rules, an attorney must violate one of the specific ethical rules. Yet even in these states, there are conservative attorneys who are as worried about apparent impropriety as they are about specific, actual impropriety.

17. Unauthorized Practice of Law

An attorney shall not assist a nonattorney in the unauthorized practice of law. Rule 5.5(b)

In Chapter 1, we saw that it is a crime in many states for a nonattorney to engage in the *unauthorized practice of law.* Our main focus in Chapter 1 was

---

[49]See Canon 9 of the *ABA Code of Professional Responsibility* (1981). "A lawyer should avoid even the appearance of professional impropriety."

the nonattorney who works for an office other than a traditional law office. An example would be a do-it-yourself divorce office that sells kits and typing services. Now our focus is the nonattorney who works under the supervision of an attorney in a law office. We want to explore the ways in which attorneys might be charged with unethically assisting *their own paralegals* engage in the unauthorized practice of law. For example, an attorney might allow a paralegal to give legal advice, to conduct depositions, or to sign court documents. These areas will be discussed below along with an overview of other major ethical issues involving paralegals.

18. Paralegals

We turn now to a more direct treatment of when attorneys can be disciplined for the unethical use of paralegals. We will cover the following topics:

(a) Paralegals, the ABA Model Code, and the ABA Model Rules

(b) Misrepresentation of paralegal identity or status

(c) Doing what only attorneys can do

(d) Absentee, shoulder, and environmental supervision

(a) Paralegals, the ABA Model Code, and the ABA Model Rules

The first major statement by the American Bar Association on the ethical use of paralegals by attorneys came in its *Model Code of Professional Responsibility:*

DR 3-101(A): A lawyer shall not aid a nonlawyer in the unauthorized practice of law.

EC 3-6: A lawyer often delegates tasks to clerks, secretaries, and other lay persons. Such delegation is proper if the lawyer maintains a direct relationship with his client, supervises the delegated work, and has complete professional responsibility for the work product. This delegation enables a lawyer to render legal services more economically and efficiently.[50]

A 1967 opinion elaborated on these standards:

American Bar Association
Formal Opinion 316 (1967)

A lawyer can employ lay secretaries, lay investigators, lay detectives, lay researchers, accountants, lay scriveners, non-lawyer draftsmen or non-lawyer researchers. In fact, he may employ non-lawyers to do any task for him except counsel clients about law matters, engage directly in the practice of law, appear in court or appear in formal proceedings as part of the judicial process, so long as it is he who takes the work and vouches for it to the client and becomes responsible for it to the client. In other words, we do not limit the kind of assistance that a lawyer can acquire in any way to persons who are admitted to the Bar, so long as the non-lawyers do not do things that lawyers may not do or do the things that lawyers only may do.

---

[50]See footnote 4 on the meaning of DR and EC in the ABA Model Code.

Hence, an attorney can hire a paralegal and is responsible for what the paralegal does. There are two levels of this responsibility: civil liability for malpractice and ethical liability for violation of ethical rules.

> Example: The law firm of Adams & Adams represents Harold Thompson in his negligence suit against Parker Co. At the firm, Elaine Stanton, Esq. works on the case with Peter Vons, a paralegal whom she supervises. Peter neglects to file an important pleading in court, and carelessly gives confidential information about Thompson to the attorney representing Parker. All of this causes Thompson great damage.

Stanton is fully responsible to the client, Thompson, who might decide to bring a malpractice suit in court against her. She cannot hide behind the fact that her paralegal was at fault. (See the discussion of malpractice liability and respondeat superior in Chapter 1.)

What about ethics? Can Stanton be reprimanded, suspended, or disbarred because of what her paralegal did? None of the materials quoted above answer this question. Responsibility to a client for malpractice often raises separate issues from responsibility to a bar association (or other disciplinary body) for unethical conduct. The two kinds of responsibility can be closely interrelated because the same alleged wrongdoing can be involved in the malpractice suit and in the disciplinary case. Yet the two proceedings are separate and should be examined separately.

In 1983, the ABA replaced the *Model Code of Professional Responsibility* with its *Model Rules of Professional Conduct*. The Model Rules, which have been our main focus in this chapter, are more helpful in telling us when attorneys are subject to ethical sanctions because of their paralegals. This is done in *Model Rule 5.3*, covering paralegals. All attorneys in the law firm are not treated the same in Rule 5.3. As you read this rule, note that different standards of ethical responsibility are imposed on the following three categories of attorneys:

- Any attorney in the firm
- A partner in the firm
- An attorney in the firm with direct supervisory authority over the paralegal

---

**Model Rules of Professional Conduct
Rule 5.3. Responsibilities
Regarding Nonlawyer Assistants**

With respect to a nonlawyer employed or retained by or associated with a lawyer:

(a) a partner in a law firm shall make reasonable efforts to ensure that the firm has in effect measures giving reasonable assurance that the person's conduct is compatible with the professional obligations of the lawyer;

(b) a lawyer having direct supervisory authority over the nonlawyer shall make reasonable efforts to ensure that the person's conduct is compatible with the professional obligations of the lawyer; and

(c) A lawyer shall be responsible for conduct of such a person that would be a violation of the Rules of Professional Conduct if engaged in by a lawyer if:

(1) the lawyer orders or ratifies the conduct involved; or

(2) the lawyer is a partner in the law firm in which the person is employed, or has direct supervisory authority over the person, and knows of the conduct at a time when its consequences can be avoided but fails to take reasonable remedial action.

Comment:

Lawyers generally employ assistants in their practice, including secretaries, investigators, law student interns, and paraprofessionals. Such assistants, whether employees or independent contractors, act for the lawyer in rendition of the lawyer's professional services. A lawyer should give such assistants appropriate instruction and supervision concerning the ethical aspects of their employment, particularly regarding the obligation not to disclose information relating to representation of the client, and should be responsible for their work product. The measures employed in supervising nonlawyers should take account of the fact that they do not have legal training and are not subject to professional discipline.

Let us analyze Rule 5.3 by applying it to Elaine Stanton, Esq. in our example. First of all, under 5.3(c)(1), *any* attorney in the firm who "orders" the paralegal to commit the wrongdoing in question is ethically responsible for that conduct. The same is true if the attorney "ratifies" (that is, approves or endorses) the wrongdoing after the paralegal commits it. There is no indication in the example that Stanton or any other attorney in the firm told Peter not to file the pleading in court, or told him to give confidential information about Thompson to the other side. Nor is there any indication that an attorney approved of Peter's conduct after it occurred.[51] Therefore, Rule 5.3(c)(1) does not apply.

We need to know whether Stanton is a partner in the firm. If so, she has an ethical obligation under 5.3(a) to "make reasonable efforts to ensure that the firm has in effect measures giving reasonable assurance" that the paralegal's conduct "is compatible with the professional obligations of the lawyer." Hence a partner cannot completely ignore office paralegals in the hope that someone else in the firm is monitoring them. Reasonable steps must be taken by every partner to establish a system of safeguards. Here are some examples:

- Make sure that all paralegals in the firm are made aware of the ethical rules governing attorneys in the state.

- Make sure that all paralegals in the firm are made aware of the importance of deadlines in the practice of law and of the necessity of using date-reminder (tickler) techniques.

In the example, Peter Vons is supervised by Elaine Stanton, Esq. Hence she is an attorney with "direct supervisory authority" over Peter. Rule 5.3(b) governs the conduct of such attorneys. This section requires her to "make reasonable efforts to ensure" that the paralegal's conduct "is compatible with the professional obligations of the lawyer."

Assume that Stanton is charged with a violation of 5.3(b) because her paralegal, Peter, failed to file an important pleading in court and disclosed confidential information about a client. At Stanton's disciplinary hearing, she would be asked supervision questions such as:

- How do you assign tasks to Peter?

- How do you know if he is capable of handling an assignment?

- How often do you meet with him after you give him an assignment?

---

[51]By Peter's conduct, we mean both what he did (disclose confidential information) and what he failed to do (file the papers in court).

- How do you know if he is having difficulty completing an assignment?
- Has he made mistakes in the past? If so, how have you handled them?

Peter might be called as a witness in her disciplinary hearing and be interrogated extensively. For example:

- How were you trained as a paralegal?
- What kinds of assignments have you handled in your paralegal career?
- How long have you worked for Elaine Stanton?
- How does she evaluate your work?
- What do you do if you have a question on an assignment but she is not available in the office?
- Why didn't you file the court document on time?
- Describe the circumstances under which you revealed confidential information to the opponent in the Thompson case.

All of these questions of Stanton and of Peter would be designed to find out if Stanton made "reasonable efforts" to ensure that Peter did not violate ethical standards. Note that attorney supervisors do not have to guarantee that a paralegal will act ethically. They simply have to "make reasonable efforts" that this will occur. The above questions are relevant to whether Stanton exerted such efforts with respect to Peter.

Another basis of ethical liability under the Model Rules is Rule 5.3(c)(2). Both a partner and a supervisory attorney can be subject to discipline if they knew about the paralegal's misconduct yet failed to take reasonable corrective steps at a time when such steps would have avoided or minimized ("mitigated") the damage. At their disciplinary hearing, a partner and/or a supervising attorney would be asked questions such as:

- When did you first find out that Peter did not file the court document?
- What did you do at that time? Why didn't you act sooner?
- When did you first find out that Peter spoke to opposing counsel?
- What did you do at that time? Why didn't you act sooner?

So, too, Peter might be asked questions at the hearing relevant to when his supervising attorney (Stanton) or any partner in the firm found out about what he had done—and what they did when they found out.

(b) Misrepresentation of Paralegal Identity or Status

"It is the lawyer's responsibility to take reasonable measures to ensure that clients, courts, and other lawyers are aware that a legal assistant, whose services are utilized by the lawyer in performing legal services, is not licensed to practice law." [52] People who come into contact with paralegals must not think that they are attorneys. Paralegals should not misrepresent their status intentionally or accidentally. The following status issues need to be covered:

---

[52]ABA *Model Guidelines*, Guideline 4, see footnote 5.

- Titles
- Disclosure of status
- Business cards
- Letterhead
- Signature on correspondence
- Advertisements, announcement cards, signs, lists, and directories
- Name on court documents

What Title Can Be Used?   There are no ethical problems with the titles *paralegal* or *legal assistant*. No one is likely to think that persons with such titles are attorneys. There are some bar associations that prefer titles that are even more explicit in communicating nonattorney status—for example, *lawyer's assistant* and *nonattorney assistant*. Yet, they are seldom used because of the widespread acceptance and clarity of the titles *paralegal* and *legal assistant*. Some years ago, the Philadelphia Bar Association said that the latter titles should be given only to employees that possessed "the requisite training and education." No state, however, is this explicit in stating who can use the titles.

It is unethical to call a paralegal an "associate" or to refer to a paralegal as being "associated" with a law firm. The title, "paralegal associate," for example, should not be used. The common understanding is that an associate is an attorney. In Iowa, similar problems exist with the title, "Certified Legal Assistant," as we shall see shortly. (See Figure 2.7).

Note on Disbarred or Suspended Attorney as Paralegal.   When attorneys have been disbarred or suspended from the practice of law for ethical improprieties, they may try to continue to work in the law as a paralegal for an attorney willing to hire them. Some states will not allow this because it shows disrespect for the court that disciplined the attorney and because of the high likelihood that the individual will engage in the unauthorized practice of law by going beyond paralegal duties. Other states are more lenient but impose other restrictions, such as not allowing a disbarred or suspended attorney to have any client contact while working as a paralegal.

Should Paralegals Disclose Their Nonattorney Status to Clients, Attorneys, Government Officials, and the General Public?   Yes, this disclosure is necessary. The more troublesome questions are: What kind of disclosure should you make and when must you make it? Compare the following communications by a paralegal:

- "I work with attorney Ward Brown at Brown & Tams."
- "I am a paralegal."
- "I am a legal assistant."
- "I am not an attorney."

The fourth statement is the clearest expression of nonattorney status. The first is totally unacceptable since you have said nothing about your status. For most contacts, the second and third statements will be ethically sufficient to overcome any misunderstanding about your nonattorney status. Yet there might be members of the public who are confused about what a paralegal or legal assistant is. Hence, the only foolproof communication in all circumstances is the fourth.

In some states, the disclosure of nonattorney status is needed only if a client, an attorney, a government official, or a member of the public is unaware of this status. Other states say that the paralegal should always disclose his or her non-attorney status at the outset of the contact. According to one state, "common sense suggests a routine disclosure at the outset of the conversation." Also, the failure to provide an oral clarification of status is *not* cured simply by using a business card that says you are a paralegal or a legal assistant.

Do not assume that a person with whom you come in contact knows you are not an attorney; the safest course is to assume the opposite!

May a Paralegal Have a Business Card? Every state allows paralegals to have their own business cards as long as their nonattorney status is clear. (See Figure 2.6.) At one time, some states wanted the word *nonlawyer* used along with the paralegal's office title. This is rarely required today. Since paralegals are not allowed to solicit business for their employer, the card may not be used for this purpose. The primary focus of the card must be to identify the paralegal rather than the attorney for whom the paralegal works. Finally, there must be nothing false or misleading printed on the card. In most states, a paralegal who is a *Certified Legal Assistant (CLA)* can include this fact on their card. In Iowa, however, this is not permitted, as we will see when we discuss signatures on correspondence. (See Figure 2.7.)

May the Letterhead of Law Firm Stationery Print the Name of a Parale-gal? States differ in their answer to this question, although most now agree that nonattorneys' names can be printed on law-firm letterhead if their title is also printed so that their nonattorney status is clear. (See Figure 2.8.) Before 1977, almost all states did *not* allow attorney stationery to print the names of nonattorney employees. The concern was that the letterhead would be used as a form of advertising by packing it with names and titles in order to make the

FIGURE 2.6 Paralegal Business Card

ABEL
MUSSER
SOKOLOSKY
&CLARK
ATTORNEYS AT LAW

DEBRA J. HOBBS
LEGAL ASSISTANT

ONE LEADERSHIP SQUARE
211 N. ROBINSON, SUITE 600
(405) 239-7046   OKLAHOMA CITY, OK 73102

Ethically proper in every state.

FIGURE 2.7   Paralegal Business Card

John Simpson, CLA
PARALEGAL

JONES, DAY, OVERTON & DAVIS, P.C.
8262 PRESTWICK DR.
WATERLOO, IA 50702

PHONE
(319) 456-9103

Ethically proper in every state *except* in Iowa.

office look impressive. This concern, however, evaporated in 1977 when the Supreme Court held that all forms of attorney advertising could not be banned.[53] After this date, most states withdrew their objection to the printing of paralegal names on attorney letterhead as long as no one would be misled into thinking that the paralegals were attorneys. In Michigan, it was recommended, but not required, that attorneys and nonattorneys be printed on different sides of the stationery to "enhance the clarification that the paraprofessional is not licensed to practice law." A few states adhere to the old view that only attorney names can be printed on law-firm letterhead. Yet, to the extent that it is still based on a prohibition of attorney advertising, this view is subject to challenge.

May a Paralegal Write and Sign Letters on Attorney Stationery?   There is never an ethical problem with a paralegal writing a letter that will be reviewed and signed by an attorney. Suppose, however, that the attorney wants the paralegal to sign his or her own name to the letter. Most states will permit this if certain conditions are met. For example, a title must be used that indicates the signer's nonattorney status, and the letter must not give legal advice.

The following formats are proper:

Sincerely,	Sincerely,	Sincerely,
Leonard Smith	Pauline Jones	Jill Strauss
Paralegal	Legal Assistant	Legal Assistant for the Firm

The following formats, however, pose difficulties:

Sincerely,	Sincerely,	Sincerely,
William Davis	John Simpson, CLA	Mary Page Certified Legal Assistant

---

[53]See footnote 47 above.

FIGURE 2.8   Attorney Letterhead that Prints Paralegal Names

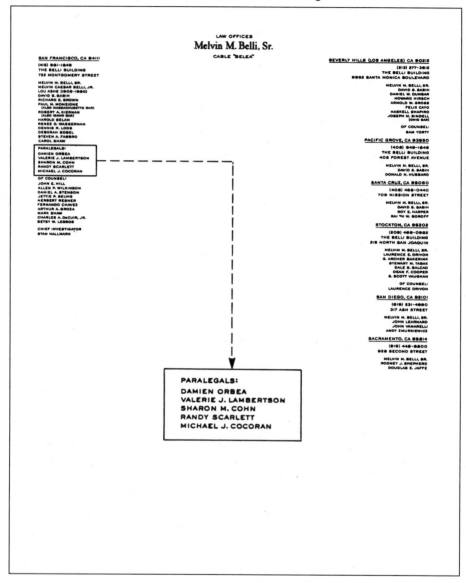

The first format is ethically improper. The lack of a title could mislead the reader into thinking that William Davis is an attorney. In most states, using the designations "CLA" or "Certified Legal Assistant" is also proper. (See Chapter 1 for a discussion of the CLA program.) In Iowa, however, they cannot be used. "A reader might think that CLA was a legal degree;" and if "Certified Legal Assistant" is used, "the public might be misled about his or her nonlawyer status." Hence, the second and third formats just shown cannot be used in Iowa. Presumably this also applies to a business card with the CLA designation. (See Figure 2.7.) This is an extreme view and is unlikely to be followed elsewhere.

In most states, there are no limitations on the persons to whom a paralegal can send letters. Yet there are a few states (such as New Jersey) where only an attorney can sign a letter to a client, to an opposing attorney, or to a court. A very minor exception to this rule would be "a purely routine request to a court clerk for a docket sheet." A paralegal can sign such a letter. This also is an extreme position. So long as the paralegal's nonattorney status is clear, and so long as an attorney is supervising the paralegal, restrictions on who can be the recipient of a paralegal-signed letter make little sense.

May an Attorney Print the Name of a Paralegal in an Advertisement, an Announcement Card, a Door Sign, an Outdoor Sign, a Law Directory or Law List, an Office Directory, or a Telephone Directory?   Attorneys communicate to the public and to each other through advertisements, law directories or lists (that print the names of practicing attorneys), office directories, general telephone directories, door signs, outdoor signs, and announcement cards (that announce that the firm has moved, opened a new branch, merged with another firm, taken on a new partner, etc.). It is relatively rare that an attorney will want to print the name of his or her paralegal in one of these vehicles of communication. In a small city or town, however, a solo practitioner or small law firm might want to do so. While several states will not allow attorneys to do this, most states that have addressed the issue say it is ethically permissible if nothing false or misleading is said about the paralegal and the latter's nonattorney status is clear.

May an Attorney Print the Name of a Paralegal on a Court Document? Formal documents that are required in litigation, such as appellate briefs, memoranda supporting a motion, complaints, or other pleadings, must be signed by an attorney representing a party in the dispute. With rare exceptions, the document cannot be signed by a nonattorney, no matter how minor the formal document may be. In most states, a paralegal can sign a letter on a routine matter to a clerk or other nonjudge, but formal litigation documents require an attorney's signature.

Suppose, however, that the attorney wishes to print on a document the name of a paralegal who worked on the document *in addition to* the attorney's name and signature. The attorney may simply want to give a measure of recognition to the efforts of this paralegal. Most states permit this as long as there is no misunderstanding as to the paralegal's nonattorney status, and no attempt is made to substitute a nonattorney's signature for an attorney's signature.

Occasionally, a court opinion will recognize the contribution of a paralegal. Before the opinion begins, the court lists the names of the attorneys who represented the parties. The name of a paralegal might be included with these attorneys. Here, for example, is the list of attorneys that includes the name of a paralegal (Becky Strickland) in the case of *United States v. Cooke*, 625 F.2d 19 (4th Cir. 1980):

> Thomas J. Keith, Winston-Salem, N.C., for appellant.
> David B. Smith, Asst. U.S. Atty. (H. M. Michaux, Jr., U.S. Atty., Durham, N.C., Becky M.

Strickland, Paralegal Specialist on brief), for appellee.

Before HALL and PHILLIPS, Circuit Judges, and HOFFMAN, Senior District Judge.

(c) Doing What Only Attorneys Can Do

There are limitations on what attorneys can ask their paralegals to do. We just examined one such limitation: paralegals should never be asked to sign court documents. The failure to abide by these limits might subject the attorney to a charge of unethically assisting a nonattorney to engage in the unauthorized practice of law. The areas we need to examine are as follows:

- Legal advice
- Nonlegal advice
- Drafting documents
- Real estate closings
- Depositions
- Executions of wills
- Settlement negotiations
- Court appearances
- Counsel's table
- Administrative hearings

May a Paralegal Give Legal Advice?   Unfortunately, it is not easy to define legal advice or the practice of law. According to the American Bar Association:

> It is neither necessary nor desirable to attempt the formulation of a single, specific definition of what constitutes the practice of law. Functionally, the practice of law relates to the rendition of services for others that call for the professional judgment of a lawyer. The essence of the professional judgment of the lawyer is his educated ability to relate the general body and philosophy of law to a specific legal problem of a client. . . . Where this professional judgment is not involved, non-lawyers, such as court clerks, police officers, abstracters, and many governmental employees, may engage in occupations that require a special knowledge of law in certain areas. But the services of a lawyer are essential in the public interest whenever the exercise of *professional judgment* is required.[54]

The major way that an attorney communicates this professional judgment is through *legal advice.* According to the ABA, it occurs when "the general body and philosophy of law" is related or applied "to a specific legal problem." You are giving legal advice when you tell a particular person how the law might affect a particular legal problem or how to achieve a particular legal result that solves or avoids such a problem. Giving such advice is the unauthorized practice of law, whether or not you charge for the advice and whether or not your advice is correct.

---

[54]EC 3–5, *ABA Model Code of Professional Responsibility* (1981).

Compare the following sets of statements:

General Information about the Law	Information about the Law as Applied to a Specific Person
"The Superior Court is located at 1223 Via Barranca."	"Your case must be heard in the Superior Court which is located at 1223 Via Barranca."
"There are several different kinds of bankruptcy."	"There are several different kinds of bankruptcy, but you should file under Chapter 13."
"The failure to pay child support will lead to prosecution."	"Your failure to pay child support will lead to prosecution."

Arguably, the statements in the second column constitute legal advice; general information about the law has been related or applied to a particular legal problem of a particular person. The legal questions or problems addressed are: What court can hear (has jurisdiction over) *your* case? What kind of bankruptcy should *you* file? Can *you* be prosecuted for not paying child support?

The statements in the first column do not appear to focus on any particular person's legal problem. Hence such statements do not constitute legal advice, at least not explicitly. But we need to examine some of these statements more closely. When you tell someone that there are "several different kinds of bankruptcy," are you, by implication, telling that person that he or she should consider, and may qualify for, at least one of the kinds of bankruptcy? When you tell someone that the "failure to pay child support will lead to prosecution," are you, by implication, telling that person that his or her failure to pay child support will lead to his or her prosecution? The moment there is a focus on a particular person's legal problem, you are in the realm of legal advice. This focus can be express or implied. Hence, whenever *any* statement about the law is made, you must ask yourself two questions:

■ Am I trying to relate legal information to any particular person's legal problem? (If so, I am giving express legal advice.)

■ Could a person reasonably interpret what I am saying as relating legal information to a particular person's legal problem even if this is not my intent? (If so, I am giving implied legal advice.)

Great care is sometimes needed to avoid giving legal advice.

There are a number of circumstances that increase the likelihood that statements can reasonably be interpreted as giving implied legal advice. For example:

■ The statement is made by someone who works in the law, such as an attorney, paralegal, or legal secretary.

■ The statement is made by someone who has helped the person with his or her legal problems in the past.

■ The statement is made by someone who knows that the person has a current legal problem.

■ The person is distressed about his or her current legal problem.

Under such circumstances, the person is likely to interpret *any* statement about the law as being relevant to his or her particular legal problem.

A number of paralegals have pointed out how easy it is to fall into the trap of giving legal advice:

> Legal assistants should be alert to all casual questions [since your answers] might be interpreted as legal advice.[55]

> Most of us are aware of the obvious, but we need to keep in mind that sometimes the most innocent comment could be construed as legal advice.[56]

> A . . . typical scenario, particularly in a small law office where legal assistants have a great deal of direct client contact, is that the clients themselves will coax you to answer questions about the procedures involved in their cases, and lead you into areas where you would be giving them legal advice. Sometimes this is done innocently—because the attorney is unavailable and they are genuinely unaware of the difference between what you can do for them and what their legal counsel is authorized to do. . . . They will press you for projections, strategy, applicable precedents—in short, legal advice. Sometimes you are placed in situations where you are not adequately supervised and your own expertise may be such that you know more about the specialized area of law than the attorney does anyway. . . . We have all walked the thin line between assisting in the provision of legal services and actually practicing law.[57]

When a paralegal gives legal advice in these circumstances, he or she is engaged in the unauthorized practice of law. An attorney who permits this to occur, or who fails to take the preventive steps required by Model Rule 5.3, is aiding the paralegal in the unauthorized practice of law—and hence is acting unethically.

There are a number of situations, however, in which a paralegal *can* give legal advice. First, a paralegal can tell a client precisely what the attorney tells the paralegal to say, even if the message constitutes legal advice. The paralegal, however, cannot elaborate on or explain this kind of message from the attorney. Paralegals "may be authorized to communicate legal advice so long as they do not interpret or expand on that advice." [58] Second, the paralegal may be working in an area of the law where nonattorneys are authorized to represent clients, such as social security hearings. (See Chapter 1.) In such areas, the authorization includes the right to give legal advice.

May a Paralegal Give a Client Nonlegal Advice?   Yes. An attorney may allow a paralegal to render specialized advice on scientific or technical topics. For example, a qualified paralegal can give accounting advice or financial advice. The danger is that the nonlegal advice might also contain legal advice or that the client might reasonably interpret the nonlegal advice as legal advice.

---

[55]King, *Ethics and the Legal Assistant*, 10 ParaGram 2 (Oregon Legal Assistants Ass'n, August 1987).

[56]DALA Newsletter 2 (Dallas Ass'n of Legal Assistants, December 1990).

[57]Spiegel, *How to Avoid the Unauthorized Practice of Law*, 8 The Journal 8–10 (Sacramento Ass'n of Legal Assistants, February 1986).

[58]ABA *Model Guidelines*, Comment to Guideline 3, see footnote 5.

May a Paralegal Draft Legal Documents?   Yes. A paralegal can draft any legal document as long as an attorney supervises and reviews the work of the paralegal. Some ethical opinions say that the document must lose its separate identity as the work of a paralegal and must leave the office as the work product of an attorney. In West Virginia, for example, "anything delegated to a nonattorney must lose its separate identity and be merged in the service of the lawyer." The key point is that an attorney must stand behind and be responsible for the document.

May a Paralegal Attend a Real Estate Closing?   The sale of property is finalized at an event called a real estate closing. Many of the events at the closing are formalities, such as signing and exchanging papers. Occasionally, however, some of these events turn into more substantive matters where negotiation, legal interpretation, and legal advice are involved.

   In most states, paralegals can attend closings in order to assist their attorney-supervisor. The tough question is whether they can attend alone and conduct the closing themselves. Chicago has one of the most liberal rules. There, paralegals can conduct the closing without the attorney-supervisor being present if no legal advice is given, if all the documents have been prepared in advance, if the attorney-supervisor is available by telephone to provide help, and if the other attorney consents. In some states, additional conditions must be met before allowing paralegals to act on their own. For example, the closing must take place in the attorney's law office with the attorney readily accessible to answer legal questions. It must be noted, however, that this is a minority position. Most states would say that it is unethical for an attorney to allow a paralegal to conduct a real estate closing alone.

May a Paralegal Conduct a Deposition?   No. Paralegals can schedule depositions, can assist in preparing a witness who will be deposed (called the deponent), can take notes at the deposition, and can summarize deposition transcripts, but they cannot conduct the deposition. Asking and objecting to questions are attorney-only functions.

May a Paralegal Supervise the Execution of a Will?   In Connecticut, the execution of a will must be supervised by an attorney. A paralegal can act as a witness to the execution, but an attorney must direct the procedure. Most other states would probably agree, although few have addressed this question.

May a Paralegal Negotiate a Settlement?   Some states allow a paralegal to negotiate with a nonattorney employee of an insurance company, such as a claims adjuster, as long as the paralegal is supervised by an attorney. Most states, however, limit the paralegal's role to exchanging messages from the supervising attorney, and do not allow any actual give-and-take negotiating by the paralegal.

May a Paralegal Make a Court Appearance?   In the vast majority of courts, a paralegal cannot perform even minor functions in a courtroom, such as asking a judge for a hearing date. As we saw in Chapter 1, very few exceptions to this rule exist. Only attorneys can act in a representative capacity before a judge. There are, however, a small number of specialized courts, like the small claims court of some states, where you do not have to be an attorney to represent parties. This exception, however, is rare. Finally, as mentioned earlier, a paralegal should not sign a formal court document that is filed in litigation.

May a Paralegal Sit at Counsel's Table During a Trial?   In many courts, only attorneys can sit at counsel's table during a trial. Yet, in some courts a paralegal is allowed to sit with the attorneys if permission of the presiding judge is obtained. This is referred to as sitting *second chair* in the courtroom.

May a Paralegal Represent Clients at Administrative Hearings?   Yes, when this is authorized at the particular state or federal agency. (See Chapter 1.)

(d) Absentee, Shoulder, and Environmental Supervision

It is difficult to overestimate the importance of attorney supervision in the arena of ethics. Almost every ethical opinion involving paralegals (and almost every attorney malpractice opinion involving paralegals) stresses the need for effective supervision. The justification for the very existence of perhaps 95% of paralegal activity is this supervision. Indeed, one of the main reasons many argue that paralegal licensing is not necessary is the protective cover of attorney supervision.

What is meant by supervision? The extremes are easy to identify. Figure 2.9 provides this spectrum of extremes. *Absentee supervision* refers to the attorney who is either never around or never available. Once tasks are assigned, paralegals are on their own. At the other extreme is *shoulder supervision,* practiced by attorneys who are afraid to delegate. When they do get up enough courage to delegate something, they constantly look over the shoulder of the paralegal, who is rarely left alone for more than two-minute intervals. Such attorneys suffer from *delegatitis,* the inordinate fear of letting anyone do anything for them.

Both kinds of supervision are misguided. If you work for an attorney who practices absentee supervision, disaster is just around the corner. You may feel flattered by the confidence placed in you; you may enjoy the challenge of independence; you may be highly compensated because of your success. But you are working in an office that is traveling 130 miles per hour in a 50 miles per hour zone. Any feeling of safety in such an office is illusory. Shoulder supervision, on the other hand, provides safety at the expense of practicality. Perpetual step-by-step surveillance will ultimately defeat the economy and efficiency motives that originally led the office to hire paralegals.

Perhaps the most effective kind of supervision is *environmental supervision,* or what might be called *holistic supervision.* It is far broader in its reach than the immediate task delegated to a paralegal. It addresses the essential ques-

FIGURE 2.9 Levels of Supervision: The Spectrum of Extremes

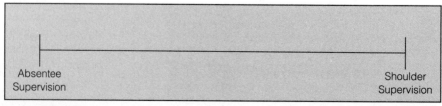

Absentee
Supervision

Shoulder
Supervision

tion: What kind of environment leads to quality paralegal work without sacrificing economy? The components of this kind of supervision are outlined in Figure 2.10. Environmental supervision requires *hiring* the right people, *training* those people, *assigning* appropriate tasks, *providing* the needed resources, *monitoring* the progress, *reviewing* the end product, and *rewarding* competence.

FIGURE 2.10   "Environmental Supervision": The Ethical Ideal

1. Before paralegals are hired, the office undertakes a study of its practice in order to identify what tasks paralegals will perform and what levels of ability will be required to perform those tasks.

2. As part of the interview process, the office conducts background checks on applicants for paralegal jobs in order to ensure that competent people are hired who already have the needed skills or who are trainable so that they can acquire these skills on the job.

3. A program of orientation and training is created to introduce paralegals to the office and to prepare them for the tasks ahead.

4. Paralegals are given a copy of the ethical rules governing attorneys in the state. In addition to reading these rules, they are given training on the meaning of the rules.

5. Paralegals are told what to do if they feel that an ethical problem exists. Lines of authority are identified if the paralegal needs to discuss the matter with someone other than, or in addition to, his or her immediate supervisor.

6. The office does not assume that every attorney knows how to supervise paralegals. Paralegals are assigned to attorneys who have the required supervisory sensitivity and skill. Furthermore, the office is always looking for ways to increase this sensitivity and skill.

7. An attorney reviews all paralegal work. While paralegals may be given discretion and asked to exercise judgment in the tasks assigned, this discretion and judgment is always subjected to attorney review.

8. No task is assigned that is beyond the capacity of the paralegal. Specialized instruction always accompanies tasks the paralegal has not performed before.

9. Once a task is assigned, the paralegal is told where to receive assistance if the immediate supervisor is not available. This lack of availability, however, is relatively rare.

10. For tasks that the office performs on a recurring basis, manuals, office procedures, checklists, or other written material are available to the paralegal to explain how the tasks are performed and where samples or models can be found. If such *systems* material does not currently exist, the office has realistic plans to create such material.

11. To cut down on misunderstanding, every paralegal assignment includes the following information:

    - A *specific due date.* ("Get to this when you can" is unacceptable and unfair.)

    - A *priority assessment.* ("Should everything else be dropped while I do this assignment?")

    - A *context.* ("How does this assignment fit into the broader picture of the case?")

    - A *financial perspective.* ("Is this billable time?")

12. At reasonable times before the due date of selected assignments, the supervisor monitors the progress of the paralegal to ensure that the work is being done professionally and accurately.

13. A team atmosphere exists at the office among the attorneys, paralegals, secretaries, and other employees. Everyone knows each other's functions, pressures, and potential as resources. A paralegal never feels isolated.

Continued

FIGURE 2.10   "Environmental Supervision": The Ethical Ideal—
Continued

14. Evaluations of paralegal performance are constructive. Both the supervisor and paralegal feel that there are opportunities for further learning.
15. The office sends the paralegal to training seminars conducted by paralegal associations and bar associations to maintain and to increase the paralegal's skills.
16. The office knows that an unhappy employee is prone to error. Hence the office ensures
that the work setting of the paralegal encourages personal growth and productivity.
This includes matters of compensation, benefits, work space, equipment, and
advancement.

Unfortunately, most law offices do *not* practice environmental supervision as outlined in Figure 2.10. The chart represents the ideal. Yet you need to know what the ideal is so that you can advocate for the conditions that will help bring it about.

Thus far, our discussion on supervision has focused on the traditional paralegal who works full time in the office of an attorney. We also need to consider the freelance paralegal who works part-time for one or more attorneys. Very often this freelance or independent paralegal works in his or her own office. (See Chapter 1.) How can attorneys fulfill their ethical obligation to supervise such paralegals?

Example: Gail Patterson has her own freelance business. She offers paralegal services to attorneys who hire her for short-term projects which she performs in her own office.

Arguably, attorneys who hire Gail often do not provide the same kind of supervision that they can provide to a full-time paralegal who works in their office. We saw earlier that Model Rule 5.3(c)(2) says that an attorney has the responsibility to take steps to avoid the consequences of an ethical violation by a paralegal or to mitigate the consequences of such a violation. Suppose that Gail commits an ethical impropriety—for example, she reveals confidential communications. Since she works in her own office, the attorney who hired her may not learn about this impropriety in time to avoid or mitigate its consequences. Conflict of interest is another potential problem. Gail works for many different attorneys and hence many different clients of those attorneys. It is possible that she could accept work from two attorneys who are engaged in litigation against each other without either attorney knowing that the other has hired Gail on the same case. (See the earlier discussion of this problem on page 93.)

A few bar associations have declared that it is ethically improper for an attorney to hire a freelance paralegal because of the difficulties of providing meaningful supervision. It is not enough that the attorney vouches for, and takes responsibility for, the final product submitted by the freelance paralegal. Ongoing supervision is also needed under Model Rule 5.3. Not many states, however, have addressed this area of ethics. In the future, we will probably see the creation of new standards to govern this kind of paralegal.

Section D. Doing Research on an Ethical Issue

1. At a law library, ask where the following two items are kept:
   - The code or rules of ethics governing the attorneys in your state
   - The ethical opinions that interpret the code or rules

2. Contact your state bar association. Ask what committee handles ethics. Contact it to find out if it has published any opinions, guidelines, or other materials on paralegals. Also ask if there is a special committee on paralegals. If so, find out what it has said about paralegals.

3. Do the same for any other bar associations in your area, such as city or county bar associations.

4. At a law library, ask where the following two items are kept:
   - The ABA's Model Rules of Professional Conduct
   - The ethical opinions that interpret these Model Rules as well as the earlier Model Code of Professional Responsibility of the ABA

5. Examine the *ABA/BNA Lawyers' Manual on Professional Conduct*. This is a loose-leaf book containing current information on ABA ethics and the ethical rules of every state.

6. Other material to check in the library:
   - C. Wolfram, *Modern Legal Ethics* (1986) (treatise)
   - *The Georgetown Journal of Legal Ethics* (periodical)
   - *Lawyers' Liability Review* (newsletter)

7. Computer research in either WESTLAW or LEXIS enables you to do research on the law of ethics in your state. Here, for example, is a query (i.e. question) you can use to ask WESTLAW to find cases in which a paralegal was charged with the unauthorized practice of law:

   > paralegal "legal assistant" /p "unauthorized practice"

   After you instructed WESTLAW to turn to the database containing the court opinions of your state, you would type this query at the keyboard in order to find out if any such cases exist.

8. Another way to find court opinions on ethics in your state is to go to the digest covering the courts in your state. Use its index to find cases on ethical issues.

Section E. Ethical Codes of the Paralegal Associations

As indicated at the beginning of this chapter, there are no binding ethical rules published by paralegal associations. Yet the two major national associations—the National Federation of Paralegal Associations (NFPA) and the National Association of Legal Assistants (NALA)—have written ethical codes.

These important documents of NFPA and of NALA are presented below, followed by a broader document of NALA, its Model Standards and Guidelines.

Affirmation of Professional Responsibility
of the National Federation of
Paralegal Associations

Preamble

The National Federation of Paralegal Associations recognizes and accepts its commitment to the realization of the most basic right of a free society, equal justice under the law.

In examining contemporary legal institutions and systems, the members of the paralegal profession recognize that a redefinition of the traditional delivery of legal services is essential in order to meet the needs of the general public. The paralegal profession is committed to increasing the availability and quality of legal services.

The National Federation of Paralegal Associations has adopted this *Affirmation of Professional Responsibility* to delineate the principles of purpose and conduct toward which paralegals should aspire. Through this Affirmation, the National Federation of Paralegal Associations places upon each paralegal the responsibility to adhere to these standards and encourages dedication to the development of the profession.

I. Professional Responsibility

A paralegal shall demonstrate initiative in performing and expanding the paralegal role in the delivery of legal services within the parameters of the unauthorized practice of law statutes.

Discussion: Recognizing the professional and legal responsibility to abide by the unauthorized practice of law statutes, the Federation supports and encourages new interpretations as to what constitutes the practice of law.

II. Professional Conduct

A paralegal shall maintain the highest standards of ethical conduct.

Discussion: It is the responsibility of a paralegal to avoid conduct which is unethical or appears to be unethical. Ethical principles are aspirational in character and embody the fundamental rules of conduct by which every paralegal should abide. Observance of these standards is essential to uphold respect for the legal system.

III. Competence and Integrity

A paralegal shall maintain a high level of competence and shall contribute to the integrity of the paralegal profession.

Discussion: The integrity of the paralegal profession is predicated upon individual competence. Professional competence is each paralegal's responsibility and is achieved through continuing education, awareness of developments in the field of law, and aspiring to the highest standards of personal performance.

IV. Client Confidences

A paralegal shall preserve client confidences and privileged communications.

Discussion: Confidential information and privileged communications are a vital part of the attorney, paralegal, and client relationship. The importance of preserving confidential and privileged information is understood to be an uncompromising obligation of every paralegal.

V. Support of Public Interests

A paralegal shall serve the public interests by contributing to the availability and delivery of quality legal services.

Discussion: It is the responsibility of each paralegal to promote the development and implementation of programs that address the legal needs of the public. A paralegal shall strive to maintain a sensitivity to public needs and to educate the public as to the services that paralegals may render.

VI. Professional Development

A paralegal shall promote the development of the paralegal profession.

Discussion: This Affirmation of Professional Responsibility promulgates a positive attitude through which a paralegal may recognize the importance, responsibility and potential of the paralegal contribution to the delivery of legal services. Participation in professional associations enhances the ability of the individual paralegal to contribute to the quality and growth of the paralegal profession.

Code of Ethics and Professional Responsibility
of the National Association of Legal Assistants

Preamble

It is the responsibility of every legal assistant to adhere strictly to the accepted standards of legal ethics and to live by general principles of proper conduct. The performance of the duties of the legal assistant shall be governed by specific canons as defined herein in order that justice will be served and the goals of the profession attained.

The canons of ethics set forth hereinafter are adopted by the National Association of Legal Assistants, Inc., as a general guide, and the enumeration of these rules does not mean there are not others of equal importance although not specifically mentioned.

Canon 1

A legal assistant shall not perform any of the duties that lawyers only may perform nor do things that lawyers themselves may not do.

Canon 2

A legal assistant may perform any task delegated and supervised by a lawyer so long as the lawyer is responsible to the client, maintains a direct relationship with the client, and assumes full professional responsibility for the work product.

Canon 3

A legal assistant shall not engage in the practice of law by accepting cases, setting fees, giving legal advice, or appearing in court (unless otherwise authorized by court or agency rules).

Canon 4

A legal assistant shall not act in matters involving professional legal judgment as the services of a lawyer are essential in the public interest whenever the exercise of such judgment is required.

Canon 5

A legal assistant must act prudently in determining the extent to which a client may be assisted without the presence of a lawyer.

Canon 6

A legal assistant shall not engage in the unauthorized practice of law and shall assist in preventing the unauthorized practice of law.

Canon 7

A legal assistant must protect the confidences of a client, and it shall be unethical for a legal assistant to violate any statute now in effect or hereafter to be enacted controlling privileged communications.

Canon 8

It is the obligation of the legal assistant to avoid conduct which would cause the lawyer to be unethical or even appear to be unethical, and loyalty to the employer is incumbent upon the legal assistant.

Canon 9

A legal assistant shall work continually to maintain integrity and a high degree of competency throughout the legal profession.

Canon 10

A legal assistant shall strive for perfection through education in order to better assist the legal profession in fulfilling its duty of making legal services available to clients and the public.

Canon 11

A legal assistant shall do all other things incidental, necessary, or expedient for the attainment of the ethics or responsibilities imposed by statute or rule of court.

Canon 12

A legal assistant is governed by the *American Bar Association Model Code of Professional Responsibility* and the *American Bar Association Model Rules of Professional Conduct.*

Model Standards and Guidelines for Utilization of Legal Assistants
of the National Association of
Legal Assistants

Preamble

Proper utilization of the services of legal assistants affects the efficient delivery of legal services. Legal assistants and the legal profession should be assured that some measures exist for identifying legal assistants and their role in assisting attorneys in the delivery of legal services. Therefore, the National Association of Legal Assistants, Inc., hereby adopts these Model Standards and Guidelines as an educational document for the benefit of legal assistants and the legal profession.

Definition

Legal assistants* are a distinguishable group of persons who assist attorneys in the delivery of legal services. Through formal education, training, and experience, legal assistants have knowledge and expertise regarding the legal system and substantive and procedural law which qualify them to do work of a legal nature under the supervision of an attorney.

Standards

A legal assistant should meet certain minimum qualifications.The following standards may be used to determine an individual's qualifications as a legal assistant:

1. Successful completion of the Certified Legal Assistant (CLA) examination of the National Association of Legal Assistants, Inc.;

2. Graduation from an ABA approved program of study for legal assistants;

3. Graduation from a course of study for legal assistants which is institutionally accredited but not ABA approved, and which requires not less than the equivalent of 60 semester hours of classroom study;

4. Graduation from a course of study for legal assistants, other than those set forth in (2) and (3) above, plus not less than six months of in-house training as a legal assistant;

5. A baccalaureate degree in any field, plus not less than six months in-house training as a legal assistant;

*Within this occupational category some individuals are known as paralegals.

6. A minimum of three years of law-related experience under the supervision of an attorney, including at least six months of in-house training as a legal assistant; or

7. Two years of in-house training as a legal assistant.

For purposes of these standards, "in-house training as a legal assistant" means attorney education of the employee concerning legal assistant duties and these Guidelines. In addition to review and analysis of assignments, the legal assistant should receive a reasonable amount of instruction directly related to the duties and obligations of the legal assistant.

Guidelines

These Guidelines relating to standards of performance and professional responsibility are intended to aid legal assistants and attorneys. The responsibility rests with an attorney who employs legal assistants to educate them with respect to the duties they are assigned and to supervise the manner in which such duties are accomplished.

Legal assistants should:

1. Disclose their status as legal assistants at the outset of any professional relationship with a client, other attorneys, a court or administrative agency or personnel thereof, or members of the general public.

2. Preserve the confidences and secrets of all clients; and

3. Understand the attorney's Code of Professional Responsibility and these Guidelines in order to avoid any action which would involve the attorney in a violation of that Code, or give the appearance of professional impropriety.

Legal assistants should not:

1. Establish attorney-client relationships, set legal fees, give legal opinions or advice, or represent a client before a court; nor

2. Engage in, encourage, or contribute to any act which could constitute the unauthorized practice of law.

Legal assistants may perform services for an attorney in the representation of a client, provided:

1. The services performed by the legal assistant do not require the exercise of independent professional legal judgment;

2. The attorney maintains a direct relationship with the client and maintains control of all client matters;

3. The attorney supervises the legal assistant;

4. The attorney remains professionally responsible for all work on behalf of the client, including any actions taken or not taken by the legal assistant in connection therewith; and

5. The services performed supplement, merge with, and become the attorney's work product.

In the supervision of a legal assistant, consideration should be given to:

1. Designating work assignments that correspond to the legal assistants' abilities, knowledge, training, and experience;

2. Educating and training the legal assistant with respect to professional responsibility, local rules and practices, and firm policies;

3. Monitoring the work and professional conduct of the legal assistant to ensure that the work is substantively correct and timely performed;

4. Providing continuing education for the legal assistant in substantive matters through courses, institutes, workshops, seminars, and in-house training; and

5. Encouraging and supporting membership and active participation in professional organizations.

Except as otherwise provided by statute, court rule or decision, administrative rule or regulation, or the attorney's Code of Professional Responsibility; and within the preceding parameters and proscriptions, a legal assistant may perform any function delegated by an attorney, including, but not limited to, the following:

1. Conduct client interviews and maintain general contact with the client after the establishment of the attorney-client relationship, so long as the client is aware of the status and function of the legal assistant, and the client contact is under the supervision of the attorney.

2. Locate and interview witnesses, so long as the witnesses are aware of the status and function of the legal assistant.

3. Conduct investigations and statistical and documentary research for review by the attorney.

4. Conduct legal research for review by the attorney.

5. Draft legal documents for review by the attorney.

6. Draft correspondence and pleadings for review by and signature of the attorney.

7. Summarize depositions, interrogatories, and testimony for review by the attorney.

8. Attend executions of wills, real estate closings, depositions, court or administrative hearings, and trials with the attorney.

9. Author and sign letters, provided the legal assistant's status is clearly indicated and the correspondence does not contain independent legal opinions or legal advice.

Section F. An Ethical Dilemma: Your Ethics or Your Job!

Throughout this chapter we have stressed the importance of maintaining your integrity through knowledge of and compliance with ethical rules. There may be times, however, when this is much easier said than done. Consider the following situations:

■ You are not sure whether an ethical violation is being committed. Nor is anyone else in the office sure. Like so many areas of the law, ethical issues can be complex.

■ You are sure that an ethical violation exists, and the violator is your supervisor!

■ You are sure that an ethical violation exists, and the violators are everyone else in the office!

You face a potential dilemma (1) if no one seems to care about the ethical problem or, worse, (2) if your supervising attorney is the one committing the ethical impropriety or (3) if the entire office appears to be participating in the impropriety. People do not like to be told that they are unethical. Rather than acknowledge the fault and mend their ways, they may turn on the accuser, the one raising the fuss about ethics. Once the issue is raised, it may be very difficult to continue working in the office.

You need someone to talk to. In the best of all worlds, it will be someone in the same office. If this is not practical, consider contacting a teacher whom you trust. Paralegal associations are also an excellent source of information and support. A leader in one paralegal association offers the following advice:

> I would suggest that if the canons, discipline rules, affirmations, and codes of ethics do not supply you with a clear-cut answer to any ethical question you may have, you should draw upon the network that you have in being a member of this association. Getting the personal input of other paralegals who may have been faced with similar situations, or who have a greater knowledge through experience of our professional responsibilities, may greatly assist you in working your way through a difficult ethical situation.[59]

Of course, you must be careful not to violate client confidentiality during discussions with someone outside the office. Never mention actual client names or any specific information pertaining to a case. You can talk in hypothetical terms. For example, "an attorney working on a bankruptcy case asks a paralegal to. . . ." Once you present data in this sterilized fashion, you can then ask for guidance on the ethical implications of the data.

If handled delicately, most ethical problems that bother you can be resolved without compromising anyone's integrity or job. Yet the practice of law is not substantially different from other fields of endeavor. There will be times when the clash between principle and the dollar or the ego cannot be resolved to everyone's satisfaction. You may indeed have to make a choice between your ethics and your job.

■ **ASSIGNMENT 2.1**

(a) What is the name of the code of ethics that governs attorneys in your state?

(b) To what body or agency does a client initially make a charge of unethical conduct against his or her attorney in your state?

(c) List the steps required to discipline an attorney for unethical conduct in your state. Begin with the complaint stage and conclude with the court that makes the final decision. Draw a flow chart that lists these steps.

---

[59]Harper, *Ethical Considerations for Legal Assistants*, Compendium (Orange County Paralegal Ass'n, April 1987).

■ ASSIGNMENT 2.2

Paul Emerson is an attorney who works at the firm of Rayburn & Rayburn. One of the firm's clients is Designs Unlimited, Inc. (DU), a clothing manufacturer. Emerson provides corporate advice to DU. Recently Emerson made a mistake in interpreting a new securities law. As a consequence, DU had to postpone for six months the issuance of a stock option. Has Paul acted unethically?

■ ASSIGNMENT 2.3

(a) Three individuals in Connecticut hire a large New York law firm to represent them in a proxy fight in which they sought control of a Connecticut bank. They lose the proxy fight. The firm then sends these individuals a $358,827 bill for 895 hours of work over a one month period. Is this bill unethical? What further facts would you like to have to help you answer this question?

(b) Victor Adams and Len Patterson are full partners in the law firm of Adams, Patterson & Kelly. A client contacts Patterson to represent him on a negligence case. Patterson refers the case to Victor Adams who does most of the work. (Under an agreement between them, Patterson will receive 40% and Adams will receive 60% of any fee paid by this client.) Patterson does not tell the client about the involvement of Adams in the case. Any ethical problems?

(c) An attorney establishes a bonus plan for her paralegals. A bonus will be given to those paralegals who bill a specified number of hours in excess of a stated minimum. The amount of the bonus will depend on the amount billed and collected. Any ethical problems?

■ ASSIGNMENT 2.4

Mary works in a law firm that charges clients $125 an hour for attorney time and $55 an hour for paralegal time. She and another paralegal, Fred, are working with an attorney on a large case. She sees all of the time sheets that the three of them submit to the firm's accounting office. She suspects that the attorney is padding his time sheets by overstating the number of hours he works on the case. For example, he lists thirty hours for a four-day period when he was in court every day on another case. Furthermore, Fred's time is being billed at the full $55 an hour rate even though he spends about 80% of his time typing correspondence, filing, and other clerical duties. Mary also suspects that her attorney is billing out Mary's time at the attorney rate rather than the paralegal rate normally charged clients for her time. Any ethical problems? What should Mary do?

■ ASSIGNMENT 2.5

Smith is an attorney who works at the firm of Johnson & Johnson. He represents Ralph Grant, who is seeking a divorce from his wife, Amy Grant. In their first meeting, Smith learns that Ralph is an experienced carpenter but is out of work and has very little money. Smith's fee is $150 an hour. Since Ralph has no money and has been having trouble finding work, Smith tells Ralph that he won't have to pay the fee if the court does not grant him the divorce. One day while Smith is working on another case involving Helen Oberlin, he learns that Helen is looking for a carpenter. Smith recommends Ralph to Helen, and she hires him for a small job. Six months pass. The divorce case is dropped when the Grants reconcile. In the meantime,

Helen Oberlin is very dissatisfied with Ralph's carpentry work for her; she claims he didn't do the work he contracted to do. She wants to know what she can do about it. She tries to call Smith at Johnson & Johnson but is told that Smith does not work there anymore. Another attorney, Georgia Quinton, Esq. helps Helen. Any ethical problems?

■ ASSIGNMENT 2.6

John Jones is a paralegal working at the XYZ law firm. The firm is handling a large class action involving potentially thousands of plaintiffs. John has been in-structed to screen the potential plaintiffs in the class. John tells those he screens out (using criteria provided by the firm) in writing or verbally that "unfortunately, our firm will not be able to represent you." Any ethical problems?

■ ASSIGNMENT 2.7

A paralegal quits the firm of Smith & Smith. When she leaves, she takes client documents she prepared while at the firm. The documents contain confidential client information. The paralegal is showing these documents to potential employers as writing samples.

(a) What is the ethical liability of attorneys at Smith & Smith under Model Rule 5.3?

(b) What is the ethical liability of attorneys at law firms where she is seeking em-ployment under 5.3?

(c) What is the paralegal's liability?

■ ASSIGNMENT 2.8

(a) Mary Smith is a paralegal at the ABC law firm. She has been working on the case of Jessica Randolph, a client of the office. Mary talks with Ms. Randolph often. Mary receives a subpoena from the attorney of the party that is suing Ms. Randolph. On the witness stand, Mary is asked by this attorney what Ms. Randolph told her at the ABC law office about a particular business transaction related to the suit. Randolph's attorney (Mary's boss) objects to the question. What result?

(b) Before Helen became a paralegal for the firm of Harris & Derkson, she was a chemist for a large corporation. Harris & Derkson is a patent law firm where Helen's technical expertise in chemistry is invaluable. Helen's next-door neigh-bor is an inventor. On a number of occasions he discussed the chemical makeup of his inventions with Helen. Regarding one of these inventions, the neighbor is being charged by the government with stealing official secrets to prepare the invention. Harris & Derkson represent the neighbor on this case. Helen also works directly on the case for the firm. In a prosecution of the neigh-bor, Helen is called as a witness and is asked to reveal the substance of all her conversations with the neighbor concerning the invention in question. Does Helen have to answer?

■ ASSIGNMENT 2.9

Bob and Patricia Fannan are separated, and they both want a divorce. They would like to have a joint-custody arrangement in which their son would spend time with each parent during the year. The only marital property is a house, which they agree should be sold, with each to get one half of the proceeds. Mary Franklin, Esq. is an attorney whom Jim and Mary know and trust. They decide to ask Franklin to represent both of them in the divorce. Any ethical problems?

▧ ASSIGNMENT 2.10

Alice is a freelance paralegal with a specialty in probate law. One of the firms she has worked for is Davis, Ritter & Boggs. Her most recent assignment for this firm has been to identify the assets of Mary Steck, who died six months ago. One of Mary's assets is a 75% ownership share in the Domain Corporation. Alice learns a great deal about this company, including the fact that four months ago it had difficulty meeting its payroll and expects to have similar difficulties in the coming year.

Alice's freelance business has continued to grow because of her excellent reputation. She decides to hire an employee with a different specialty so that her office can begin to take different kinds of cases from attorneys. She hires Bob, a paralegal with four years of litigation experience. The firm of Jackson & Jackson hires Alice to digest a series of long deposition documents in the case of Glendale Bank v. Ajax Tire Co. Jackson & Jackson represents Glendale Bank. Peterson, Zuckerman & Morgan represents Ajax Tire Co. Alice assigns Bob to this case. Ajax Tire Co. is a wholly owned subsidiary of the Domain Corporation. Glendale Bank is suing Ajax Tire Co. for fraud in misrepresenting its financial worth when Ajax Tire Co. applied for and obtained a loan from Glendale Bank.

Any ethical problems?

▧ ASSIGNMENT 2.11

Assume that you owned a successful freelance business in which you provided paralegal services to over 150 attorneys all over the state. How should your files be organized in order to avoid a conflict of interest?

▧ ASSIGNMENT 2.12

Joan is a paralegal who works for the XYZ law firm, which is representing Goff in a suit against Barnard, who is represented by the ABC law firm. Joan calls Barnard and says, "Is this the first time that you have ever been sued?" Barnard answers, "Yes it is. Is there anything else that you would like to know?" Joan says *no* and the conversation ends. Any ethical problems?

▧ ASSIGNMENT 2.13

Mary is a paralegal who is a senior citizen. She works at the XYZ legal service office. One day she goes to a senior citizens center and says the following:

> All of you should know about and take advantage of the XYZ legal service office where I work. Let me give you just one example why. Down at the office there is an attorney named Armanda Morris. She is an expert on insurance company cases. Some of you may have had trouble with insurance companies that say one thing and do another. Our office is available to serve you.

Any ethical problems?

■ ASSIGNMENT 2.14

(a) What restrictions exist on advertising by attorneys in your state? Give an example of an ad on TV or in the newspaper that would be unethical. On researching an ethical issue, see page 115.

(b) In *Bates v. State Bar of Arizona,* 433 U.S. 350 (1970), the United States Supreme Court held that a state could not prohibit all forms of lawyer advertising. Has *Bates* been cited by state courts in your state on the advertising issue? If so, what impact has the case had in your state? To find out, shepardize *Bates.*

■ ASSIGNMENT 2.15

Mary Jackson is a paralegal at Rollins & Rollins. She is supervised by Ian Gregory. Mary is stealing money from the funds of one of the firm's clients. The only attorney who knows about this is Dan Roberts, Esq., who is not a partner at the firm and who does not supervise Mary. Dan says and does nothing about Mary's actions. What ethical obligations does Dan have under Model Rule 5.3?

■ ASSIGNMENT 2.16

John Smith is a paralegal at Beard, Butler, and Clark. John's immediate supervisor is Viola Butler, Esq. With the latter's OK, John Smith sends a letter to a client of the firm (Mary Anders). Has Viola Butler acted unethically in permitting John to send out the following letter?

Law Offices of
Beard, Butler, and Clark
310 High St.
Maincity, Ohio 45238
512-663-9410

Attorneys at Law
Ronald Beard
Viola Butler
Wilma Clark

Paralegal
John Smith

May 14, 1991

Mary Anders
621 S. Randolph Ave.
Maincity, Ohio 45238

Dear Ms. Anders:

Viola Butler, the attorney in charge of your case, asked me to tell you that your hearing has been changed to May 2. If you have any questions don't hesitate to call me.

Sincerely,

John Smith
Legal Intern

JS:wps

■ ASSIGNMENT 2.17

Under what circumstances, if any, would it be appropriate for you to refer to a client of the office where you work as "my client"?

■ ASSIGNMENT 2.18

John Jones is a paralegal who works for an attorney named Linda Sunders. Linda is away from the office one day and telephones John, who is at the office. She dictates a one-line letter to a client of the office. The letter reads, "I advise you to sue." Linda asks John to sign the letter for her. The bottom of the letter reads as follows:

Linda Sunders
by John Jones

Any ethical problems?

■ ASSIGNMENT 2.19

Mary is a paralegal who works at the XYZ law firm. She specializes in real estate matters at the firm. Mary attends a real estate closing in which her role consists of exchanging documents and acknowledging the receipt of documents. Analyze this problem on the basis of the following variations:

(a) The closing takes place at the XYZ law firm.

(b) The closing takes place at a bank.

(c) Mary's supervising attorney is not present at the closing.

(d) Mary's supervising attorney is present at the closing.

(e) Mary's supervising attorney is present at the closing except for thirty minutes, during which time Mary continued to exchange documents and acknowledge the receipt of documents.

(f) During the closing, the attorney for the other party says to Mary, "I don't know why my client should have to pay that charge." Mary responds: "In this state that charge is always paid in this way."

■ ASSIGNMENT 2.20

John is a paralegal who works for the XYZ law firm, which is representing a client against the Today Insurance Company. The Company also employs paralegals who work under the Company's general counsel. One of these paralegals is Mary. In an effort to settle the case, Mary calls John and says, "We offer you $200.00." John says, "We'll let you know." Any ethical problems?

■ ASSIGNMENT 2.21

John Smith is a paralegal who works for Beard, Butler, and Clark. He sends out the following letter. Any ethical problems?

John Smith
Paralegal
310 High St.
Maincity, Ohio 45238
512-663-9410

June 1, 1991

State Unemployment Board
1216 Southern Ave.
Maincity, Ohio 45238

Dear Gentlepeople:

I work for Beard, Butler, and Clark, which represents Mary Anders, who has a claim before your agency. A hearing originally scheduled for June 8, 1991 has been postponed. We request that the hearing be held at the earliest time possible after the 8th.

Sincerely,

John Smith

JS:wps

■ ASSIGNMENT 2.22

Give five examples of tasks that would be unethical for a paralegal to perform. Give five examples of unethical comments made by a paralegal when performing tasks that otherwise would be ethical for a paralegal to perform.

■ ASSIGNMENT 2.23

Compare the Affirmation of Professional Responsibility of NFPA with the Code of Ethics and Professional Responsibility of NALA, page 116. Make a list of the topics or themes covered in one of the documents but not in the other. Is there a difference in emphasis between the two documents?

■ ASSIGNMENT 2.24

Draft your own paralegal code as a class project. First, have a meeting in which you make a list of all the issues that you think should be covered in the code. Divide up the issues by the number of students in the class so that every student has roughly the same number of issues. Each student should draft a proposed rule on each of the issues to which he or she is assigned. Accompany each rule with a brief commentary on why you think the rule should be as stated. Draft alternative versions of the proposed rule if different versions are possible and you want to give the class the chance to examine all of them. The class then meets to vote on each of the proposed rules. Students will make presentations on the proposed rules they have drafted. If the class is not happy with the way in which a particular proposed rule was drafted by a student, the latter will redraft the rule for later consideration by the class. One member of the class should be designated the "code reporter," who records the rules accepted by the class by majority vote.

After you have completed the code, you should consider inviting attorneys from the local bar association to your class in order to discuss your proposed code. Do the same with officials of the closest paralegal association in your area.

☐ Chapter Summary

Attorneys are regulated by the highest court in the state, often with the extensive involvement of the state bar association. Since paralegals cannot practice law and cannot become full members of a bar association, they cannot be punished for a violation of the ethical rules governing attorneys. The American Bar Association is a voluntary association; no attorney must be a member. The ABA publishes ethical rules which the states are free to adopt, modify, or reject.

The current rules of the ABA are found in its *Model Rules of Professional Conduct*. These ethical rules require attorneys to be competent, to act with reasonable diligence and promptness, to charge fees that are reasonable, to avoid conduct that is criminal and fraudulent, to avoid asserting claims and defenses that are frivolous, to safeguard the property of clients, to avoid making false statements of law and fact to a tribunal, to withdraw from a case for appropriate reasons, to maintain the confidentiality of client information, to avoid conflicts of interest, to avoid improper communications with an opponent, to avoid improper solicitation of clients, to avoid improper advertising, to report serious professional misconduct of other attorneys, to avoid assisting nonattorneys engaged in the unauthorized practice of law, and to supervise paralegal employees appropriately.

Ethical opinions and guidelines exist in almost every state on the proper use of a paralegal by an attorney. All states agree that the title used for this employee must not mislead anyone about his or her nonattorney status, and that the employee must disclose his or her nonattorney status when necessary to avoid misunderstanding. Rules also exist on other aspects of the attorney-paralegal relationship, but not all states agree on what these rules should be. The following apply in most states:

Under attorney approval and supervision, paralegals in most states:

- can have their own business card
- can have their name printed on the law firm letterhead
- can sign law firm correspondence
- can give nonlegal advice
- can draft legal documents
- can attend a real estate closing
- can represent clients at agency hearings if authorized by the agency

With few exceptions, paralegals in most states:

- cannot give legal advice
- cannot conduct a deposition
- cannot sign formal court documents
- cannot supervise the execution of a will
- cannot make an appearance in court

Separate ethical rules and guidelines have been adopted by the National Association of Legal Assistants and by the National Federation of Paralegal Associations.

Key Terms

ethics
sanctions
national bar association
state bar association
local bar association
integrated bar
    association
mandatory bar
    association
unified bar association
registration
self-regulation
Model Rules of
    Professional
    Conduct
Model Code of
    Professional
    Responsibility
DR
EC
disbarment
suspension
interim suspension
reprimand
private reprimand
censure
public censure
admonition
probation
competence
malpractice
6th amendment
reasonable diligence
reasonable fee
retainer
minimum fee schedule
antitrust law
contingent fee

fee splitting
referral fee
forwarding fee
double billing
padding time sheets
insider trading
pirated software
frivolous positions
commingle funds
adversarial system
withdrawal
cured
impaired attorney
privileged
confidentiality
attorney-client privilege
work-product rule
discoverable
waiver
conflict of interest
divided loyalty
multiple representation
common representation
adverse interests
friendly divorce
switching sides
imputed disqualification
vicarious disqualification
Chinese wall
ethical wall
cone of silence
tainted/contaminated
    employee
quarantined paralegal
conflicts check
lateral hire
disinterested

in-person solicitation
barratry
ambulance chasing
attorney advertising
runner/capper
unauthorized practice of
    law
model rule 5.3
tickler
associate/associated
business card
CLA
law-firm letterhead
law directory
legal advice
professional judgment
separate identity of
    document
real estate closing
deposition/deponent
supervision
delegatitis
second chair
freelance paralegal
Affirmation of
    Professional
    Responsibility
    (NFPA)
Code of Ethics and
    Professional
    Responsibility
    (NALA)
Model Standards and
    Guidelines for
    Utilization of Legal
    Assistants (NALA)

■ Post Script

■ Change: Deregulation of the Legal Profession?

The rules on the unauthorized practice of law described in this book reflect the legal profession as it exists today. What about the future? It is unlikely that we will soon see any significant change in the essential structure of the system by which the legal profession and paralegals are regulated.

But calls for change will continue to emerge. Some of the proposals for change are nothing short of revolutionary as demonstrated in the following dramatic speech:

W. Durant, "Maximizing Access to Justice: A Challenge to the Legal Profession"

(Mr. Durant was the Chairman of the Legal Services Corporation, a federal agency that funds programs that provide legal services to the poor. Mr. Durant made the following comments in a speech before the American Bar Association on February 12, 1987.)

The greatest barrier to widely dispersed low cost dispute resolution services for the poor, and for all people, could very well be the laws protecting our profession. They make it a cartel . . . .

The legal monopoly rests on two major pillars. The first are laws that set aside specific work exclusively for lawyers. Anyone else who performs "lawyer's work" may be prosecuted for the Unauthorized Practice of Law [UPL statutes]. The second is a series of restrictions on how one may become a lawyer. These restrictions are really barriers to competition, not guardians of competence.

Stanford Law School Assistant Professor Deborah Rhode concluded an exhaustive study of UPL statutes and practice by observing that "at every level of enforcement, the consumer's need for protection has been proclaimed rather than proven." The use of UPL prosecutions is "inconsistent, incoherent, and, from a policy perspective, indefensible," she says.

We should encourage at every turn the ability of entrepreneurs, paraprofessionals and lay people to be a part of the delivery of legal services for the poor and for all people. I've met many eligible clients around the country who can quite capably be advocates in resolving disputes if barriers to practice did not exist. How can doors be open to others to participate in this profession? In serving others a private sector deregulated legal profession can deliver a good quality product in much the same way that a good commercial enterprise does. How do some of our most common necessities get most widely distributed, even to the least of our brethren, at the lowest price and best service? We let the free competitive energies of creative and energetic people in the private sector provide and deliver for us. And, for the most part they do. Such people exist for the delivery of legal services but are blocked by UPL statutes and aggressive Bar efforts to halt them.

Peggy Ann Muse in Oregon, Rose Palmer in Pennsylvania, Richard Grimes in Denver, Colorado; Cecile Browning in Kansas, Virginia Cramer in Michigan, Peter Anderson in Wisconsin, Benny Bonanno in Ohio, Phil Lydic in Washington, Barry Wood in New Jersey, Donald Erickson in Missouri and, of course, Rosemary Furman in Florida are just some of the people who are trying to bring lower cost legal services to poor people and others but are or have been aggressively prosecuted by the organized Bar to prevent them from delivering services or "practicing law."

Peggy Muse's firm in Oregon helped arbitrate claims, collect small debts, and service other cases too small to justify hiring an attorney. Her fees were ⅓ or less than those charged by a lawyer. The State Bar, not her clients, complained. The Bar goes after her.

Rose Palmer who founded Legal Advocacy for Women is not a lawyer but she is typical of people harassed by the organized Bar. She goes to court to give encouragement, advice, and help to women, many who are poor, who are trying to get alimony, child support, and just plain fairness in divorce proceedings. She should be a hero. She is; but not to the local Bar in Pittsburgh. She is receiving city funding for her good work but other possible funding was cancelled after an attorney who represents husbands in divorce proceedings filed a UPL complaint against her.

There are many organizations growing up around the country like Rose Palmer's which can help people use the legal system correctly.

Lori Morelock is the product of one. She enforced her court ordered child support without the use of a lawyer. Virginians Organized To Insure Children's Entitlement to Support gave her training and encouragement. Morelock says that several attorneys urged her to accept welfare payments and stop fighting the child support system. She fired her lawyers and tackled the tasks alone. She was discouraged by both judges and lawyers. But in the end she prevailed.

An attorney in Pittsburgh said it simply. "Many in the Bar are afraid of losing control, of people finding ways to do things on their own without their help. If they let women's groups get away with it, other, more lucrative sectors could do the same thing. And then they would lose money."

There are approximately 1.2 million cases handled annually by programs associated with the Legal Services Corporation. A high degree of specialization for these cases seems not to be required. Almost 30 percent are in the Family Law area common to almost any general practice: divorce, separation, annulment, custody, visitation rights, spouse abuse, and support. Housing cases constitute another 19 percent of legal services cases and less than 3 percent involve public housing. Medicaid and Medicare cases that affect the elderly poor represent less than 2 percent of our cases. Further, about one-third of our cases are closed with no more than brief advice being given. These statistics, like all statistics, do not reveal the whole truth. But they do suggest that a broader array of people from all walks of life could be a part of the delivery of legal services.

The second feature of the legal monopoly restricts how one becomes a lawyer and what you can do when you are one.

In all states, you must pass a bar exam to practice law, though the specific tests vary greatly in terms of length, subjects covered and grading standards. The detailed knowledge necessary for someone to answer a question on constitutional law, for example, may be critical for a law professor or a specialized practitioner, but is probably not required for an attorney specializing in the small claims that normally arise in a neighborhood practice. In many states, a Board of Law Examiners can and do vary the pass/fail rate as if operating a medieval drawbridge.

Two-thirds of the state allow someone to sit for the bar exam *only* if he or she has graduated from a school accredited by the ABA; the rest, except for California, require prospective attorneys to attend a school approved by the ABA *or* the state Bar. Law school accreditation by the ABA reduces the number of law schools, the number of law students, and produces students trained in a particular way that may or may not be just what the consumer wants, or needs, in resolving disputes. This is not a quality control issue. It is an issue of control under the pretext of quality. The automotive industry or the Society of Automotive Engineers does not accredit engineering schools. The industry hires the best qualified people from a wide variety of schools. A relevant basic skills test is fine. Let there be many schools which train lawyers or dispute resolvers in their own way, for their own niche in the market. They can probably do it in significantly less time and at less cost.

Think for a moment if you will of the sea of transactions that exist between people. Think of the millions of disputes that will inevitably arise. They can be resolved in almost an infinite number of ways. An entrepreneur sees an opportunity, an opportunity to give and to serve. Perhaps all one wanted to do all his or her life was to provide easier access for people to enforce their rights or to resolve landlord tenant matters, or domestic or consumer claims. Such a person should not have to spend three years in law school, spend so many thousands of dollars to graduate and then pass comprehensive exams on subjects hardly related in order to provide basic service. Competent practitioners who are not looking for Wall Street but simply wish to handle the simpler, less costly cases, cases most often handled for the poor, and the majority of people, are locked out.

In the market place where millions of transactions take place every day, entrepreneurs are coming up with alternatives to the option of high-priced lawyers. High volume, low price legal clinics have proliferated; more than 12 million consumers (and the number grows daily) are now served by prepaid legal plans. Alternative Dispute Resolutions (ADR) centers have jumped from 20 a decade ago to some 330 today. Hyatt Legal Services and Jacoby & Meyers are some of the most entrepreneurial lawyers in existence. They have established hundreds of these effective low cost legal clinics throughout the country. Attorney Van O'Steen in Arizona has developed very effective and low cost self-help legal packets on very routine but important legal services. They all perform a wonderful service because they are taking something as important as justice and making it widely available at a low cost to poor and middle class people. Ten years ago, such would not be possible. You could not advertise legal services, hence you could not develop volume, economies of sale, or effectively provide price competition. While price fixing was once the rule and advertising prohibited until a decade ago, solicitation, broader advertising, reciprocity among states, and other normal competitive practices in any other business are still tightly controlled. Even membership in the lawyer's guild is mandatory in many states. The ABA is voluntary and look at its strength. State bars should be voluntary.

The overall effect of this system created and operated by lawyers is to limit entry into the profession, to discourage competition, to increase prices, delays and costs and ultimately to deny access to justice for the poor, for all of us. The legal cartel's heaviest burden falls on the poor. They are denied choices and access. They are denied advocates and opportunities.

State Unauthorized Practice of Law statutes simply should be repealed. The legal business should be like any other business subject to the usual consumer protections.

On a federal level, Congress and the President can initiate legislation or executive orders to make it possible for lay people to appear in administrative hearings before administrative boards, and agencies, to prepare necessary documents and advise clients in such matters.

The most effective method for change is the power of a shared vision. Here, it is simply a vision to unleash the tremendous energies of a free and creative people to bring about an open and competitive system of resolving disputes and providing access to justice for all people. It is a vision that offers to entrepreneurs, eligible clients, teachers, ministers, paralegals, social workers, legal secretaries, and so many others a chance to be involved in opening up our profession to develop a broader array of service mechanisms for resolving disputes between people and for providing access to justice. It is a vision to empower communities, individuals and local associations of all sorts, . . . to be involved in the resolution and reconciliation of disputes and people.

The question is really whether we truly want to maximize access to justice and in what ways. Shakespeare is wrong. We need not kill all the lawyers. We simply need to de-regulate them. Open up the profession. Broaden the base. Let more people, let more institutions deliver the services. Costs will come down, services will be expanded and alternatives in resolving disputes will be developed. Deregulation in the trucking, airline, and railroad industries, and even, to some extent the accounting profession, to name but a few, all reflect this positive development for consumers. Justice likewise is too important to be left bottled up by laws protecting the legal profession.

■ Review

When you complete this book you should:

1. Know the ten commandments of an ethical conservative.
2. Know what is meant by ethics and how they are enforced.
3. Know why a paralegal cannot be disciplined by a bar association for unethical conduct.
4. Know why paralegals need to understand the ethical rules that govern attorneys.
5. Know the kinds of bar associations that exist.
6. Know the relationship between the American Bar Association and other bar associations.
7. Know how attorneys are regulated. Know the process by which an attorney can be disciplined.
8. Know the sanctions that can be imposed on attorneys for unethical conduct.
9. Distinguish between (a) the ABA Model Rules of Professional Conduct, and (b) the ABA Model Code of Professional Responsibility.
10. Know the standard used to determine whether an attorney has complied with the ethical obligation to be competent.
11. Know how paralegals can fulfill their ethical obligation to be competent.
12. Know the standard used to determine whether an attorney has complied with the ethical obligation to act with reasonable diligence and promptness in representing a client.
13. Know the standard used to determine whether attorney fees are ethically unreasonable.
14. Know why minimum fee schedules are illegal.
15. Know when contingent fees are unethical.
16. Know the rule against an attorney unethically splitting a fee with a paralegal.
17. Be able to identify ethical problems, if any, concerning a paralegal's participation in the retirement program of a firm.
18. Understand the pressures on paralegals to engage in unethical double billing and padding of time sheets.
19. Know the attorney's obligation to avoid criminal or fraudulent conduct.
20. Know the kinds of activities that can involve a paralegal in criminal or fraudulent conduct.
21. Know the standard used to determine whether an attorney has unethically aided a client to engage in criminal or fraudulent conduct.

22. Know the standard used to determine whether an attorney has unethically asserted a frivolous claim or defense.

23. Know the attorney's ethical obligation to avoid commingling funds and to safeguard client property.

24. Know the attorney's ethical obligation to avoid false statements and to disclose facts and laws that support the other side.

25. Know the common rationales used by attorneys to justify deception.

26. Know when an attorney must withdraw from a case and when he or she has the option of withdrawing.

27. Know the standard used to determine whether an attorney has unethically violated client confidentiality.

28. Know the attorney-client privilege and its relationship to the ethical obligation to maintain client confidentiality.

29. Know the attorney work-product rule and its relationship to the ethical obligation to maintain client confidentiality.

30. Know the circumstances under which paralegals can fall into the trap of violating client confidentiality.

31. Know the definition of conflict of interest.

32. Know the standards used to determine whether an attorney has an unethical conflict of interest by (a) entering a business transaction with a client, (b) making a loan to a client, (c) accepting a gift from a client, and (d) engaging in multiple representation.

33. Know the standard used to determine whether an attorney can ethically represent someone opposed to a former client.

34. Know when there can be an imputed disqualification of an entire law firm.

35. Know the screening components of a Chinese Wall and when they might avoid imputed disqualification.

36. Know the objective and methods of accomplishing a conflicts check.

37. Know how a paralegal might cause the imputed disqualification of a new employer, and how to avoid such a disaster.

38. Know the standard used to determine whether attorneys and their staffs have unethically communicated with the other side.

39. Know the standard used to determine whether an attorney has unethically solicited clients.

40. Know the standard used to determine whether an attorney has unethically advertised his or her services.

41. Know the standard used to determine whether an attorney has unethically failed to report the misconduct of another attorney.

42. Know the consequences of an attorney engaging in conduct that appears to be improper.

43. Be able to state the essence of the following documents that directly

pertain to the use of paralegals: (a) DR-101, (b) EC 3-6, and (c) ABA Formal Opinion 316.

44. Be able to state the separate ethical standards imposed on the three categories of attorneys covered in Model Rule 5.3.

45. Know the kinds of questions a paralegal might be asked in a hearing against an attorney who has been charged with a violation of Model Rule 5.3.

46. Be able to identify ethical problems, if any, concerning the title of this new career in law.

47. Know the danger that exists when a disbarred or suspended attorney functions as a paralegal.

48. Know when paralegals must disclose their nonattorney status to others.

49. Be able to identify ethical problems, if any, concerning business cards for paralegals.

50. Be able to identify ethical problems, if any, concerning a paralegal's name printed on law firm stationery.

51. Be able to identify ethical problems, if any, concerning signing letters on law firm stationery.

52. Be able to identify ethical problems, if any, concerning a paralegal's name printed in an advertisement, on an announcement card, on a door, in a directory, on a law list, or on a court document.

53. Be able to identify express and implied legal advice.

54. Be aware of the pressures on a paralegal to give legal advice.

55. Know when a paralegal can give legal and nonlegal advice.

56. Be able to identify ethical problems, if any, concerning a paralegal drafting legal documents.

57. Be able to identify ethical problems, if any, concerning paralegal attendance at a real estate closing.

58. Be able to identify ethical problems, if any, concerning paralegal involvement in depositions.

59. Be able to identify ethical problems, if any, concerning a paralegal (a) executing a will, (b) negotiating a settlement, (c) making court appearances, (d) sitting at counsel's table, and (e) representing clients at administrative hearings.

60. Know the basic components of "environmental supervision:" the ethical ideal.

61. Be able to identify the potential ethical difficulties that attorneys face when they use freelance paralegals.

62. Be able to list the main sets of books that you would use to research an ethical issue.

63. Be able to state the major provisions of NFPA's Affirmation of Professional Responsibility.

64. Be able to state the major provisions of NALA's Code of Ethics and Professional Responsibility.

65. Be able to state the major provisions of NALA's Model Standards and Guidelines for Utilization of Legal Assistants.

66. Know what resources are available when a paralegal faces an ethical dilemma on the job.

State and Local Bar Associations

ALABAMA

Alabama State Bar
P.O. Box 671
Montgomery, AL 36104
205-269-1515

Birmingham Bar Association
109 N. 20th St., 2nd Fl.
Birmingham, AL 35203
205-251-8006

ALASKA

Alaska Bar Association
P.O. Box 100279
Anchorage, AK 99501
907-272-7469

ARIZONA

Maricopa County Bar Association
333 W. Roosevelt St.
Phoenix, AZ 85003
602-257-4200

State Bar of Arizona
363 N. 1st Ave.
Phoenix, AZ 85003
602-252-4804

ARKANSAS

Arkansas Bar Association
400 W. Markham
Little Rock, AR 72201
501-375-4605

CALIFORNIA

Alameda County Bar Association
405 14th St., Suite 208
Oakland, CA 94612
415-893-7160

Bar Association of San Francisco
685 Market St., #700
San Francisco, CA 94105
415-764-1600

Beverly Hills Bar Association
300 S. Beverly Dr., #201
Beverly Hills, CA 90212
213-553-6644

Lawyers Club of Los Angeles
700 S. Flower St.
Los Angeles, CA 90017
213-624-2525

Lawyers' Club of San Francisco
685 Market St., #750
San Francisco, CA 94105
415-882-9150

Los Angeles County Bar Association
617 S. Olive St.
Los Angeles, CA 90014
213-627-2727

Orange County Bar Association
601 Civic Center Dr. West
Santa Ana, CA 92701
714-541-6222

San Diego County Bar Association
1333 7th Ave.
San Diego, CA 92101
619-231-0781

Santa Clara County Bar Association
2001 Gateway P1., #220 West
San Jose, CA 95110
408-453-3448

State Bar of California
555 Franklin St.
San Francisco, CA 94102
415-561-8200

COLORADO

Colorado Bar Association
1900 Grant St., #950
Denver, CO 80203-4309
303-860-1115

Denver Bar Association
1900 Grant St., Suite 950
Denver, CO 80201-4309
303-860-1115

CONNECTICUT

Connecticut Bar Association
101 Corporate Pl.
Rocky Hill, CT 06067
203-721-0025

DELAWARE

Delaware Bar Association
708 Market Street
Wilmington, DE 19899
302-658-5278

DISTRICT OF COLUMBIA

Bar Association of the District of
  Columbia
1819 H. St. NW, 12th F1.
Wash. D.C. 20006
202-293-6600

District of Columbia Bar
1707 L. St. NW, 6th F1.
Wash. D.C. 20036
202-331-3883

FLORIDA

Florida Bar
650 Apalachee Parkway
Tallahassee, FL 32399-2300
904-561-5600

Dade County Bar Association
111 N.W. First Ave.
Miami, FL 33128
305-371-2220

GEORGIA

Atlanta Bar Association
100 Peachtree St. NW
Atlanta, GA 30303
404-521-0781

State Bar of Georgia
800 The Hurt Bldg.
Atlanta, GA 30303
404-527-8700

HAWAII

Hawaii State Bar
1001 Bishop St., Suite 950
Honolulu, HI 96813
808-537-1868

IDAHO

Idaho State Bar
P.O. Box 895
Boise, ID 83702
208-342-8958

ILLINOIS

Chicago Bar Association
321 S. Plymouth Ct.
Chicago, IL 60603-1575
312-782-7348

Chicago Council of Lawyers
220 S. State St., Rm. 800
Chicago, IL 60604
312-427-0710

Illinois State Bar Association
424 S. Second St.
Springfield, IL 62701
217-525-1760

800-252-8908
312-726-8775 (Chicago)
800-442-ISBA

Illinois Trial Lawyers Association
110 W. Edwards St.
P.O. Box 5000
Springfield, IL 62705
217-798-0755
800-252-8501

INDIANA

Indianapolis Bar Association
10 West Market St.
Indianapolis, IN 46204
317-632-8240

Indiana State Bar Association
230 E. Ohio St., 6th Fl.
Indianapolis, IN 46204
317-639-5465

IOWA

Iowa State Bar Association
1101 Fleming Bldg.
Des Moines, IA 50309
515-243-3179

KANSAS

Kansas Bar Association
1200 Harrison St.
Topeka, KS 66612
913-234-5696

KENTUCKY

Kentucky Bar Association
West Main at Kentucky River
Frankfort, KY 40601
502-564-3795

Louisville Bar Association
707 W. Main St., #200
Louisville, KY 40202
502-583-5314

LOUISIANA

Louisiana State Bar Association
601 St. Charles Ave.

New Orleans, LA 70130
504-566-1600

Louisiana Trial Lawyers Association
442 Europe St.
P.O. Drawer 4289
Baton Rouge, LA 70821
504-383-5554

MAINE

Maine State Bar Association
124 State St.
P.O. Box 788
Augusta, ME 04330
207-622-7523

MARYLAND

Bar Association of Baltimore City
111 N. Calvert St.
Baltimore, MD 21202
301-539-5936

Maryland State Bar Association
520 W. Fayette St.
Baltimore, MD 21201
301-685-7878

MASSACHUSETTS

Boston Bar Association
16 Beacon St.
Boston, MA 02108
617-742-0615

Massachusetts Bar Association
20 West St.
Boston, MA 02111
617-542-3602

MICHIGAN

Detroit Bar Association
2380 Penobscot Bldg.
Detroit, MI 48226
313-961-6120

Michigan Trial Lawyers Association
501 S. Capitol Ave., Suite 405
Lansing, MI 48933-2327
517-482-7740

Oakland County Bar Association
1200 N. Telegraph Rd., Suite 532

Pontiac, MI 48053
313-338-2100

State Bar of Michigan
306 Townsend St.
Lansing, MI 48933-2083
517-372-9030

MINNESOTA

Hennepin County Bar Association
430 Marquette Ave., No. 402
Minneapolis, MN 55487
612-340-0022

Minnesota State Bar Association
430 Marquette Ave., Suite 403
Minneapolis, MN 55401
612-333-1183
800-292-4152

MISSISSIPPI

Mississippi State Bar
643 N. State St.
Jackson, MS 39202
601-948-4471

MISSOURI

Bar Association of Metropolitan Saint
    Louis
One Mercantile Center #3600
St. Louis, MO 63101
314-421-4134

Kansas City Metropolitan Bar
    Association
1125 Grand Ave.
Kansas City, MO 64106
816-474-4322

Missouri Bar
326 Monroe
Jefferson City, MO 65102
314-635-4128

MONTANA

State Bar of Montana,
46 N. Last Chance Gulch
P.O. Box 577
Helena, MT 59624
406-442-7660

NEBRASKA

Nebraska State Bar Association
635 S. 14th St.
Lincoln, NE 68508
402-475-7091

NEVADA

State Bar of Nevada
295 Holcomb Ave., Suite 2
Reno, NV 89502-1085
702-382-0502

NEW HAMPSHIRE

New Hampshire Bar Association
112 Pleasant Street
Concord, NH 03301
603-224-6942

NEW JERSEY

Essex County Bar Association
5 Becker Farm Road
Roseland, NJ 07068
201-622-6207

New Jersey State Bar Association
1 Constitution Sq.
New Brunswick, NJ 08901-1500
201-249-5000

NEW MEXICO

State Bar of New Mexico
121 Tijeras St. NE
Albuquerque, NM 87102
505-842-6132
800-876-6227

New Mexico Trial Lawyers' Association
    Foundation
P.O. Box 301
Albuquerque, NM 87103
505-243-6003

NEW YORK

Association of the Bar of the City of New
    York
42 W. 44th St.

New York, NY 10036
212-382-6600

New York County Lawyers Association
14 Vesey St.
New York, NY 10007
212-267-6646

New York State Bar Association
1 Elk St.
Albany, NY 12207
518-463-3200

New York State Trial Lawyers
   Association
132 Nassau St.
New York, NY 10038
212-349-5890

NORTH CAROLINA

North Carolina Bar Association
1312 Annapolis Dr.
Raleigh, NC 27611
919-828-0561

North Carolina State Bar
1312 Annapolis Dr.
Raleigh, NC 27611
919-828-0561

NORTH DAKOTA

State Bar Association of North Dakota
515½ E. Broadway, Suite 101
Bismarck, ND 58501
701-255-1404
800-472-2685

OHIO

Cincinnati Bar Association
35 E. 7th St., 8th Fl.
Cincinnati, OH 45202-2411
513-381-8213

Cleveland Bar Association
118 St. Clair Ave., NE
Cleveland, OH 44114-1523
216-696-3525

Columbus Bar Association
40 S. 3rd St., 6th Fl.
Columbus, OH 43215-5134
614-221-4112

Cuyahoga County Bar Association
1228 Euclid Ave., No. 370
Cleveland, OH 44115
216-621-5112

Ohio State Bar Association
33 W. 11th Ave.
Columbus, OH 43201
614-421-2121

OKLAHOMA

Oklahoma Bar Association
1901 N. Lincoln
Oklahoma City, OK 73105
405-524-2365
800-522-8065

Oklahoma County Bar Association
119 W. Robinson #240
Oklahoma City, OK 73102
405-236-8421

Tulsa County Bar Association
1446 S. Boston
Tulsa, OK 74119-3613
918-584-5243

OREGON

Multnomah Bar Association
711 SW Adler, Suite 311
Portland, OR 97205
503-222-3275

Oregon State Bar
5200 S.W. Meadows Rd.
P.O. Box 1689
Lake Oswego, OR 97035
503-620-0222

PENNSYLVANIA

Allegheny County Bar Association
420 Grant Bldg.
Pittsburgh, PA 15219
412-261-6161

Pennsylvania Bar Association
100 South St.
P.O. Box 186
Harrisburg, PA 17108
717-238-6715

Philadelphia Bar Association
One Reading Bldg.
Philadelphia, PA 19107
215-238-6300

PUERTO RICO

Puerto Rico Bar Association
P.O. Box 1900
San Juan, PR 00908
809-721-3358

Puerto Rican Bar Association
888 Grand Concourse, Suite 1-0
Bronx, NY 10451
212-292-8201

RHODE ISLAND

Rhode Island Bar Association
91 Friendship St.
Providence, RI 02903
401-421-5740

SOUTH CAROLINA

South Carolina Bar Association
950 Taylor St.
Columbia, SC 29202
803-799-6653

SOUTH DAKOTA

State Bar of South Dakota
222 E. Capitol
Pierre, SD 57501
605-224-7554

TENNESSEE

Tennessee Bar Association
3622 Westend Ave.
Nashville, TN 37205
615-383-7421

TEXAS

Dallas Bar Association
2101 Ross Ave.
Dallas, TX 75201
214-969-7066

Houston Bar Association
1001 Fannin, Suite 1300

Houston, TX 77002
713-759-1133

State Bar of Texas
1414 Colorado
Austin, TX 78711
512-463-1463

UTAH

Utah Bar Association
645 S. 200 East
Salt Lake City, UT 84111
801-531-9077

VERMONT

Vermont Bar Association
P.O. Box 100
Montpelier, VT 05602
802-223-2020
800-642-3153

VIRGINIA

Virginia Bar Association
701 E. Franklin St., Suite 1515
Richmond, VA 23219
804-644-0041

Virginia State Bar
801 E. Main St., Suite 1000
Richmond, VA 23219
804-786-2061

VIRGIN ISLANDS

Virgin Islands Bar Association
46 King St.
Christiansted, VI 00822
809-778-7497

WASHINGTON

Seattle-King County Bar
900 4th Ave., #600
Seattle, WA 98164
206-624-9365

Washington State Bar Association
2001 6th Ave.
Seattle, WA 98121-2599
206-448-0441

WEST VIRGINIA

West Virginia Bar Association
100 Capitol St.
Charleston, WV 25301
304-342-1474

West Virginia Sate Bar
E-400 State Capitol
Charleston, WV 25305
304-346-8414

West Virginia Trial Lawyers Association
P.O. Box 3968
Charleston, WV 25339
304-344-0692

WISCONSIN

Milwaukee Bar Association
533 E. Wells St.

Milwaukee, WI 53202
414-274-6760

State Bar of Wisconsin
402. W. Wilson
Madison, WI 53703
608-257-3838
800-362-8906

WYOMING

Wyoming State Bar
500 Randall Ave.
Cheyenne, WY 82001
307-632-9061

Bar Association and Court Opinions on Paralegals

Chicago Bar Association
Real Property Law Committee Recommendations
4/5/83

THE USE OF PARALEGALS IN
REAL ESTATE TRANSACTIONS

The paralegal may perform such tasks in connection with a real estate transaction as are assigned by the employing attorney, provided that the tasks are performed under the direction and supervision of, and are reviewed by, the attorney and do not involve the giving of legal advice. The paralegal may attend a closing with the employing attorney. A paralegal may close a real estate transaction, unaccompanied by the employing attorney, only (i) if all documents have been prepared and approved by all parties in advance of the closing, (ii) with prior consent of other counsel, and (iii) with the employing attorney being available for consultation and instructions by telephone. Within the foregoing limitations, the use of a paralegal to close a real estate transaction, unaccompanied by the employing attorney, should be approached with caution, having regard to the skill and experience of the paralegal, the complexity of the transaction and the client-attorney relationship, and bearing in mind that the employing attorney retains ultimate responsibility for the transaction.

Florida Bar Association
Committee on Professional Ethics
Advisory Opinion No. 73-43

. . . .

2. Whether the employee may attend closings of sales of condominium units to be held in the firm's office but without any attorneys in the firm being present. She will give no legal advice.

. . . .

We answer the second question in the negative. The question itself recognizes that the employee may not give legal advice or perform any acts that would amount to practicing law. The committee, one member dissenting in part, is of the opinion that there is no reason for the employee to attend the closings except to give legal advice and that her presence could be construed as answering unasked questions about the propriety or legality of documents. One committeeman is of the opinion that the employee may properly attend such closings provided she does nothing more than distribute documents for signature.

. . . .

Below you will find two opinions of the New Jersey Bar Association and one of the New York State Bar Association. Note the differences in the approaches taken by the two bar associations. New Jersey is quite restrictive. New York was also once restrictive, but became considerably less so when the U.S. Supreme Court decided *Bates v. State of Arizona,* 433 U.S. 350 (1977). The *Bates* opinion sent shock waves throughout the legal profession. It struck down laws that prohibited all forms of lawyer advertising. One effect of *Bates* was to cause some bar associations, such as New York, to allow paralegals to have their names printed on law firm stationery. Before *Bates,* this practice was frowned upon as a practice that was contrary to professional dignity and etiquette. It also suggested commercialization and a form of publicity for the firm. Once advertising was permitted after *Bates,* however, the practice was no longer considered unacceptable. Some states, however, such as New Jersey, still adhere to the more conservative position.

New Jersey Bar Association
Supreme Court of New Jersey's Advisory Committee
on Professional Ethics, Opinion 296
(98 N.J.L.J. 105, Feb. 6, 1975)

PARALEGAL EMPLOYEES—IDENTIFICATION WITH LAW FIRMS

Three inquiries have been submitted to this Committee relating to investigators and paralegal employees of a law firm.

Question One

Is it ethically proper for an attorney or firm to permit an investigator-paralegal full-time employee to sign correspondence on the attorney's or firm's letterhead where he identifies himself as a nonlawyer?

A paralegal employee is a lay person employed by an attorney to perform certain law office functions for which legal training and bar admission are not required.

Disciplinary Rule 3–101(A) reads as follows:

"A lawyer shall not aid a non-lawyer in the unauthorized practice of law."

Attorneys should avoid not only unprofessional conduct but also the appearance of such conduct. Our *Opinion 8,* 86 N.J.L.J. 718 (1963) and 9, 86 N.J.L.J. 617 (1963).

If a staff investigator were permitted to sign correspondence on the firm letterhead, such a seemingly innocent practice could foster myriad abuses, not the least of which might be the unauthorized practice of law in violation of *DR* 3–101(A). Such signed correspondence, even accompanied by an identification of the investigatory position of the signatory, might be taken as a representation that the layman is involved in the firm's practice in a manner contrary to *DR* 3-101(A) and *DR* 3–103(A). Given such a possible consequence, it is our conclusion that such practice cannot be sanctioned.

Question Two

May a firm include on its letterhead the name of a full-time investigative employee along with his title as staff investigator?

The American Bar Association, Standing Committee on Professional Ethics, *Informal Opinion* 619 (1962), quoting *Drinker, Legal Ethics* (1953) 228, refused to allow a secretary's name to appear on a lawyer's letterhead stating:

> A lawyer's letterhead may not carry the name of a client or of a patent agent associate, non-lawyer, notary or engineer or clerk or student or other layman, or give the names of references, or state that a layman's association is associated with him in handling collections. . . ."

Similarly, ABA *Informal Opinion* 845 (1965) held that the inclusion of a name on a letterhead with the designation "office manager" would be improper. Likewise, ABA *Informal Opinion* 1000 (1967), citing both *Informal Opinions* 619 and 845, supra held:

> ". . . that it would be improper to list your salaried investigator on your firm letterhead as 'Staff Investigator' or in any other manner."

Disciplinary Rule 2-102(A)(4) stipulates that an attorney or firm can use no letterhead except one of a prescribed content and dignified form. Additionally *DR* 2–101 inveighs generally against self-laudation, an inescapable effect should we allow the inclusion of a staff investigator's name and title on the letterhead. In ABA *Informal Opinion* 845, supra, it was stated that use of such a letterhead would:

> ". . . impress upon those seeing the letterhead the size, importance and efficiency of the firm. . . ."

Clearly, such a letterhead would have a self-laudatory effect, contravening the spirit of *DR* 2–101 in addition to offending the letter of *DR* 2-102(A)(4), and therefore it cannot be permitted.

Question Three

We are also called upon to consider whether the use by such an investigator-paralegal employee of a business card in the following form would be ethically proper:

> John Doe
> Investigator
> Firm Name & Address Tel. No. 123–4567

We considered this question in our *Opinion 9*, supra, and answered it in the negative. Parenthetically, it might be added, that we maintain this position in full cognizance of the American Bar Association Committee on Professional

Ethics, *Informal Opinion* 909 (1966) which saw fit to sanction such cards, though the committee admitted:

"... It is true, of course, that the card is a physical article and that possibilities of its improper use or effect are far greater than in the case of an oral identification. ..."

As was stated in *Opinion 9*, supra, of this Committee:

"There are, of course, other ways of identification besides the suggested means, without any possible abuse or misrepresentation."

Therefore, such cards may not be used as they are in possible derogation of the general integrity of the legal profession.

Supreme Court of New Jersey's Advisory Committee on Professional Ethics, Opinion 296 (Supplement) (99 N.J.L.J. 113, Feb. 12, 1976)

PARALEGAL EMPLOYEES— IDENTIFICATION WITH LAW FIRMS

The Professional Economics Committee of the New Jersey State Bar Association and several law firms of this State have petitioned that we reconsider *Opinion 296*, 98 N.J.L.J. 105 (1975), relating to the use of paralegals in law offices.

The original opinion dealt with three inquiries. The petition for reconsideration was limited to Question One.

In response to Questions Two and Three, we had held that the names of nonlawyers may not be included on a firm letterhead and the use of the firm business card identifying a nonlawyer was improper.

For convenience we repeat Question One in full:

"Is it ethically proper for an attorney or firm to permit an investigator-paralegal full-time employee to sign correspondence on the attorney's or firm's letterhead where he identifies himself as a non-lawyer?"

The inquiry as posed called for the approval of the únrestricted right of a paralegal employee to sign correspondence on the attorney's or firm's letterhead.

A hearing was held before this Committee on the petition for review to decide the propriety of our determination and whether it should be modified. The use of paraprofessionals was described as being in a state of development, a development which the petitioners urged as being in the best interests of the public and practicing lawyers.

The American Bar Association has recently concluded extensive hearings concerning the use of paraprofessionals and the subject is still under discussion.

There are two kinds of legal paraprofessionals:

1. Those who assist lawyers on behalf of clients, performing a variety of tasks, such as investigation, drafting, tax return preparation and research, which are performed under the supervision of a lawyer who is completely responsible for that work to a client. See American Bar Association, Committee on Profes-

sional Ethics, *Opinion* 316 (1967) and Code of Professional Responsibility *EC* 3–6. These paralegals cannot counsel clients, interpret the law, or represent people in adversary proceedings.

2. Individuals involved in the management of law firms who are not involved in the rendition of legal services, but who assist the partners in the conduct of their practice.

As noted, the original inquiry was unrestricted and made no differentiation between the kinds of paraprofessionals. As to the latter, the ministerial or office-type matters not involving the practice of law, we see no objection to the paralegal's signing such correspondence, since it does not in any way involve the practice of law. As to the former, we believe that routine requests for documents from officials, court stenographers, and the like would not constitute the practice of law and should be permitted.

However, we believe that any interaction with other attorneys, law firms, parties, or agents of parties would tend to aid in the practice of law by laymen. Parenthetically, in the course of the hearings, one of the firms described its use of paraprofessionals in "adjusting" property claims. Whether that would constitute the unauthorized practice of law is a point which we need not decide here, but it is an apt illustration of the difficulty in permitting the unrestricted use of paraprofessional assistance.

It is not the function of this Committee to undertake to designate every particular act or function of lay employees which would constitute the unauthorized practice of law. Whenever any question might reasonably arise, it seems to us that the profession's duty to the public and the recognition of the need to preserve the dignity of the profession suggest that correspondence ought to be signed by the responsible lawyer in the firm. Since the ultimate responsibility must reside with the attorney in the firm, the burden of signing the correspondence ought not to be intolerable.

. . .

In summary, we conclude that *Opinion* 296 should be modified by amending the answer to Question One, to permit the paraprofessional to sign the letter if his identity is clearly stated and under the guidelines noted in this opinion.

We reiterate that a paralegal should never perform services which involve the exercise of the professional judgment of a lawyer, nor should he advise clients with respect to their legal rights, nor should the activities of a paralegal in any way modify or interfere with direct attorney-client relationships or those between an attorney and his opposing attorney.

Our modification of *Opinion* 296 does not extend to Questions Two and Three which are not being amended by this opinion. Accordingly, we would modify our original opinion as follows:

1. A lay assistant may sign letterhead stationery of a law firm involving administrative communications not involving the practice of law to ministerial officials, vendors, and others.

2. A lay assistant may sign letterhead stationery of the law firm addressed to other administrative personnel, such as court printers, stenographers, court clerks, record custodians, and the like.

New York State Bar Association

New York State Bar Association, Committee on
Professional Ethics, Opinion #500 (12/6/78)(52–78)

Question

May the letterhead of a law firm list certain non-lawyer employees such as registered patent agents and paralegals?

Opinion

Prior to the recent amendment of our Code of Professional Responsibility, DR 2–102(A)(4) rigidly circumscribed the information that could be disclosed on a lawyer's professional letterhead. The former Disciplinary Rule did far more than prohibit the inclusion of untruthful or misleading information. It was intended to set a standard of professional dignity which standard was, in turn, thought to encourage public confidence in both the profession and the administration of justice. See, *e.g.,* former EC 2–9 and EC 2–10.

Under this standard, as well as those of former Canon 27, the listing of all non-lawyer employees on a lawyer's letterhead was prohibited. See, *e.g.,* N.Y. State 261 (1972) (paralegals), N.Y. County 589 (1971) (patent agents), N.Y. City 545 (1940) (non-lawyer patent attorney), N.Y. City 829 (1937) (patent agents), ABA Inf. 1367 (1976) (paralegals), ABA Inf. 845 (1965) (office manager), ABA Inf. 619 (1962) (lawyer's secretary); *cf.,* N.Y. State 85 (1968) and ABA Inf. 571(b) (1962) (involving potentially misleading information concerning lawyers).

The Supreme Court's decision in *Bates* v. *State of Arizona,* 433 U.S. 350 (1977), led to the adoption in this State of major amendments to the Ethical Considerations and Disciplinary Rules under Canon 2. These amendments not only incorporated the court adopted uniform rules governing lawyer advertising and publicity, but included a number of other court authorized liberalizing amendments permitting the free flow of reliable and useful information about lawyers and their services. See, N.Y. State 487 (1978).

The basic impact of these amendments was to bring about a revolutionary shift of emphasis in favor of the dissemination of information "designed to educate the public to an awareness of legal needs and to provide information relevant to the selection of the most appropriate counsel." DR 2–101(D), as amended. Disciplinary Rules which had seemed to interfere with the dissemination of such information primarily for reasons of professional dignity and etiquette were either repealed or substantially modified. In place of the former broad prohibitions on publicity and commercial advertising, the amendments essentially narrowed the ambit of proscription to specified practices which in themselves were thought to be injurious to both the profession and the public. See, amended DR 2–101(A) and (B); see also, amended EC 2–10.

The only explicit references to professional letterheads contained in the amended Code are now set forth in DR 2–102(A)(4) and (D)* Except for the requirements of DR 2–102(D) relating to lawyers not admitted to practice in all jurisdictions listed on a firm's letterhead, the only limitation on information appearing on letterheads is that the information be "in accordance with DR 2–101." The most important of the standards established by amended DR 2–101 are set forth in subdivisions (A), (B) and (D) which now provide:

A. A lawyer on behalf of himself or herself or partners or associates, shall not use or disseminate or participate in the preparation or dissemination of any public communication containing statements or claims that are false, deceptive, misleading or cast reflection on the legal profession as a whole.

B. Advertising or other publicity by lawyers, including participation in public functions, shall not contain puffery, self-laudation, claims regarding the quality of the lawyers' legal services, or claims that cannot be measured or verified.

* * *

D. Advertising and publicity shall be designed to educate the public to an awareness of legal needs and to provide information relevant to the selection of the most appropriate counsel. Information other than that specifically authorized in subdivision (C) that is consistent with these purposes may be disseminated providing that it does not violate any other provisions of this rule."

The effect of these amendments is to permit lawyers to include on their letterheads the names of their non-lawyer employees whenever the inclusion of such names would not be deceptive and might reasonably be expected to supply information relevant to the selection of counsel.

While non-lawyer status will no longer preclude the use of a person's name on a firm's letterhead, his name should be accompanied by language that makes clear his non-lawyer status. *Cf.,* DR 2–102(D) (requiring a clear statement concerning the "jurisdictional limitations" of a firm's "members and associates"

---

*As amended, DR 2–102 now provides in relevant part:

A. A lawyer or law firm may use professional cards, professional announcement cards, office signs, letterheads or similar professional notices or devices, provided the same do not violate any statute or court rule, and are in accordance with DR 2–101, including the following:

* * *

4. A letterhead identifying the lawyer by name and as a lawyer, and giving the addresses, telephone numbers, the name of the law firm, associates and any information permitted under DR 2–105. A letterhead of a law firm may also give the names of members and associates, and names and dates relating to deceased and retired members. A lawyer may be designated 'Of Counsel' on a letterhead if there is a continuing relationship with a lawyer or law firm, other than as a partner or associate. A lawyer or law firm may be designated as 'General Counsel' or by similar professional reference on stationery of a client if the lawyer or the firm devotes a substantial amount of professional time in the representation of that client. The letterhead of a law firm may give the names and dates of predecessor firms in a continuing line of succession.

Amended DR 2–102(D) provides:

D. A partnership shall not be formed or continued between or among lawyers licensed in different jurisdictions unless all enumerations of the members and associates of the firm on its letterhead and in other permissible listings makes clear the jurisdictional limitations on those members and associates of the firm not licensed to practice in all jurisdictions; however, the same firm name may be used in each jurisdiction.

who appear on its letterhead). Thus, for example, the term "registered patent agent" should be qualified by a designation such as "nonlawyer." Even then, to avoid deception, such persons should only be listed when their non-lawyer status is relevant to the work of the firm. See, DR 2–101(A) and DR 2–102(A).

(Unlike the term "registered patent agent," the term "paralegal," albeit somewhat imprecise, is sufficient without further qualification to make clear the employee's non-lawyer status. Whether use of the term "paralegal" is appropriate to the actual status enjoyed by the employee is another question to be determined under the standards established by DR 2–101(A).)

Our prior opinion in N.Y. State 261, *supra,* is overruled to the extent that the same is inconsistent with the foregoing.

For the reasons stated, and subject to the qualifications hereinabove set forth, the question posed is answered in the affirmative.

United States v. Kovel

United States Court of Appeals, Second Circuit, 1961
296 F.2d 918.

FRIENDLY, Circuit Judge.

This appeal from a sentence for criminal contempt for refusing to answer a question asked in the course of an inquiry by a grand jury raises an important issue as to the application of the attorney-client privilege to a non-lawyer employed by a law firm.

Kovel is a former Internal Revenue agent having accounting skills. Since 1943 he has been employed by Kamerman & Kamerman, a law firm specializing in tax law. A grand jury in the Southern District of New York was investigating alleged Federal income tax violations by Hopps, a client of the law firm; Kovel was subpoenaed to appear on September 6, 1961. The law firm advised the Assistant United States Attorney that since Kovel was an employee under the direct supervision of the partners, Kovel could not disclose any communications by the client or the result of any work done for the client, unless the latter consented; the Assistant answered that the attorney-client privilege did not apply to one who was not an attorney.

On September 7, the grand jury appeared before Judge Cashin. The Assistant United States Attorney informed the judge that Kovel had refused to answer "several questions * * * on the grounds of attorney-client privilege"; he proffered "respectable authority * * * that an accountant, even if he is retained or employed by a firm of attorneys, cannot take the privilege." The judge answered "You don't have to give me any authority on that." A court reporter testified that Kovel, after an initial claim of privilege had admitted receiving a statement of Hopps' assets and liabilities, but that, when asked "what was the purpose of your receiving that," had declined to answer on the ground of privilege "Because the communication was received with a purpose, as stated by the client"; later questions and answers indicated the communication was a letter addressed to Kovel. After verifying that Kovel was not a lawyer, the judge directed him to answer, saying "You have no privilege as such." The reporter then read another question Kovel had refused to answer, "Did you ever discuss with

Mr. Hopps or give Mr. Hopps any information with regard to treatment for capital gains purposes of the Atlantic Beverage Corporation sale by him?" The judge again directed Kovel to answer reaffirming "There is no privilege—you are entitled to no privilege, as I understand the law."

Later on September 7, they and Kovel's employer, Jerome Kamerman, now acting as his counsel, appeared again before Judge Cashin. The Assistant told the judge that Kovel had "refused to answer some of the questions which you had directed him to answer." A reporter reread so much of the transcript heretofore summarized as contained the first two refusals. The judge offered Kovel another opportunity to answer, reiterating the view, "There is no privilege to this man at all." Counsel referred to New York Civil Practice Act, § 353, which we quote in the margin.*

Counsel reiterated that an employee "who sits with the client of the law firm * * * occupies the same status * * * as a clerk or stenographer or any other lawyer * * * "; the judge was equally clear that the privilege was never "extended beyond the attorney." The court held [Kovel] in contempt, sentenced him to a year's imprisonment, ordered immediate commitment and denied bail. Later in the day, the grand jury having indicted, Kovel was released until September 12, at which time, without opposition from the Government, I granted bail pending determination of this appeal.

Here the parties continue to take generally the same positions as below— Kovel, that his status as an employee of a law firm automatically made all communications to him from clients privileged; the Government, that under no circumstances could there be privilege with respect to communications to an accountant. The New York County Lawyers' Association as *amicus curiae* has filed a brief generally supporting appellant's position.

Decision under what circumstances, if any, the attorney-client privilege may include a communication to a nonlawyer by the lawyer's client is the resultant of two conflicting forces. One is the general teaching that "The investigation of truth and the enforcement of testimonial duty demand the restriction, not the expansion, of these privileges," 8 Wigmore, Evidence (McNaughton Rev. 1961), § 2192, p. 73. The other is the more particular lesson "That as, by reason of the complexity and difficulty of our law, litigation can only be properly conducted by professional men, it is absolutely necessary that a man * * * should have recourse to the assistance of professional lawyers, and * * * it is equally necessary * * * that he should be able to place unrestricted and unbounded confidence in the professional agent, and that the communications he so makes to him should be kept secret * * *," Jessel, M.R. in Anderson v. Bank, 2 Ch.D. 644, 649 (1876). Nothing in the policy of the privilege suggests that attorneys, simply by placing accountants, scientists or investigators on their payrolls and maintaining them in their offices, should be able to invest all communications by clients to such persons with a privilege the law has not seen fit to extend when the latter are operating under their own steam. On the other

---

* "An attorney or counselor at law shall not disclose, or be allowed to disclose, a communication, made by his client to him, or his advice given thereon, in the course of his professional employment, nor shall any clerk, stenographer or other person employed by such attorney or counselor * * * disclose, or be allowed to disclose any such communication or advice."

hand, in contrast to the Tudor times when the privilege was first recognized, the complexities of modern existence prevent attorneys from effectively handling clients' affairs without the help of others; few lawyers could now practice without the assistance of secretaries, file clerks, telephone operators, messengers, clerks not yet admitted to the bar, and aides of other sorts. "The assistance of these agents being indispensable to his work and the communications of the client being often necessarily committed to them by the attorney or by the client himself, the privilege must include all the persons who act as the attorney's agents." 8 Wigmore, Evidence, § 2301; Annot., 53 A.L.R. 369 (1928).

Indeed, the Government does not here dispute that the privilege covers communications to non-lawyer employees with "a menial or ministerial responsibility that involves relating communications *to an attorney*." We cannot regard the privilege as confined to "menial or ministerial" employees. Thus, we can see no significant difference between a case where the attorney sends a client speaking a foreign language to an interpreter to make a literal translation of the client's story; a second where the attorney, himself having some little knowledge of the foreign tongue, has a more knowledgeable non-lawyer employee in the room to help out; a third where someone to perform that same function has been brought along by the client; and a fourth where the attorney, ignorant of the foreign language, sends the client to a non-lawyer proficient in it, with instructions to interview the client on the attorney's behalf and then render his own summary of the situation, perhaps drawing on his own knowledge in the process, so that the attorney can give the client proper legal advice. All four cases meet every element of Wigmore's famous formulation, § 2292, "(1) Where legal advice of any kind is sought (2) from a professional legal advisor in his capacity as such, (3) the communications relating to that purpose, (4) made in confidence (5) by the client, (6) are at his instance permanently protected (7) from disclosure by himself or by the legal advisor, (8) except the protection be waived," . . . § 2301 of Wigmore would clearly recognize the privilege in the first case and the Government goes along to that extent; § 2301 would also recognize the privilege in the second case and § 2301 in the third unless the circumstances negated confidentiality. We find no valid policy reason for a different result in the fourth case, and we do not read Wigmore as thinking there is. Laymen consulting lawyers should not be expected to anticipate niceties perceptible only to judges—and not even to all of them.

This analogy of the client speaking a foreign language is by no means irrelevant to the appeal at hand. Accounting concepts are a foreign language to some lawyers in almost all cases, and to almost all lawyers in some cases. Hence the presence of an accountant, whether hired by the lawyer or by the client, while the client is relating a complicated tax story to the lawyer, ought not destroy the privilege, any more than would that of the linguist in the second or third variations of the foreign language theme discussed above; the presence of the accountant is necessary, or at least highly useful, for the effective consultation between the client and the lawyer which the privilege is designed to permit. By the same token, if the lawyer has directed the client, either in the specific ca[s]e or generally, to tell his story in the first instance to an accountant engage[d] the lawyer, who is then to interpret it so that the lawyer may better gi[ve] advice, communications by the client reasonably related to that purp[ose] fall within the privilege; there can be no more virtue in requiring the lawyer to sit by while the client pursues these possibly tedious preliminary conversations with the accountant than in insisting on the lawyer's physical presence while the client dictates a statement to the lawyer's secretary or is interviewed by a clerk not yet admitted to practice. What is vital to the privilege is that the communication be made *in confidence* for the purpose of obtaining *legal* advice *from the lawyer.* If what is sought is not legal advice but only accounting service, or if the advice sought is the accountant's rather than the lawyer's, no privilege exists. We recognize this draws what may seem to some a rather arbitrary line between a case where the client communicates first to his own accountant (no privilege as to such communications, even though he later consults his lawyers on the same matter, Gariepy v. United States, 189 F.2d 459, 463 (6 Cir. 1951)),‡ and others, where the client in the first instance consults a lawyer who retains an accountant as a listening post, or consults the lawyer with his own accountant present. But that is the inevitable consequence of having to reconcile the absence of a privilege for accountants and the effective operation of the privilege of client and lawyer under conditions where the lawyer needs outside help. We realize also that the line we have drawn will not be so easy to apply as the simpler positions urged on us by the parties—the district judges will scarcely be able to leave the decision of such cases to computers; but the distinction has to be made if the privilege is neither to be unduly expanded nor to become a trap.

The judgment is vacated and the cause remanded for further proceedings consistent with this opinion.

UNITED STATES v. CABRA

United States Court of Appeals, Fifth Circuit, 1980.
622 F.2d 182.

AINSWORTH, Circuit Judge:
This appeal raises the novel question whether a district judge can impound notes taken during a criminal trial by a paralegal employed by defense counsel to assist in preparation of the defense. We hold that in this case, the district judge acted improperly in impounding the notes.

Appellants Edwin L. Cabra and Claude "Buddy" Leach were tried in district court on charges of vote buying in connection with the November 7, 1978 general election. After three weeks of trial, appellants were acquitted on all counts. Other charges against Leach alleging illegal receipt of campaign contributions are still pending.

During the trial, the district judge, on his own motion, called a bench conference to ask defense counsel if anyone associated with the defense was taking notes on the proceedings. Defense counsel informed the court that Ms. Mary

---

‡We do not deal in this opinion with the question under what circumstances, if any, such communications could be deemed privileged on the basis that they were being made to the accountant as the client's agent for the purpose of subsequent communication by the accountant to the lawyer; unications by the client's agent to the attorney are privileged, 8 Wigmore, Evidence,

Jane Marcantel, a paralegal employed by the defense, was taking shorthand notes of portions of the testimony. Counsel stated that the purpose of the note-taking was to assist in the preparation of cross-examination, to provide summaries of testimony, and to aid in the preparation of the defense in anticipated criminal prosecutions in related cases. Ms. Marcantel was not present during the entirety of the trial and thus her notes did not reflect a complete account of the proceedings. The shorthand notes were not verbatim, but merely reflected, as accurately as possible, the substance of the testimony.

After ascertaining the character of the notes, the district judge, over defense counsel's objection, ordered that Ms. Marcantel could continue to take notes but that at the completion of the trial the notes were to be submitted to the court and sealed. After trial, the district judge sent a letter requesting compliance with the order. Appellants moved to vacate the order and filed a memorandum of law supporting their position. The district judge denied the motion, but stayed the order pending this appeal.

The district judge based the order on the court's duty "to insure the orderly process of a case." He stated that since the notes could be considered as an unofficial transcript the validity of the official transcript was at stake. "The court feels that there should only be one official transcript and that such unofficial transcripts should not be allowed. The court by this does not mean that these particular defendants would make any improper use of these notes. Rather this order is required to protect the integrity of the official court reporter's transcript." (R. 1140)

A district judge has the power to issue appropriate orders regulating conduct in the courtroom in order to assure an orderly trial. *See, e.g., United States v. Columbia Broadcasting System, Inc.,* 497 F.2d 102, 104 (5th Cir. 1974); *Seymour v. United States,* 373 F.2d 629 (5th Cir. 1967). *See also United States v. Dinitz,* 538 F.2d 1214, 1223–24 (5th Cir. 1976), *cert. denied,* 429 U.S. 1104, 97 S.Ct. 1133, 51 L.Ed.2d 556 (1977). Often the basis of the power is the need to insure that a defendant obtains a fair trial free from unnecessary disruption. *See United States v. Schiavo,* 504 F.2d 1, 6 (3rd Cir.) (*en banc*) ("The Sixth Amendment imposes a duty on the district courts . . . to take reasonable measures to ensure defendants fair trials, free of prejudice and disruption"), *cert. denied sub. nom. Ditter v. Philadelphia Newspapers, Inc.,* 419 U.S. 1096, 95 S.Ct. 690, 42 L.Ed.2d 688 (1974). *See generally Sheppard v. Maxwell,* 384 U.S. 333, 349–51, 86 S.Ct. 1507, 1515–16, 16 L.Ed.2d 600 (1966).

This case is similar to the facts presented in *Columbia Broadcasting System.* There, the district court issued an order prohibiting any sketching of the proceedings. Sketches were made by artists employed by the media for subsequent showing on television news programs. This court, while acknowledging the district court's power to control its proceedings, rejected the order as overly broad. "We are unwilling . . . to condone a sweeping prohibition of in-court sketching when there has been no showing whatsoever that sketching is in any way obtrusive or disruptive." *Columbia Broadcasting System, supra,* 497 F.2d at 107 (footnote omitted). As in *Columbia Broadcasting System,* we cannot understand how Ms. Marcantel's note-taking resulted in any disruption of the courtroom proceedings. There is no evidence that her work had any disturbing or disruptive effect. It appeared that her actions did not differ from the note-taking activities of the press covering the trial or of opposing counsel. Certainly, the note-taking did not interfere with or infringe appellants' rights to a fair trial as the task was performed on their behalf.

The district court placed great weight on the fact that Ms. Marcantel's notes were verbatim. There is no evidence, however, that this was true. Defense counsel stated that the notes were incomplete and that while Ms. Marcantel strived for accuracy, the notes were not always taken in question and answer form. Even assuming that the notes were verbatim, however, we do not believe that the district judge's action was proper. Note-taking at trial is an acknowledged function of paralegals, see W. P. Statsky, *Introduction to Paralegalism*, 356 (West 1974). [First edition] A court should not penalize a party on account of the proficiency of its paralegal's performance. The district court's concern for the sanctity of the official transcript is misplaced. While it is the court's responsibility to assure that the official transcript is prepared in accordance with the Court Reporter's Act, 28 U.S.C. § 753, see *United States v. Garner*, 581 F.2d 481, 488 (5th Cir. 1978), the Act explicitly states that "[n]o transcripts of the proceedings of the court shall be considered as official except those made from the records taken by the reporter." Moreover, defense counsel stated that they had no intention of relying on the notes as an official summary of the testimony. Thus, the district court was operating under the mistaken assumption that the paralegal's notes challenged the validity of the official transcript.

Since the district court's reasons for impounding the notes were based on unwarranted concerns, the order was an improper exercise of the court's discretionary authority to control courtroom proceedings. Accordingly, the order is reversed.

REVERSED.

APPENDIX

C

Survey of Nonlawyer Practice before Federal Administrative Agencies

Standing Committee on Lawyers' Responsibility for Client Protection and the American Bar Association Center for Professional Responsibility

February, 1985

I. Background

The American Bar Association Standing Committee on Lawyers' Responsibility for Client Protection disseminated this survey to thirty-three (33) federal administrative agencies in late August, 1984. The survey was intended to provide background information on the experiences of agencies permitting non-lawyer practice (other than for purposes of self-representation). During September and October ninety-seven percent (97%) of the agencies responded either over the phone or by mail following initial contact with their Offices of General Counsel. The ABA Center for Professional Responsibility tabulated the results in October, 1984.

II. Brief Analysis and Conclusions

We found that the overwhelming majority of agencies studied permit non-lawyer representation in both adversarial and nonadversarial proceedings.* However, most of them seem to encounter lay practice very infrequently (in less than 5% of adjudications), while only a few encounter lay practice as often as lawyer practice. Thus, although universally permitted, lay practice before federal agencies rarely occurs.

Few of the responding agencies comprehensively monitor or control the lay practice that does occur. Only about twenty percent (20%) require nonlawyers to register with the agency before permitting them to practice. Registration pro-

(continued on p. 170)

---

*A proceeding is adversarial if there is an opposing side in the controversy, whether or not the other side is represented. A proceeding is nonadversarial if only one side is appearing before the agency official.

CHART I Regulations Governing Nonlawyer Representation, Frequency, and Type of Practice

Agency	Statute/ Regulation Permitting Appearance	Permits Nonlawyer Adversarial Representation	Permits Nonlawyer Nonadversarial Representation	Provisions Limiting or Governing Practice	Frequency of Nonlawyer Representation	Change in Frequency of Nonlawyer Rep. w/in Past 6 Years	Most Common Type(s) of Nonlawyer Representation
Bd. of Immigration Appeals: Immigration and Naturalization Serv.	8 CFR § 292.1-3	Yes	Yes	"Accredited representative"[1] working for "recognized organization"[2] may charge only nominal fees. "Reputable individual"[3] may not charge fees	No statistics available	No statistics available	One time only by family member/ friend; charitable, religious or social service organization
Civil Aeronautics Bd.	14 CFR § 300.1-6 14 CFR § 302.11	Yes	Yes	None	Fewer than 6 appearances per yr., less than 1% of appearances[4]	None	Economic consultants for corporations
Comptroller of the Currency	12 CFR § 19.3	Yes[5]	Yes	Nonlawyer may be required to file a power of attorney or show to the satisfaction of the Comptroller the possession of requisite qualifications	None	None	None

							Non-fee by industry rep., consultant, or private service agency
Consumer Product Safety Comm'n	16 CFR § 1025.61 et seq.	Yes	Yes	Filing and approval of proof of qualifications. See 16 CFR § 1025.65	Very infrequent, 2–5% of appearances	None	Non-fee by industry rep., consultant, or private service agency
Dep't of Agric., Agricultural Marketing Serv.	7 CFR § 50.27	Yes	Yes	None	Fewer than 3 appearances per yr., less than 1% of appearances	Decreased,[6] no statistics available	Economist/accountant providing assistance prior to appearance

[1] May become accredited by the Department of Immigration Appeals (D.I.A.) by submitting an application through a recognized organization for review of character and fitness and experience with and knowledge of immigration law. No formal testing requirement or licensing fee.

[2] Typically a religious, charitable or social service organization becomes recognized by submitting an application for approval to the D.I.A. assuring that it will charge only nominal fees and assess no representation charges.

[3] Typically a family member or friend submits declaration that he or she charges no fee, has a preexisting relationship with immigrant-applicant, and appears only on individual basis at request of immigrant-applicant.

[4] Although nonlawyer practice [is] not discouraged, complexity of agency proceedings tends to require specialized legal practice. Typical parties, large corporations or businesses, tend to hire lawyers.

[5] Permitted but lay representation rare because of complex proceedings and substantial rights or amounts of money involved.

[6] In agency's early history, economists provided a substantial amount of representation because of the economic nature of agency proceedings. As proceedings become more sophisticated, economists began aiding lawyers rather than assuming primary responsibility for legal representation. Representation by economists is now rare, and lawyers handle the bulk of representation.

CHART I Regulations Governing Nonlawyer Representation, Frequency, and Type of Practice—*Continued*

Agency	Statute/ Regulation Permitting Appearance	Permits Nonlawyer Adversarial Representation	Permits Nonlawyer Nonadversarial Representation	Provisions Limiting or Governing Practice	Frequency of Nonlawyer Representation	Change in Frequency of Nonlawyer Rep. w/in Past 6 Years	Most Common Type(s) of Nonlawyer Representation
Dep't of Commerce, Office of Secretary	Those of other agencies governing appearances before administrative bodies, e.g., MSPB, 5 CFR Part 1201	Yes	Yes	Reasonable atty's fees for litigated matters set by agency; maximum atty's fees for settlement set at $75./hr.; government pays fees to winning atty	No statistics available	No statistics available	Non-fee by union reps.
Dep't of Commerce, Patent and Trademark Office	35 U.S.C. §§ 31-33	Yes	Yes	Only registered[7] practitioners permitted to practice	Less than 16% of appearances[8]	None	Repeated practice for a fee by registered agents
Dep't of Health and Human Services, Food and Drug Admin.	32 CFR §§ 12.40, 12.45	Yes	Yes	None	No appearances in recent years	None	None
Dep't of Justice, Drug Enforcement Admin.	21 CFR § 1316.50	Yes	N/A, all proceedings adversarial	None	2 to 3 appearances per yr., 5% of appearances[9]	None	One time only by officer/employee of small family-owned business

Dep't of Justice, Foreign Claims Settlement Comm'n	45 CFR § 500.1-6	No	No[10]	Lawyer's fees set by statute at 10% of claim award and deducted from award	N/A[11]	N/A[11]	Family member providing assistance prior to appearance
Dep't of Labor, Benefits Review Bd.	20 CFR § 802.201(b) 20 CFR § 802.202	Yes	N/A, all proceedings adversarial	Employer pays fee for successful claimant represented by lawyer; claimant pays fee when represented by nonlawyer; lawyer may acquire lien against award; nonlawyers may not.[12] Professional status is criterion for determining fees.[13]	2–4% of appearances	None	Repeated practice for fee

[7] Nonlawyers become registered by passing a character and fitness review and an examination. Nonlawyers having served four years in the examining corps of the Patent and Trademark Office (P.T.O.) may waive the exam. See 57 CFR § 1.341.

[8] Nonlawyers comprise about 16% of registered practitioners, but not all registered practitioners appear before P.T.O., so that nonlawyers probably appear in less than 16% of patent applications filed with P.T.O.

[9] Appearances are by the employees or officers of small family-owned businesses, analogous to pro se appearances.

[10] The agency only allows "representation" by bar members. Family members may sometimes assist in preparation of claims or at oral hearings, typically where elderly parent has language barrier problems.

[11] No nonlawyer representation allowed.

[12] These policies may tend to discourage lay representation.

[13] Typically approved rates for nonlawyers are less than half of those attorneys receive.

CHART I Regulations Governing Nonlawyer Representation, Frequency, and Type of Practice—*Continued*

Agency	Statute/ Regulation Permitting Appearance	Permits Nonlawyer Adversarial Representation	Permits Nonlawyer Nonadversarial Representation	Provisions Limiting or Governing Practice	Frequency of Nonlawyer Representation	Change in Frequency of Nonlawyer Rep. w/In Past 6 Years	Most Common Type(s) of Nonlawyer Representation
Dep't of Labor, Employees Compensation Appeals Bd.	20 CFR § 501.11	Yes	N/A, all proceedings adversarial	All fees approved by board	Appear as frequently as lawyers	None	One time only by family member/ friend; repeated practice for a fee
Dep't of Labor, National Railroad Adjustment Bd.	45 U.S.C. § 3153	Yes	N/A	Only entities identified in 45 U.S.C. § 151 allowed to practice	Almost 100% of appearances	None	Industry employees

Dep't of Labor, Wage and Appeals Bd.	20 CFR § 725.362(a) 20 CFR § 725.365 20 CFR § 725.366(b)	Yes	N/A	Fees must be reasonably commensurate with services performed;[14] attorney's fee deducted from award; employer pays fee for successful claimant represented by lawyer; claimant prep fee when represented by nonlawyer; lawyer may require lien against award, nonlawyers may not.[15]	3% of appearances; as in 180 case/ yr.	Decrease due to investigations by Office of Inspector General into unauthorized receipt of fees	One time only by family member or friend; repeated practice for fee; assistance prior to appearance
Dep't of Transportation, Maritime Admin.	46 CFR § 201.21	Yes	Yes	Only registered nonlawyers permitted to practice	Very infrequent	None	
Federal Deposit Ins. Corp.	12 CFR § 308.04	Yes	Yes	Only qualified nonlawyers permitted to represent	10 to 20 appearances per yr., 5% of appearances	50% decrease	One time only by family member/ friend; nonlawyer assistance prior to appearance

[14] *See* 20 CFR § 725.366(b) (black lung) and 20 CFR § 702.132 (longshore).
[15] These policies may tend to discourage lay representation.

CHART I Regulations Governing Nonlawyer Representation, Frequency, and Type of Practice—*Continued*

Agency	Statute/ Regulation Permitting Appearance	Permits Nonlawyer Adversarial Representation	Permits Nonlawyer Nonadversarial Representation	Provisions Limiting or Governing Practice	Frequency of Nonlawyer Representation	Change in Frequency of Nonlawyer Rep. w/in Past 6 Years	Most Common Type(s) of Nonlawyer Representation
Federal Energy Regulatory Comm'n	18 CFR § 385.2101	Yes	Yes	None	1 or 2 per yr.	None	Engineering firm assisting in technical nonadversarial proceeding
Federal Maritime Comm'n	46 CFR § 502.30	Yes	Yes	Only registered nonlawyers permitted to appear[16]	.5 to 1% of appearances	None	One time only by family member/ friend; non-fee by industry rep., consultant or private service agency

					5–10% of appearances	None	Non-fee by industry rep., consultant or private service agency
Federal Mine Safety & Health Review Comm'n	29 CFR § 2700.3(b)	Yes, at trial hearings before Administrative Law Judges (ALJ); at appellate reviews before commissioners	N/A	Nonlawyer may practice only if party, "representative of miners,"[17] or owner, partner, full time officer or employee of party-business entity; otherwise permitted to appear for limited purpose in special proceedings	5–10% of appearances	None	
General Accounting Office	31 U.S.C. § 731-732; 4 CFR §§ 11 and 28; GAO Orders 2713.2, 2752.1, and 2777.1	Yes, in adverse actions, grievance proceedings, and discrimination complaints	Yes	Nonlawyers not permitted fees; government pays fees to winning representatives[18]	Very infrequent	Not aware of any	

[16] Certificates of registration are issued on payment of $13.00 processing fee and completion of application form indicating sufficient educational qualifications and recommendations. There is no testing or formal licensing.

[17] See generally 30 CFR § 40.1(b).

[18] As provided in discrimination statutes, backpay act, and appeals authorized by law.

CHART I Regulations Governing Nonlawyer Representation, Frequency, and Type of Practice—*Continued*

Agency	Statute/ Regulation Permitting Appearance	Permits Nonlawyer Adversarial Representation	Permits Nonlawyer Nonadversarial Representation	Provisions Limiting or Governing Practice	Frequency of Nonlawyer Representation	Change in Frequency of Nonlawyer Rep. w/in Past 6 Years	Most Common Type(s) of Nonlawyer Representation
Internal Revenue Serv.	13 CFR Part 10; 31 U.S.C. § 330; Treasury Dept. Circular 230	Yes	Yes	Noncertified public accountant and nonlawyer must become enrolled agent[19] to practice	As frequent as lawyer representation[20]	Increased, no statistics available	Repeated practice for fee by certified public accountant or enrolled agent
Interstate Commerce Comm'n	49 CFR § 1103	Yes	Yes	Fee limitations;[21] only registered nonlawyer permitted to practice,[22] however, self-representation is allowed without registration	1,600 nonlawyers now registered and account for 5% of appearances.[23]	Decreased,[24] no statistics available	Repeated practice for a fee
National Credit Union Admin.	12 CFR § 747	Yes	Yes	None	No statistics available	Decreased, no statistics available	Credit union representatives
National Labor Relations Bd.		Yes	Yes	None	Infrequent	None	

					200 appearances per yr., appear twice as frequently as lawyers	Decreased, no statistics available	Union representatives
National Mediation Bd.	None, agency governed by 29 CFR § 1200 et seq.	N/A, all proceedings adversarial	Yes	None	200 appearances per yr., appear twice as frequently as lawyers	Decreased, no statistics available	
National Transportation Safety Bd.	49 CFR § 821 49 CFR § 831 49 CFR § 845	Yes	Yes	In adjudication lawyer representation encouraged; in investigation lawyer participation discouraged because technical expertise required; parties[25] participate in investigations	Very infrequent except at investigatory levels	None	Manufacturers at investigatory levels

[19] Nonlawyers and noncertified public accountants become enrolled agents by 1) passing a character and fitness review, and 2) successful completion of special enrollment examination testing on federal taxation and related matters, or 3) former employment with the IRS, provided duties qualify the individual. Lawyers and certified public accountants may practice without enrollment.

[20] Includes representation by certified public accountants as well as enrolled agents.

[21] Practitioners may not overestimate the value of services, accept compensation from party other than client, make contingent fee arrangements or divide fees with laypersons. *See* 49 CFR § 1103.70.

[22] To become registered applicant must 1) meet educational and experience requirements, 2) undergo character and fitness review, 3) pass exam administered by the agency testing knowledge in the field of transportation, and 4) take an oath. *See* 49 CFR § 1103.3.

[23] Figure includes appearances in rulemaking as well as adjudicatory proceedings.

[24] Deregulation has reduced the caseload while proceedings have become more complex, creating a greater need for legal expertise.

[25] "Parties" includes manufacturers, unions, operators and other regulatory agencies.

CHART I Regulations Governing Nonlawyer Representation, Frequency, and Type of Practice—*Continued*

Agency	Statute/ Regulation Permitting Appearance	Permits Nonlawyer Adversarial Representation	Permits Nonlawyer Nonadversarial Representation	Provisions Limiting or Governing Practice	Frequency of Nonlawyer Representation	Change in Frequency of Nonlawyer Rep. w/in Past 6 Years	Most Common Type(s) of Nonlawyer Representation
Occupational Safety and Health Review Comm'n	29 CFR § 2200.22	Yes	N/A, all proceedings adversarial	Optional simplified procedures to encourage self-representation by small businesses	20% of appearances[26]	20% decrease[27]	Nonlegal employee representing employer; union representative
Small Business Admin.	13 CFR § 121.11 13 CFR § 134.16	Yes	N/A, all proceedings adversarial	None	Less than 1% of appearances[28]	None	
Social Security Admin.	42 USC § 406(a) 29 CFR	Yes, tentatively as part of experiment; generally agency has no adversarial proceedings	Yes	Claimants advised of advantages of representation at hearing level;[29] fees set by agency;[30] attorneys' fees withheld from awards[31]	Appear in 13% of total hearings or in 25–30% of hearings with representation	None, although lawyer representation increased by 56% since 1978[32]	One time only by family member/ friend; repeated practice for fee; non-fee rep. by legal services paralegal
U.S. Customs Serv.	None	Yes	Yes	None	5 to 15% of caseload volume	None	Repeated practice for fee by licensed customs brokers and former customs officials

U.S. Environmental Protection Agency	40 CFR § 124 40 CFR § 164.30 40 CFR § 22.10	Yes	N/A	None	No appearances	None	None

[26] Statistic includes pro se representation.

[27] Nonlawyer practice accounted in 1980 for 40% of the agency's caseload but decreased in 1982–83 to 20%. Decrease may result from increasing complexity in cases causing claimants to seek legal representation.

[28] Figure excludes pro se appearances in size and Standard Industrial Classification (SIC) Appeals. Approximately 50% of size and SIC appeals are conducted pro se by nonlawyers.

[29] When hearing request [is] filed, agency sends a letter to unrepresented claimant describing advantages of representation. Attached to letter is a list of organizations which may provide representation. The list includes lawyer referral services, legal aid groups, law schools, etc.

[30] The agency sets all fees based on criteria listed in 20 CFR § 404.1725(b), including extent and type of services, complexity of case, level of skill and competence required in performing services, time spent, results achieved, level at which representative became involved, and amount requested.

[31] When decision is entered in favor of a claimant represented by a lawyer in a Title II or Black Lung case, normally 25% of the benefits awarded are withheld. After agency has set the fee it forwards fee directly to the lawyer from the amount withheld. If attorney's fees exceed the amount withheld, the lawyer must seek the remainder from the claimant. If the attorney's fees are less than the amount withheld, the claimant receives the remainder. Nonlawyer representatives do not have this withholding benefit.

[32] In fiscal year 1978 lawyers appeared in 32% of hearings; nonlawyers in 12%. In fiscal year 1983 lawyers appeared in 50% of hearings; nonlawyers in 13%. Though the letter discussed in footnote 29 does not exclusively reference lawyers' services, this list may attribute to the increase in lawyer representation. Lawyers also have a high success rate before the agency as well as the advantage of award withholdings to secure fees in Title II and Black Lung cases (see footnote 31).

cedures may range from simply listing nonlawyers' names to more formalized certifying or licensing procedures which may include testing and character reviews. Proceedings in most of these agencies tend to require highly technical or specialized knowledge. Registration insures that lay representation meets an appropriate level of quality and competence. In at least one agency, registration insures that nonlawyer representatives will charge only nominal fees or no fees at all.

No agencies indicated that they would discipline nonlawyers differently from lawyers, although they clearly have an additional ability to pursue sanctions against lawyers through external disciplinary mechanisms. Only a few agencies indicated any special need for nonlawyer discipline. Most reported they had not encountered any problems with misconduct by nonlawyers or any inability of nonlawyers to meet appropriate ethical standards (though fewer than a third of the agencies studied have actually defined any specific ethical standards). Of those that voiced complaints about nonlawyers' skills in representation, most indicated that the problem they encounter most frequently is nonlawyers' lack of familiarity with procedural rules and tactics. The majority of responses suggest that nonlawyers do not pose any special practice problems, nor do they receive any special disciplinary consideration. Overall, the concern for nonlawyers' competence and ethical conduct seems limited, perhaps because nonlawyer practice is not widespread.

III. Methodology

Throughout the survey our questions focused on lay representation (other than self-representation) occurring in adjudicatory proceedings. In question 1, in which we asked whether agencies permitted nonlawyer representation, we attempted to distinguish between adversarial and nonadversarial proceedings. Our distinction did not prove particularly informative because all agencies permitting nonlawyer practice (97%) allow such practice in both arenas.

Question 2 sought the methods by which agencies control or limit those practicing before them. The responses vary considerably from agency to agency. Questions 3 and 4 requested statistics concerning the frequency of nonlawyer practice. Many of the agencies indicated that statistics were unavailable. These responses also vary considerably. The results of questions 1 through 4 are tabulated in Chart I beginning on page 158.

Paralegal Associations

 PARALEGAL ASSOCIATIONS (NATIONAL)

(Membership statistics, where known, are presented in brackets.)

National Association of Legal Assistants
[15,000]
1601 S. Main St., Suite 300
Tulsa, OK 74119
918-587-6828

National Federation of Paralegal
Associations [17,500]
P.O. Box 33108
Kansas City, MO 64114
816-941-4000

(NALA and NFPA have numerous affiliated local paralegal associations. NALA affiliates are indicated by one asterisk (*) below; NFPA affiliates are indicated by two asterisks below (**). The addresses of these local associations change frequently. If the address given below turns out to be incorrect, contact the national office of NALA or NFPA for a more current address. Local associations without an asterisk are unaffiliated at the time of publication.)

 PARALEGAL ASSOCIATIONS (STATE)

ALABAMA

Alabama Association of Legal Assistants
(*) [215]
P.O. Box 55921
Birmingham, AL 35255

Huntsville Association of Paralegals
P.O. Box 244
Huntsville, AL 35804-0244

Mobile Association of Legal Assistants
[75]
P.O. Box 1988
Mobile, AL 36633

ALASKA

Alaska Association of Legal Assistants
(**) [130]
P.O. Box 101956
Anchorage, AK 99510-1956

Fairbanks Association of Legal Assistants
(*)
P.O. Box 73503
Fairbanks, AK 99707

Juneau Legal Assistants Association (**)
[20]
P.O. Box 22336
Juneau, AK 99802

ARIZONA

Arizona Association of Professional
  Paralegals (**) [50]
P.O. Box 25111
Phoenix, AZ 85002

Arizona Paralegal Association (*)
P.O. Box 392
Phoenix, AZ 85001
602-258-0121

Legal Assistants of Metropolitan Phoenix
  (*)
P.O. Box 13005
Phoenix, AZ 85002

Southeast Valley Association of Legal
  Assistants (*)
% Sandy Slater
1707 N. Temple
Mesa, AZ 85203

Tucson Association of Legal Assistants
  (*)
P.O. Box 257
Tucson, AZ 85702-0257

ARKANSAS

Arkansas Association of Legal Assistants
  (*)
P.O. Box 2162
Little Rock, AR 72203-2162

CALIFORNIA

California Alliance of Paralegal
  Associations [4000]
P.O. Box 2234
San Francisco, CA 94126
415-576-3000

California Association of Freelance
  Paralegals [94]
P.O. Box 3267
Berkeley, CA 94703-0267
213-251-3826

Central Coast Legal Assistant Association
  (**) [70]
P.O. Box 93
San Luis Obispo, CA 93406

Central Valley Paralegal Association
P.O. Box 4086
Modesto, CA 95352

East Bay Association of Paralegals [200]
P.O. Box 29082
Oakland, CA 94604

Inland Counties Paralegal Association
P.O. Box 292
Riverside, CA 92502-0292

Kern County Paralegal Association [63]
P.O. Box 2673
Bakersfield, CA 93303

Legal Assistants Association of Santa
  Barbara (*)
P.O. Box 2695
Santa Barbara, CA 93120
805-965-7319

Los Angeles Paralegal Association (**)
  [1150]
P.O. Box 241928
Los Angeles, CA 90024
213-251-3755

Marin Association of Legal Assistants
P.O. Box 13051
San Rafael, CA 94913-3051
415-456-6020

Orange County Paralegal Association
  [490]
P.O. Box 8512
Newport Beach, CA 92658-8512
714-744-7747

Paralegal Association of Santa Clara
  County (*)
P.O. Box 26736
San Jose, CA 95159

Redwood Empire Association of Legal
  Assistants
P.O. Box 143
Santa Rosa, CA 95402

Sacramento Association of Legal
  Assistants (**) [271]
P.O. Box 453
Sacramento, CA 95812-0453

San Diego Association of Legal Assistants
  (**) [450]
P.O. Box 87449
San Diego, CA 92138-7449
619-491-1994

San Francisco Association of Legal
  Assistants (**) [975]
P.O. Box 26668

San Francisco, CA 94126-6668
415-777-2390

San Joaquin Association of Legal
   Assistants
P.O. Box 1306
Fresno, CA 93715

Sequoia Paralegal Association
P.O. Box 3884
Visalia, CA 93278-3884

Ventura County Association of Legal
   Assistants (*)
P.O. Box 24229
Ventura, CA 93002

COLORADO

Association of Legal Assistants of
   Colorado (*) [106]
% Alma Rodrigues
4150 Novia Dr.
Colorado Springs, CO 80911

Rocky Mountain Legal Assistants
   Association (**) [440]
P.O. Box 304
Denver, CO 80201
303-369-1606

CONNECTICUT

Central Connecticut Association of Legal
   Assistants (**) [290]
P.O. Box 230594
Hartford, CT 06123-0594

Connecticut Association of Paralegals,
   Fairfield County (**) [135]
P.O. Box 134
Bridgeport, CT 06601

Connecticut Association of Paralegals,
   New Haven (**) [100]
P.O. Box 862
New Haven, CT 06504-0862

Legal Assistants of Southeastern
   Connecticut (**) [55]
P.O. Box 409
New London, CT 06320

DELAWARE

Delaware Paralegal Association (**)
   [295]

P.O. Box 1362
Wilmington, DE 19899

DISTRICT OF COLUMBIA

National Capital Area Paralegal
   Association (**) [620]
1155 Connecticut Ave. N.W.
Wash. D.C. 20036-4306
202-659-0243

FLORIDA

Broward County Paralegal Association
% Leigh Williams
Ruden, Barnett, McClosky
P.O. Box 1900
Ft. Lauderdale, FL 33302

Dade Association of Legal Assistants (*)
% Maxine Stone
14027 S.W. 84th St.
Miami, FL 33183

Florida Legal Assistants (*) [1500]
% Nancy Martin
P.O. Box 503
Bradenton, FL 34206

Jacksonville Legal Assistants (*)
P.O. Box 52264
Jacksonville, FL 32201

Orlando Legal Assistants (*)
% Roxane MacGillivray
Akerman, Senterfitt & Eidson
P.O. Box 231
Orlando, FL 32802

Pensacola Legal Assistants (*)
% Deborah Johnson
Levin, Middlebrooks & Mabie
226 S. Palafox St.
Pensacola, FL 32581

Volusia Association of Legal Assistants
   (*)
P.O. Box 15075
Daytona Beach, FL 32115-5075

GEORGIA

Georgia Association of Legal Assistants
   (**) [820]
P.O. Box 1802
Atlanta, GA 30301

Southeastern Association of Legal
  Assistants of Georgia (*)
% Debra Sutlive
2215 Bacon Park Drive
Savannah, GA 31406

South Georgia Association of Legal
  Assistants (*)
% Martha Tanner
L. Andrew Smith, P.C.
P.O. Box 1026
Valdosta, GA 31603-1026

HAWAII

Hawaii Association of Legal Assistants
  (**) [150]
P.O. Box 674
Honolulu, HI 96809

IDAHO

Idaho Association of Legal Assistants (*)
  [54]
P.O. Box 1254
Boise, ID 83701

ILLINOIS

Central Illinois Paralegal Association (*)
% Debra Monke
GTE North Inc.
1312 E. Empire St.
Bloomington, IL 61701

Illinois Paralegal Association (**) [1100]
P.O. Box 857
Chicago, IL 60690
312-939-2553

Independent Contractors Association of
  Illinois
6400 Woodward Ave.
Downers Grove, IL 60516

Peoria Paralegal Association
% Sharon Moke
1308 Autumn Lane
Peoria, IL 60604

INDIANA

Indiana Legal Assistants (*)
% Dorothy French

14669 Old State Rd.
Evansville, IN 47711

Indiana Paralegal Association (**) [300]
P.O. Box 44518, Federal Station
Indianapolis, IN 46204

Michiana Paralegal Association (**) [40]
P.O. Box 11458
South Bend, IN 46634

IOWA

Iowa Association of Legal Assistants
  [400]
P.O. Box 335
Des Moines, IA 50302-0337

Paralegals of Iowa, Ltd.
P.O. Box 1943
Cedar Rapids, IA 52406

KANSAS

Kansas Association of Legal Assistants (*)
  [138]
% Jimmie Sue Marsh
Foulston & Siefkin
700 Fourth Financial Center
Wichita, KS 67202

Kansas City Association of Legal
  Assistants (**)
P.O. Box 13223
Kansas City, MO 64199
913-381-4458

Kansas Legal Assistants Society (**)
  [190]
P.O. Box 1657
Topeka, KS 66601

KENTUCKY

Kentucky Paralegal Association [232]
P.O. Box 2675
Louisville, KY 40201-2657

Lexington Paralegal Association (**) [80]
P.O. Box 574
Lexington, KY 40586

Louisville Association of Paralegals (**)
  [182]
P.O. Box 962
Louisville, KY 40201

LOUISIANA

Baton Rouge Paralegal Association
P.O. Box 306
Baton Rouge, LA 70821

Lafayette Paralegal Association
P.O. Box 2775
Lafayette, LA 70502

Louisiana State Paralegal Association
[200]
P.O. Box 56
Baton Rouge, LA 70821-0056

New Orleans Paralegal Association (**)
[190]
P.O. Box 30604
New Orleans, LA 70190

Northwest Louisiana Paralegal
Association (*)
P.O. Box 1913
Shreveport, LA 71166-1913

Southwest Louisiana Association of
Paralegals
P.O. Box 1143
Lake Charles, LA 70602-1143

MAINE

Maine Association of Paralegals (*)
P.O. Box 7554
Portland, ME 04112

MARYLAND

Baltimore Association of Legal
Assistants (**) [140]
P.O. Box 13244
Baltimore, MD 21203
301-576-BALA

MASSACHUSETTS

Berkshire Association for Paralegals and
Legal Secretaries
% Nancy Schaffer
Stein, Donahue & Zuckerman
54 Wendell Ave.
Pittsfield, MA 01201

Central Massachusetts Paralegal
Association (**) [80]
P.O. Box 444
Worcester, MA 01614

Massachusetts Paralegal Association (**)
[440]
P.O. Box 423
Boston, MA 02102
617-642-8338

Western Massachusetts Paralegal
Association (**) [50]
P.O. Box 30005
Springfield, MA 01102-0005

MICHIGAN

Legal Assistants Association of Michigan
(*)
% Cora Webb
Woll, Crowley, Berman
315 S. Woodward
Royal Oak, MI 48067

Legal Assistant Section [400]
State Bar of Michigan
440 E. Congress, 4th Fl.
Detroit, MI 48226

Legal Assistants Section
State Bar of Michigan
306 Townsend St.
Lansing, MI 48933-2083
517-372-9030

MINNESOTA

Minnesota Association of Legal
Assistants (**) [972]
P.O. Box 15165
Minneapolis, MN 55415

Minnesota Paralegal Association (*)
% Tracy Blanshan
Kennedy Law Office
724 SW First Ave.
Rochester, MN 55902

MISSISSIPPI

Gulf Coast Paralegal Association
942 Beach Drive
Gulfport, MS 39507

Mississippi Association of Legal
Assistants (*)
P.O. Box 996
600 Heritage Bldg.
Jackson, MS 39205

Paralegal Association of Mississippi
P.O. Box 22887
Jackson, MS 39205

MISSOURI

Gateway Paralegal Association
P.O. Box 50233
St. Louis, MO 63105

Kansas City Association of Legal
  Assistants (**) [470]
P.O. Box 13223
Kansas City, MO 64199
913-381-4458

Southwest Missouri Paralegal Association
  [80]
2148 South Oak Grove
Springfield, MO 65804-2708

St. Louis Association of Legal Assistants
  (*) [434]
P.O. Box 9690
St. Louis, MO 63122

MONTANA

Big Sky Paralegal Association
P.O. Box 2753
Great Falls, MT 59403

Montana Paralegal Association
P.O. Box 693
Billings, MT 59101

NEBRASKA

Nebraska Association of Legal Assistants
  (*)
P.O. Box 24943
Omaha, NE 68124

NEVADA

Clark County Organization of Legal
  Assistants (*)
% Angel A. Price
3800 S. Nellis #235
Las Vegas, NV 89121

Sierra Nevada Association of Paralegals
  (*)
P.O. Box 40638
Reno, NV 89504

NEW HAMPSHIRE

Paralegal Association of New Hampshire
  (*)
% Frances Dupre
Wiggin & Nourie
P.O. Box 808
Manchester, NH 03105

NEW JERSEY

Central Jersey Paralegal Association
P.O. Box 1115
Freehold, NJ 07728

Legal Assistants Association of New
  Jersey (*) [260]
P.O. Box 142
Caldwell, NJ 07006

South Jersey Paralegal Association (**)
  [170]
P.O. Box 355
Haddonfield, NJ 08033

NEW MEXICO

Legal Assistants of New Mexico (**)
  [200]
P.O. Box 1113
Albuquerque, NM 87103-1113
505-260-7104

NEW YORK

Adirondack Paralegal Association
% Maureen Provost
Bartlett, Pontiff, Stewart
One Washington Street
Box 2168
Glen Falls, NY 12801

Legal Professionals of Dutchess County
51 Maloney Rd.
Wappingers Falls, NY 12590

Long Island Paralegal Association (**)
  [130]
P.O. Box 31
Deer Park, NY 11729

Manhattan Paralegal Association [515]
200 Park Ave., Suite 303 East
New York, NY 10166
212-986-2304

Paralegal Association of Rochester (**)
[170]
P.O. Box 40567
Rochester, NY 14604

Southern Tier Association of Paralegals
(**) [45]
P.O. Box 2555
Binghamton, NY 13902

Western New York Paralegal Association
(**) [275]
P.O. Box 207
Buffalo, NY 14202
716-862-6132

West/Roc Paralegal Association (**)
[130]
Box 101
95 Mamaroneck Ave.
White Plains, NY 10601

NORTH CAROLINA

Cumberland County Paralegal
Association
P.O. Box 1358
Fayetteville, NC 28302

Metrolina Paralegal Association
P.O. Box 36260
Charlotte, NC 28236

North Carolina Paralegal Association (*)
% T. William Tewes
Fuller & Corbett
P.O. Box 1121
Goldsboro, NC 27533-1121

Professional Legal Assistants
P.O. Box 31951
Raleigh, NC 27622
919-821-7762

Raleigh Wake Paralegal Association
P.O. Box 1427
Raleigh, NC 27602

Triad Paralegal Association
Drawer U
Greensboro, NC 27402

NORTH DAKOTA

Red River Valley Legal Assistants (*)
P.O. Box 1954
Fargo, ND 58106

Western Dakota Association of Legal
Assistants (*)
P.O. Box 7304
Bismarck, ND 58502

OHIO

Cincinnati Paralegal Association (**)
[380]
P.O. Box 1515
Cincinnati, OH 45201
513-244-1266

Cleveland Association of Paralegals (**)
[480]
P.O. Box 14247
Cleveland, OH 44114

Greater Dayton Paralegal Association
(**) [160]
P.O. Box 515, Mid City Station
Dayton, OH 45402

Legal Assistants of Central Ohio (**)
[270]
P.O. Box 15182
Columbus, OH 43215-0812
614-224-9700

Northeastern Ohio Paralegal Association
P.O. Box 9236
Akron, OH 44305

Toledo Association of Legal Assistants (*)
[176]
P.O. Box 1322
Toledo, OH 43603

OKLAHOMA

Oklahoma Paralegal Association (*)
P.O. Box 18476
Oklahoma City, OK 73154

Tulsa Association of Legal Assistants (*)
P.O. Box 1484
Tulsa, OK 74101

OREGON

Oregon Legal Assistants Association (**)
[340]
P.O. Box 8523
Portland, OR 97207

Pacific Northwest Legal Assistants (*)
P.O. Box 1835
Eugene, OR 97440

PENNSYLVANIA

Berks County Paralegal Association
544 Court St.
Reading, PA 19601
215-375-4591

Central Pennsylvania Paralegal
   Association (**) [70]
P.O. Box 11814
Harrisburg, PA 17108

Keystone Legal Assistant Association (*)
% Catrine Nuss
3021 Guineveer Drive, Apt. B4
Harrisburg, PA 17110

Lancaster Area Paralegal Association
% Rosemary Merwin
Gibble, Kraybill & Hess
41 East Orange St.
Lancaster, PA 17602

Paralegal Association of Northwestern
   Pennsylvania (**) [40]
P.O. Box 1504
Erie, PA 16507

Philadelphia Association of Paralegals
   (**) [775]
1411 Walnut St., Suite 200
Philadelphia, PA 19102
215-564-0525

Pittsburgh Paralegal Association (**)
   [400]
P.O. Box 2845
Pittsburgh, PA 15230

Wilkes-Barre Area Group
% Tom Albrechta
6 East Green St.
West Hazelton, PA 18201

RHODE ISLAND

Rhode Island Paralegal Association (**)
   [200]
P.O. Box 1003
Providence, RI 02901

SOUTH CAROLINA

Charleston Association of Legal
   Assistants
P.O. Box 1511
Charleston, SC 29402

Columbia Association of Legal Assistants
   (**)
P.O. Box 11634
Columbia, SC 29211-1634

Greenville Association of Legal Assistants
   (*)
P.O. Box 10491 F.S.
Greenville, SC 29603

Paralegal Association of the Pee Dee [31]
P.O. Box 5592
Florence, SC 29502-5592

SOUTH DAKOTA

South Dakota Legal Assistants
   Association (*) [61]
% Louise Peterson
May, Johnson, Doyle
P.O. Box 1443
Sioux Falls, SD 57101-1443

TENNESSEE

Memphis Paralegal Association (**)
   [105]
P.O. Box 3646
Memphis, TN 38173-0646

Middle Tennessee Paralegal Association
   (**) [145]
P.O. Box 198006
Nashville, TN 37219

Southeast Tennessee Paralegal
   Association
% Calecta Veagles
P.O. Box 1252
Chattanooga, TN 37401

Tennessee Paralegal Association (*)
P.O. Box 11172
Chattanooga, TN 37401

TEXAS

Alamo Area Professional Legal Assistants
   [245]

P.O. Box 524
San Antonio, TX 78292

Capital Area Paralegal Association (*)
[252]
% Chris Hemingson
Pope, Hopper, Roberts & Warren
111 Congress, Suite 1700
Austin, TX 78701

Dallas Association of Legal Assistants
(**) [799]
P.O. Box 117885
Carrollton, TX 75011-7885

El Paso Association of Legal Assistants
(*) [106]
P.O. Box 121
El Paso, TX 79941-0121

Fort Worth Paralegal Association [226]
P.O. Box 17021
Fort Worth, TX 76102

Houston Legal Assistants Association
P.O. Box 52266
Houston, TX 77052
713-580-7722

Legal Assistant Division [2046]
State Bar of Texas
P.O. Box 12487
Austin, TX 78711
512-463-1383

Legal Assistants Association/Permian
Basin (*)
P.O. Box 10683
Midland, TX 79702

Legal Assistants Professional Association
(Brazos Valley)
P.O. Box 925
Madisonville, TX 79702

Northeast Texas Association of Legal
Assistants (*) [29]
P.O. Box 2284
Longview, TX 75606

Nueces County Association of Legal
Assistants (*)
% Joyce Hoffman
Edwards & Terry
P.O. Box 480
Corpus Christi, TX 78403

Southeast Texas Association of Legal
Assistants (*) [130]
% Janie Boswell
8335 Homer
Beaumont, TX 77708

Texarkana Association of Legal
Assistants (*) [40]
P.O. Box 6671
Texarkana, TX 75505

Texas Panhandle Association of Legal
Assistants (*) [63]
% Lisa Clemens
Morgan, Culton
P.O. Box 189
Amarillo, TX 79105

Tyler Area Association of Legal
Assistants [94]
P.O. Box 1178
Tyler, TX 75711-1178

West Texas Association of Legal
Assistants (*) [44]
P.O. Box 1499
Lubbock, TX 79408

UTAH

Legal Assistants Association of Utah (*)
P.O. Box 112001
Salt Lake City, UT 84147-2001
801-531-0331

VERMONT

Vermont Paralegal Association [80]
% Trudy Seeley
Langrock, Sperry & Wool
P.O. Drawer 351
Middlebury, VT 05753

VIRGINIA

American Academy of Legal Assistants
1022 Paul Avenue N.E.
Norton, VA 24273

Peninsula Legal Assistants (*)
% Diane Morrison
Jones, Blechman, Woltz & Kelly
P.O. Box 12888
Newport News, VA 23612

Richmond Association of Legal Assistants
(*) [318]
% Vicki Roberts
McGuire, Woods, Battle & Boothe
One James Center
Richmond, VA 23219

Roanoke Valley Paralegal Association
(**) [70]
P.O. Box 1505
Roanoke, VA 24001
703-224-8000

Tidewater Association of Legal Assistants
(*)
% Claire Isley
Wilcox & Savage
1800 Sovran Center
Norfolk, VA 23510

VIRGIN ISLANDS

Virgin Islands Paralegals (*)
% Eloise Mack
P.O. Box 6276
St. Thomas, VI 00804

WASHINGTON

Washington Legal Assistants Association
(**) [453]
2033 6th Ave., Suite 804

Seattle, WA 98121
206-441-6020

WEST VIRGINIA

Legal Assistants of West Virginia (*)
% Mary Hanson
Hunt & Wilson
P.O. Box 2506
Charleston, WV 25329-2506

WISCONSIN

Paralegal Association of Wisconsin (**)
[380]
P.O. Box 92882
Milwaukee, WI 53202
414-272-7168

WYOMING

Legal Assistants of Wyoming (*)
% Nancy Hole
Brown & Drew
123 West First St.
Casper, WY 82601

Glossary

AAfPE American Association for Paralegal Education.

ABA American Bar Association.

Accreditation The process by which an organization evaluates and recognizes a program of study (or an institution) as meeting specified qualifications or standards.

Adjudication The process by which a court resolves a legal dispute through litigation. The verb is *adjudicate*.

Administrative Agency A unit of government whose primary mission is to carry out or administer the statutes of the legislature and the executive orders of the chief of the executive branch.

Administrative Code A collection of administrative regulations organized by subject matter.

Administrative Hearing A proceeding at an administrative agency presided over by a hearing officer (e.g., an Administrative Law Judge) to resolve a controversy.

Administrative Law Judge A hearing officer who presides over a hearing at an administrative agency.

Administrative Procedure Act The statute that governs aspects of procedure before administrative agencies.

Administrative Regulation A law of an administrative agency designed to explain or carry out the statutes and executive orders that govern the agency. Also called a *rule*.

Admonition A nonpublic declaration that the attorney's conduct was improper. This does not affect his or her right to practice. Also called a private reprimand.

ADR Alternative dispute resolution.

Adversarial Hearing A proceeding in which both parties to a controversy appear before a judge.

Adversarial System Justice and truth have a greater chance of emerging when parties to a controversy appear before a neutral judge and jury to argue their conflicting positions.

Adverse Interests Opposing purposes or claims.

Adverse Judgment A judgment or decision against you.

Advice *See* Professional Judgment.

Advocacy An attempt to influence actions of others.

Affiant *See* Affidavit.

Affidavit A written statement of fact in which a person (called the affiant) swears that the statement is true.

Affiliate Member *See* Associate Member.

Affirmation of Professional Responsibility A statement of the ethical guidelines of the National Federation of Paralegal Associations.

Agency Practitioner An individual authorized to practice before an administrative agency. This individual often does not have to be an attorney.

ALA Association of Legal Administrators.

Allegation A claimed fact.

Ambulance Chasing Aggressively going to individuals with potentially good claims as plaintiffs (e.g., personal-injury victims) to encourage them to hire a particular attorney. If the attorney uses someone else to do the soliciting, the latter is called a *runner*. If this other person uses deception or fraud in the solicitation, he or she is sometimes called a *capper*.

Analogous Sufficiently similar in the facts and law being applied. Also referred to as *on point.*

Annotate To provide notes or commentary. A text is annotated if such notes and commentary are provided along with the text.

Annotated Code/Annotated Statutes A collection of statutes organized by subject matter, along with notes and commentary.

Answer The pleading that responds to or answers the allegations of the complaint.

Antitrust Law The law governing unlawful restraints of trade, price fixing, and monopolies.

APA *See* Administrative Procedure Act.

Appearance Going to court to act on behalf of a party to the litigation. The first time this is done, the attorney files a *notice of appearance.*

Appellant The party bringing an appeal because of dissatisfaction with something the lower tribunal did.

Appellate Brief A document submitted to an appellate court containing arguments on whether a lower court made errors of law.

Appellate Jurisdiction The power of a court to hear an appeal of a case from a lower tribunal to determine whether it made any errors of law.

Appellee The party against whom an appeal is brought. Also called the *respondent.*

Apprentice A person in training for an occupation under the supervision of a full member of that occupation.

Approval The recognition that comes from accreditation, certification, licensure, or registration. The ABA uses *approval* as a substitute for the word *accreditation.*

Approval Commission A group of individuals who investigate whether a paralegal school meets the criteria for approval established by the ABA.

Arbitration In lieu of litigation, both sides agree to allow a neutral third party to resolve their dispute.

Assigned Counsel An attorney appointed by the court and paid with government funds to represent an individual who cannot afford to hire an attorney.

Associate An attorney employee of a law firm who hopes eventually to become a partner.

Associated Pertaining to an attorney who is an associate in a law firm.

Associate Member A nonattorney who is allowed to become part of—but not a full member of—a bar association. Sometimes called *affiliate member.*

Attestation Clause A clause stating that a person saw a witness sign a document.

Attorney Attestation A signed statement by an attorney that a paralegal applying for membership in a paralegal association meets designated criteria of the association, e.g., is employed as a paralegal.

Attorney-Client Privilege A client and an attorney can refuse to disclose communications between them whose purpose was to facilitate the provision of legal services for the client.

Attorney General The chief attorney for the government. *See also* Opinion of the Attorney General.

Authority Anything that a court could rely on in reaching its decision.

Authorized Practice of Law Services that constitute the practice of law which a non-attorney has authorization to provide. *See also* Practice of Law, Professional Judgment.

Bailiff A court employee who keeps order in the courtroom and renders general administrative assistance to the judge.

Bar Prevent or stop.

Barratry Stirring up quarrels or litigation; illegal solicitation of clients.

Barrister A lawyer in England who represents clients in the higher courts.

Bar Treaties Agreements between attorneys and other occupations on what law-related activities of these other occupations do and do not constitute the unauthorized practice of law.

Below (1) The lower tribunal that heard the case before it was appealed. (2) Later in the document.

Bill A proposed statute.

Billable Tasks Those tasks requiring time that can be charged to a client.

Board of Appeals The unit within an administrative agency to which a party can appeal a decision of the agency.

Bond A sum of money deposited in court to ensure compliance with a requirement.

Capper *See* Ambulance Chasing.

Case (1) A legal matter in dispute or potential dispute. (2) The written decision of a court. *See also* Opinion.

Casebook A law-school textbook containing numerous edited court opinions.

Case Clerk An assistant to a paralegal; an entry-level paralegal.

Case Manager An experienced legal assistant who can coordinate or direct legal assistant activities on a major case or transaction.

Cause of Action A legally acceptable reason for suing.

Censure A formal disapproval or declaration of blame. *See also* Reprimand.

Certificated Having met the qualifications for certification from a school or training program.

Certification The process by which a nongovernmental organization grants recognition to an individual who has met qualifications specified by that organization. *See also* Specialty Certification.

Certified Having complied with or met the qualifications for certification.

Certified Legal Assistant (CLA) The title bestowed by the National Association of Legal Assistants on a paralegal who has passed the CLA exam and has met other criteria of NALA. *See also* Specialty Certification.

Certified PLS A Certified Professional Legal Secretary. This status is achieved after passing an examination and meeting other requirements of NALS, the National Association of Legal Secretaries.

CFLA Certified Florida Legal Assistant. To earn this title, a paralegal must first pass the CLA (Certified Legal Assistant) exam of NALA, and then pass a special exam on Florida law.

Chinese Wall Steps taken to prevent a tainted employee (attorney, paralegal, or secretary) from having any contact with the case of a particular client in the office. The employee is tainted because he or she has a conflict of interest with that client. A Chinese wall is also called an *ethical wall*. A tainted employee is also called a *contaminated employee*. Once the Chinese wall is set up around the tainted employee, the latter is referred to as a *quarantined employee*.

Citation A reference to any written material. It is the "address" where the material can be found in the library. Also called a *cite*.

Cite (1) A citation. (2) To give the volume and page number, name of the book, etc. where written material can be found in a library.

Civil Dispute One private party suing another, or a private party suing the government, or the government suing a private party for a matter other than the commission of a crime.

CLA *See* Certified Legal Assistant.

Claims-Made Policy Insurance that covers only claims actually filed (i.e., made) during the period in which the policy is in effect.

CLAS Certified Legal Assistant Specialist (an advanced certification status of NALA).

CLE Continuing Legal Education. Undertaken after an individual has received his or her primary education or training in a law-related occupation.

Closing The event during which steps are taken to finalize the transfer of an interest in property.

Code A set of rules, organized by subject matter.

Codefendant More than one defendant being sued in a civil case (or prosecuted in a criminal case) in the same litigation.

Code of Ethics and Professional Responsibility A statement of the ethical guidelines of the National Association of Legal Assistants.

Codified Cite The citation to a statute that has been printed in a code and, therefore, has been organized by subject matter. *See also* Session Law Cite.

Codify To arrange material by subject matter.

Commingling Mixing general law firms funds with client funds in a single account.

Common Law Judge-made law in the absence of controlling statutory law or other higher law. *See also* Enacted Law.

Common Representation *See* Multiple Representation.

Competence, Attorney Having the knowledge and skill that is reasonably necessary to represent a particular client.

Complaint The pleading filed by the plaintiff that tries to state a claim or cause of action against the defendant.

Confidential That which should not be revealed; pertaining to information that others do not have a right to receive.

Conflict of Interest Divided loyalty that actually or potentially places one of the participants to whom undivided loyalty is owed at a disadvantage. *See also* Divided Loyalty.

Conflicts Check A check of the client files of a law firm to help determine whether a conflict of interest might exist between a prospective client and current or past clients. The person performing this check is often called a *conflicts specialist*.

Conflicts of Law An area of the law that determines what law applies when a choice must be made between the laws of different, coequal legal systems, e.g., two states.

Constitution The fundamental law that creates the branches of government and that identifies basic rights and obligations.

Contaminated Paralegal *See* Chinese Wall.

Contest To challenge.

Contingent Fee A fee that is dependent on the outcome of the case.

Contract Attorney *See* Project Attorney.

Contract Paralegal A self-employed paralegal who often works for several different attorneys on a freelance basis. *See also* Freelance Paralegal.

Corporate Counsel The chief attorney of a corporation. Also called the *general counsel*.

Corporate Legal Department The law office within a corporation containing salaried attorneys (in-house attorneys) who advise and represent the corporation.

Counterclaim A claim or cause of action against the plaintiff stated in the defendant's answer.

Court of First Instance A trial court; a court with original jurisdiction.

Credentialization A form of official recognition based on one's training or employment status.

Credible Believable.

Criminal Dispute A suit brought by the government for the alleged commission of a crime.

Cross-claim Usually, a claim by one codefendant against another.

Cross-examination   Questioning the witness called by the other side after direct examination.

Cured   Corrected.

Damages   An award of money paid by the wrongdoer to compensate the person who has been harmed.

Declaratory Judgment   A court decision establishing the rights and obligations of the parties but not ordering them to do or to refrain from doing anything.

Deep Pocket   Slang for the person or organization with enough money or other assets to be able to pay a judgment.

Default Judgment   A judgment for the plaintiff because the defendant failed to appear or to file an answer before the deadline.

Defense   An allegation of fact or the presentation of a legal theory that is offered to offset or defeat a claim or demand.

Demurrer   Even if the plaintiff proved all the facts stated in the complaint, a cause of action would not be established.

Deponent   *See* Deposition.

Deposition   A pretrial discovery device consisting of a question-and-answer session involving a party or witness designed to assist the other party prepare for trial. The person who is questioned is called the *deponent.*

Dictum   A statement made by a court that was not necessary to resolve the specific legal issues before the court. The plural of dictum is dicta.

Digesting   Summarizing discovery documents. *See also* Depo Summarizer.

Digests   (1) Volumes that contain summaries of court opinions. These summaries are sometimes called *abstracts* or *squibs.* (2) Volumes that contain summaries of annotations in A.L.R., A.L.R.2d, etc.

Disbarment   The temporary or permanent termination of the right to practice law.

Disciplinary Rule (DR)   *See* Model Code of Professional Responsibility.

Discovery   Pretrial devices designed to assist a party prepare for trial. *See* Deposition, Interrogatories.

Disinterested   Not working for one side or the other in a controversy or other legal matter; not deriving benefit if one of the sides prevails.

Disqualification   *See* Vicarious Disqualification.

Dissenting Opinion   An opinion that disagrees with the result and the reasoning used by the majority.

District Court   *See* United States District Court.

Divided Loyalty   The responsibility of protecting the interest of parties who are competitors or are otherwise at odds with each other. *See also* Conflict of Interest.

Docket Number   The number assigned to a case by the court.

DR   Disciplinary Rule. *See* Model Code of Professional Responsibility.

Draft   Write.

EC   Ethical Consideration. *See* Model Code of Professional Responsibility.

Element   A portion of a rule which is a precondition of the applicability of the entire rule. The *element in contention* is the element of the rule about which the parties cannot agree. The disagreement may be over the meaning of the element or how it applies to a given set of facts.

Enacted Law   Law written by the legislature (statutes), by the people (constitutions), and by an administrative agency (regulations). Law that is not the product of adjudication. *See* Adjudication.

En Banc   By the entire court.

Enrolled Agent   An individual authorized to represent taxpayers at all administrative proceedings within the Internal Revenue Service—this person does not have to be an attorney.

Enrollment *See* Registration.

Entry-Level Certification Certification of individuals who have just begun their careers.

Estate All the property left by a decedent from which his or her debts can be paid.

Et al. And others.

Ethical Wall *See* Chinese Wall.

Ethical Consideration (EC) *See* Model Code of Professional Responsibility.

Ethics Rules embodying standards of behavior to which members of an organization are expected to conform.

Evidence That which is offered to help establish or disprove a factual position. A separate determination must be made on whether a particular item of evidence is relevant or irrelevant, admissible or inadmissible, etc.

Execution Carrying out or enforcing a judgment.

Exempt Employee An employee who is not entitled to overtime compensation under the Fair Labor Standards Act because the employee is a professional, administrative, or executive employee. Paralegals are nonexempt, except for paralegal managers.

Ex Parte Hearing A hearing at which only one party is present. A court order issued at such a hearing is an *ex parte order*.

External/Adversary Memorandum of Law A memorandum written primarily for individuals outside of the office to convince them to take a certain course of action. *See also* Memorandum of Law.

Facts & Findings A periodical of the National Association of Legal Assistants.

Fair Labor Standards Act The federal statute that regulates conditions of employment such as when overtime compensation must be paid. *See also* Exempt Employee.

Federalism The coexistence of, and the interrelationships among, the state governments and the federal government, particularly with respect to the powers of each of these levels of government.

Federal Question A legal question that arises from the application of the United States Constitution, a statute of Congress, or a federal administrative regulation.

Fee-Generating Case The case of a client who can pay a fee out of the damages awarded or from his or her independent resources.

Fee Splitting A single client bill covering the fee of two or more attorneys who are not in the same firm.

Felony A crime punishable by a sentence of one year or more.

Filed Formally presented to a court.

First Instance, Court of A trial court; a court with original jurisdiction.

Fixed Fee A flat fee for services. A set amount paid regardless of the outcome of the case or the amount of time needed to complete it.

Formbook A manual that contains forms, checklists, practice techniques, etc. Also called a *practice manual* or *handbook*.

Forum The court where the case is to be tried.

Forwarding Fee *See* Referral Fee.

FRCP Federal Rules of Civil Procedure.

Freedom of Information Act A statute that gives citizens access to certain information in the possession of the government.

Freelance Paralegal A self-employed paralegal who works for several different attorneys, or a self-employed paralegal who works directly for the public. Also referred to as an *independent paralegal.*

Friendly Divorce A divorce proceeding in which the parties have no significant disputes between them.

General Counsel The chief attorney in a corporate law department.

General Practitioner An attorney who handles any kind of case.

Go Bare To engage in an occupation or profession without malpractice insurance.

GOD The "Great Overtime Debate." *See* Exempt Employee.

Grounds Reasons.

Group Legal Services A form of legal insurance in which members of a group pay a set amount on a regular basis, for which they receive designated legal services. Also called *prepaid legal services*.

Guideline Suggested conduct that will help an applicant obtain accreditation, certification, licensure, registration, or approval.

HALT Help Abolish Legal Tyranny, an organization that seeks to reform the legal profession, primarily by eliminating the monopoly of attorneys over the practice of law.

Handbook *See* Formbook.

Heading The beginning of a memorandum that lists who the memo is for, who wrote it, what it is about, etc.

Hearing Examiner One who presides over an administrative hearing.

Hearing Memorandum A memorandum of law submitted to a hearing officer.

Holding A court's answer to one of the legal issues in the case. Also called a *ruling*.

Hornbook A treatise that summarizes an area of the law.

Id. Same citation as immediately above.

Impaired Attorney An attorney with a drug or alcohol problem.

Impeach To challenge; to attack the credibility of.

Imputed Disqualification *See* Vicarious Disqualification.

Independent Contractor One who operates his or her own business and contracts to do work for others who do not control the details of how that work is performed.

Independent Paralegal *See* Freelance Paralegal.

Indigent Poor, unable to pay for needed services.

Inferior Court A lower court.

Infra Below, mentioned or referred to later in the document.

In-house Attorney An attorney who is an employee of a business corporation. *See* Corporate Legal Department.

In Issue In dispute or question.

Instrument A formal document that gives expression to a legal act or agreement, e.g., a mortgage.

Integrated Bar Association A state bar association to which an attorney must belong in order to practice law in the state. Also called a *mandatory* or *unified bar association*.

Interim Suspension A temporary suspension, pending the imposition of final discipline.

Internal/Interoffice Memorandum of Law A memorandum written for members of one's own office. *See also* Memorandum of Law.

Interrogatories A pretrial discovery device consisting of written questions sent by one party to another to assist the sender of the questions to prepare for trial.

Jailhouse Lawyer A paralegal in prison, usually self-taught, who has a limited right to practice law and to give legal advice to fellow inmates if the prison does not provide adequate alternatives for legal services. Also known as a *writ writer*.

Jargon Technical language; language that does not have an everyday meaning.

Judgment The decision of the court on the controversy before it.

Judicial Branch The branch of government with primary responsibility for interpreting laws and resolving disputes that arise under them.

Jurisdiction   The power of a court. *See also* Geographic Jurisdiction, Subject-Matter Jurisdiction.

LAMA   Legal Assistant Management Association.

Lateral Hire   An attorney, paralegal, or secretary who has been hired from another law office.

Law Clerk   An employee of an attorney who is in law school studying to become an attorney or who has graduated from law school and is waiting to pass the bar examination. In Ontario, Canada, a law clerk is a trained professional doing independent legal work, which may include managerial duties, under the direction and guidance of a lawyer, and whose function is to relieve a lawyer of routine and administrative matters and to assist a lawyer in the more complex ones.

Law Directory   A list of attorneys.

Legal Administrator   An individual, usually a nonattorney, with broad management responsibility for a law office.

Legal Advice   *See* Professional Judgment.

Legal Analysis   The process of connecting a rule of law to a set of facts in order to determine how that rule might apply to a particular situation. The goal of the process is to solve a legal dispute or to prevent one from arising.

Legal Assistant   *See* Paralegal.

Legal Assistant Clerk   A person who assists a legal assistant in clerical tasks such as document numbering, alphabetizing, filing, and any other project that does not require substantive knowledge of litigation or of a particular transaction. *See also* Document Clerk.

Legal Assistant Division   A few state bar associations, e.g., Texas, have established special divisions which paralegals can join as associate members.

Legal Assistant Manager   A person responsible for recruiting, interviewing, and hiring legal assistants who spends little or no time working on client cases as a legal assistant. He or she may also be substantially involved in other matters pertaining to legal assistants, e.g., training, monitoring work assignments, designing budgets, and overseeing the billing of paralegal time. Also known as a *paralegal manager*.

Legal Issue   A question of law; a question of what the law is, or what the law means, or how the law applies to a set of facts. If the dispute is over the truth or falsity of the facts, it is referred to as a *question of fact* or a *factual dispute*.

Legal Technician   A self-employed paralegal who works for several different attorneys, or a self-employed paralegal who works directly for the public. Sometimes called an *independent paralegal* or a *freelance paralegal*.

Legislation   (1) The process of making statutory law. (2) A statute.

Legislative Branch   The branch of government with primary responsibility for making or enacting the law.

Letterhead   The top part of stationery which identifies the name and address of the office (often with the names of selected employees).

LEXIS   The legal research computer service of Mead Data Co.

Liable   Legally responsible.

Licensed Independent Paralegal   A paralegal who holds a limited license. *See* Limited Licensure.

Licensure   The process by which an agency of government grants permission to persons meeting specified qualifications to engage in an occupation and to use a particular title.

Limited Licensure   The process by which an agency of government grants permission to persons meeting specified qualifications to engage in designated activities that are now customarily (although not always exclusively) performed by another license holder, i.e., that are part of someone else's monopoly.

Limited Practice Officer A nonattorney in Washington state who has the authority to select and prepare designated legal documents pertaining to real estate closings.

Litigation The formal process of resolving legal controversies through special tribunals established for this purpose. The major tribunal is a court.

Magistrate A judicial officer having some but not all the powers of a judge.

Majority Opinion The opinion whose result and reasoning is supported by at least half plus one of the judges on the court.

Malpractice Serious wrongful conduct committed by an individual, usually a member of a profession.

Mandatory Bar Association *See* Integrated Bar Association.

Martindale–Hubbell A national directory of attorneys.

Memorandum of Law A memorandum is simply a note, a comment, or a report. A legal memorandum is a written explanation of what the law is and how it might apply to a fact situation.

Minimum-Fee Schedule A published list of fees recommended by a bar association.

Misdemeanor A crime punishable by a sentence of less than a year.

Model Code of Professional Responsibility An earlier edition of the ethical rules governing attorneys recommended by the American Bar Association. The Model Code consisted of Ethical Considerations (ECs), which represented the objectives toward which each attorney should strive, and Disciplinary Rules (DRs), which were mandatory statements of the minimum conduct below which no attorney could fall without being subject to discipline.

Model Rules of Professional Conduct The current set of ethical rules governing attorneys recommended by the American Bar Association. These rules revised the ABA's earlier rules found in the Model Code of Professional Responsibility.

Model Standards and Guidelines for Utilization of Legal Assistants A statement of ethical and related guidelines of the National Association of Legal Assistants.

Monitoring Legislation Finding out current information on the status of a proposed statute in the legislature.

Multiple Representation Representing more than one side in a legal matter or controversy. Also called *common representation.*

NALA National Association of Legal Assistants.

NALS National Association of Legal Secretaries. *See also* Certified PLS.

National Paralegal Reporter A periodical of the National Federation of Paralegal Associations.

Neighborhood Legal Service Office A law office that serves the legal needs of the poor, often publicly funded.

NFPA National Federation of Paralegal Associations.

NJC Neighborhood Justice Center.

Nonadversarial Proceeding Only one party appears in the proceeding, or both parties appear but they have no real controversy between them.

Nonbillable task A task for which an office cannot bill a client.

Nonexempt Employee *See* Exempt Employee.

Notary Public A person who witnesses (i.e., attests to the authenticity of) signatures, administers oaths, and performs related tasks. In Europe, a notary often has more extensive authority.

Oath A sworn statement that what you say is true.

Occurrence Policy Malpractice insurance that covers all occurrences (e.g., a negligent error or omission) during the period the policy is in effect, even if the claim is not actually filed until after the policy expires.

Of Counsel   An attorney with a special status in the firm, e.g., a semiretired partner.

Office Sharing   Attorneys with their own independent practices who share the use and cost of administration such as rent, copy machine, etc.

Opinion   A court's written explanation of how and why it applied the law to the specific facts before it to reach its decision. Also called a *case*. Opinions are printed in volumes called *reporters*.

Padding   Adding something without justification.

Paralegal   A person with legal skills who works under the supervision of an attorney or who is otherwise authorized to use those skills; this person performs tasks that do not require all the skills of an attorney and that most secretaries are not trained to perform. Synonymous with *legal assistant*.

Paralegal Manager   *See* Legal Assistant Manager.

Paralegal Specialist   A job classification in the federal government.

Percentage Fee   The fee is a percentage of the amount involved in the transaction or award.

Personal Jurisdiction   The court's power over a particular person. Also called *in personam jurisdiction*.

Personal Liability   Being responsible because of what you wrongfully did or wrongfully failed to do. *See also* Vicarious Liability.

Plaintiff   The party initiating the lawsuit.

Plead   To deliver a formal statement or response.

Pleading   A paper or document filed in court stating the position of one of the parties on the cause(s) of action or on the defense(s).

PLS   Professional Legal Secretary. *See also* Certified PLS.

Practical Manual   *See* Formbook.

Practice of Law   Engaging in any of the following activities on behalf of another: representation in court, representation in an agency proceeding, preparation of legal documents, or providing legal advice.

Private Law Firm   A law firm that generates its income from the fees of individual clients.

Private Reprimand   *See* Admonition.

Private Sector   An office where the funds come from client fees or the corporate treasury.

Private Statute   *See* Statute.

Procedural Law   The rules that govern the mechanics of resolving a dispute in court or in an administrative agency, e.g., a rule on the time a party has to respond to a complaint.

Professional Corporation   The organization of a law practice as a corporation.

Professional Judgment   Relating or applying the general body and philosophy of law to a specific legal problem. When communicated to a client, the result is known as *legal advice*.

Project Attorney   An attorney who works either part-time or full time over a relatively short period. Also referred to as a *contract attorney*.

Prosecution   (1) Bringing a criminal case. (2) The attorney representing the government in a criminal case. (3) Going through the steps to litigate a civil case.

Prosecutor   The attorney representing the government in a criminal case.

Public Benefits   Government benefits.

Public Censure.   *See* Reprimand.

Public Defender   An attorney who is paid by the government to represent low-income people charged with crimes.

Public Law   *See* Statute.

Public Sector An office where the funds come from charity or the government.

Public Statute *See* Statute.

Quarantined Paralegal *See* Chinese Wall.

Quasi-adjudication An administrative decision of an administrative agency which has characteristics of a court opinion.

Quasi-judicial Like or similar to a court.

Quasi-legislation A regulation of an administrative agency that has characteristics of the legislation (statutes) of a legislature.

Question of Law/Question of Fact *See* Legal Issue.

RE Concerning

Reasonable Fee A fee that is not excessive in light of the amount of time and labor involved, the complexity of the case, the experience and reputation of the attorney, the customary fee charged in the locality for the same kind of case, etc.

Record (1) The official collection of all the trial pleadings, exhibits, orders, and word-for-word testimony that took place during the trial. (2) A collection of data fields that constitute a single unit, e.g., employee record.

Referral Fee A fee received by an attorney from another attorney to whom the first attorney referred a client. Also called a *forwarding fee*.

Registered Agent An individual authorized to practice before the United States Patent Office. He or she does not have to be an attorney.

Registration The process by which individuals or institutions list their names on a roster kept by an agency of government or by a nongovernmental organization. The agency or organization will often establish qualifications for the right to register, and determine whether applicants meet these qualifications. Also called *enrollment*.

Regulation Any governmental or non-governmental method of controlling conduct. *See also* Administrative Regulation.

Reporters Volumes containing the full text of court opinions.

Reprimand A public declaration that an attorney's conduct was improper. This does not affect his or her right to practice. Also called a *censure* and a *public censure*.

Respondeat Superior Let the superior answer. An employer is responsible for the wrongs committed by an employee within the scope of employment.

Respondent *See* Appellee.

Retainer (1) The contract of employment between attorney and client. (2) An amount of money paid by a client to make certain that an attorney will be available to work for him or her. (3) The amount of money or other assets paid by the client as a form of deposit or advance payment against future fees and costs.

Review To examine in order to determine whether any errors of law were made. *See also* Appellate Jurisdiction.

Rule *See* Administrative Regulation, Rules of Court.

Rule of Three Gross revenue generated through paralegal billing should equal three times a paralegal's salary.

Rules of Court Rules of procedure that govern the conduct of litigation before a particular court.

Runner *See* Ambulance Chasing.

Sanction (1) A penalty or punishment imposed for unacceptable conduct. (2) To authorize or give approval.

Second Chair A seat at the counsel's table in the courtroom used by an assistant to the trial attorney during the trial.

Section (§) A portion of a statute, regulation, or book.

Self-Regulation A process by which members of an occupation or profession establish and administer the rules on who can become a member and when members should be disciplined.

Senior Legal Assistant An experienced legal assistant with the ability to supervise or train other legal assistants. He or she may have developed a specialty in a practice area.

Service of Process The delivery of a formal notice to a defendant ordering him or her to appear in court to answer the allegations of the plaintiff.

Sole Practice A single attorney owns and manages the law firm.

Solicitor (1) A lawyer in England who handles day-to-day legal problems of clients with only limited rights to represent clients in certain lower courts. *See also* Barrister. (2) In the United States, some high government attorneys are called solicitors, e.g., the Solicitor-General of the United States who argues cases before the United States Supreme Court for the federal government.

Special Interest Group An organization that serves a particular group of people, e.g., a union.

Specialty Certification Official recognition of competency in a particular area of law. The National Association of Legal Assistants, for example, has a specialty certification program to recognize a person as a Certified Legal Assistant Specialist (CLAS). A paralegal must first become a Certified Legal Assistant (CLA), and then pass one of NALA's specialty exams. *See also* Certified Legal Assistant.

Staff Attorney A full-time attorney who has no expectation of becoming a full partner. Sometimes called a *second-tiered* attorney.

Standard Form A preprinted form used frequently for various kinds of transactions or proceedings.

Standard of Proof A statement of how convincing a version of a fact must be before the trier of facts can accept it as true.

State Question A legal question that arises from the application of the state constitution, a state statute, or a state administrative regulation.

Statute A law passed by the legislature declaring, commanding, or prohibiting something. The statute is contained in a document called an *act*. If the statute applies to the general public or to a segment of the public, it is called a *public law* or *public statute*. If the statute applies to specifically named individuals or to groups— and has little or no permanence or general interest—it is called a *private law* or *private statute*.

Statutory Code A collection of statutes organized by subject matter.

Stay To delay the enforcement or the execution of a judgment.

Stipulated Agreed to.

Subject-Matter Jurisdiction The power of the court to resolve a particular category of dispute.

Subscription The signature of the attorney who prepared the complaint.

Substantive Law The nonprocedural rules that govern rights and duties.

Summary Quick, expedited, without going through a full adversarial hearing.

Summary Judgment, Motion for A request by a party that a decision be reached on the basis of the pleadings alone, without going through an entire trial, because there is no dispute on any material facts.

Summons A formal notice from the court ordering the defendant to appear.

Superior Court Usually a trial court.

Supervising Legal Assistant Someone who spends about fifty percent of his or her time supervising other legal assistants and about fifty percent on client cases as a legal assistant.

Supplemented Added to.

Supra Above, mentioned or referred to earlier in the document.

Supremacy Clause The clause in the United States Constitution that gives the federal government supremacy over state and local governments in regulating designated areas.

Supreme Court   The highest court in a judicial system. (In New York, however, the supreme court is a trial court.)

Suspension   The removal of an attorney from the practice of law for a specified minimum period, after which the attorney can apply for reinstatement.

Sustain   To affirm the validity of.

System   An organized method of performing a recurring task.

Tainted Paralegal   *See* Chinese Wall.

Tickler   A reminder system that helps office staff remember important deadlines.

Tort   A private wrong or injury other than a breach of contract or the commission of a crime, although some breaches of contract and crimes can also constitute torts.

Transcribed   Copied or written out word for word.

Transcript   A word-for-word account.

Treatise, Legal   A book written by a private individual (or by a public official writing as a private citizen) that provides an overview, summary, or commentary of a legal topic.

Trial Book   *See* Trial Brief.

Trial Brief   An attorney's set of notes on how to conduct a trial, often placed in a *trial notebook*. Sometimes called a *trial manual* or *trial book*.

Trial de Novo   A totally new fact-finding hearing.

Trial Manual   *See* Trial Brief.

Trial Memorandum   *See* Points and Authorities Memorandum.

Trial Notebook   A collection of documents, arguments, and strategies that an attorney plans to use during a trial. Sometimes referred to as the *trial brief*. (It can mean the notebook in which the trial brief is placed.)

Unauthorized Practice of Law   Services that constitute the practice of law, which a nonattorney has no authorization to provide. *See also* Practice of Law, Professional Judgment.

Unified Bar Association   *See* Integrated Bar Association.

United States Court of Appeals   The main federal appellate court just below the United States Supreme Court.

United States District Court   The main federal trial court.

United States Supreme Court   The highest court in the federal judicial system.

Venue   The place of the trial.

Verdict   The final conclusion of the jury.

Verification   An affidavit stating that a party has read the complaint and swears that it is true to the best of his or her knowledge.

Vicarious Disqualification   A law firm cannot continue to represent a client or cannot accept a new client because it has hired someone (attorney, paralegal, or secretary) who has a conflict of interest with that client.

Vicarious Liability   Being responsible because of what someone else has wrongfully done or wrongfully failed to do. *See also* Personal Liability.

Wage and Hour Division   The unit within the U.S. Department of Labor that administers the Fair Labor Standards Act, which governs overtime compensation and related matters. *See also* Exempt Employee, Fair Labor Standards Act.

Waiver   The loss of a right or privilege because of an explicit rejection of it or because of a failure to claim it at the appropriate time.

WESTLAW   The legal research computer service of West Publishing Co.

Work-Product Rule   Notes, working papers, memoranda, or similar documents and tangible things prepared by the attorney in anticipation of litigation are not discoverable. *See also* Discoverable.

Writ of Certiorari   An order by an appellate court requiring a lower court to certify the record of a lower court proceeding and to send it up to the appellate court which has decided to accept the appeal.

Writ Writer   *See* Jailhouse Lawyer.

Index

A

■ B

■ E

▪ M

■ P

▪ S

U

V

W

Y